PENGUI

off the grid

Nick Rosen is a rising authority on living off the grid and has written extensively on the subject for the *Times* (London), the *Guardian*, and Reuters. He is also an award-winning documentary filmmaker. He edits the Web site Off-Grid.net in back of his RV, using a laptop plugged into the cigar lighter (and a wireless modem plugged into the laptop). His hobbies include cooking, diving, and trespassing, and he has a part-time, off-grid home on the island of Majorca.

off the grid

Inside the Movement for More Space,
Less Government, and True Independence
in Modern America

NICK ROSEN

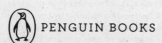 PENGUIN BOOKS

PENGUIN BOOKS

Published by the Penguin Group

Penguin Group (USA) Inc., 375 Hudson Street, New York, New York 10014, U.S.A.

Penguin Group (Canada), 90 Eglinton Avenue East, Suite 700, Toronto,
   Ontario, Canada M4P 2Y3 (a division of Pearson Penguin Canada Inc.)

Penguin Books Ltd, 80 Strand, London WC2R 0RL, England

Penguin Ireland, 25 St Stephen's Green, Dublin 2, Ireland (a division of
   Penguin Books Ltd)

Penguin Group (Australia), 250 Camberwell Road, Camberwell,
   Victoria 3124, Australia (a division of Pearson Australia Group Pty Ltd)

Penguin Books India Pvt Ltd, 11 Community Centre, Panchsheel Park,
   New Delhi – 110 017, India

Penguin Group (NZ), 67 Apollo Drive, Rosedale, North Shore 0632,
   New Zealand (a division of Pearson New Zealand Ltd)

Penguin Books (South Africa) (Pty) Ltd, 24 Sturdee Avenue, Rosebank,
   Johannesburg 2196, South Africa

Penguin Books Ltd, Registered Offices:
80 Strand, London WC2R 0RL, England

First published in Penguin Books 2010

10   9   8   7   6   5   4   3   2   1

LIBRARY OF CONGRESS CATALOGING-IN-PUBLICATION DATA
Rosen, Nick.
Off the grid : inside the movement for more space, less government, and true
independence in modern America / Nick Rosen.
p. cm.
ISBN 978-0-14-311738-4
1. Self-reliant living—United States.   I. Title.
GF78.R67 2010
640—dc22   2010013334

Printed in the United States of America
Set in ITC Giovanni Book
Designed by Sabrina Bowers

for Caitlin Jett

Contents

off the grid

1 Another Way

> "People are becoming less self-reliant and more dependent than ever before ... they cannot really do anything for themselves. They depend utterly on vastly complex organizations, on fantastic machinery, on larger money income...."
>
> E. E. Schumacher

> "Simplify, simplify."
>
> Henry David Thoreau, *Walden*

Sequoia had been both feared and loved by the residents of Greenfield. Her temper was legendary, and yet, according to Mike, who also settled here in the 1970s, "She could have had any man on this ranch."

In her heyday and beyond, several mourners told me, she would stride around the back roads wearing nothing but cowboy boots, her flame-red hair reaching down to her ass, a joint hanging from her pouting lips, boyfriend du jour at her side.

And now here she was in the dim light, lying in state on the clubhouse table, dressed in white and cream, like Titania from *A Midsummer Night's Dream*, surrounded by piles of flowers, her face heavily made up, her long tresses combed straight down.

A cross section of the ranch's 185 residents were busy demolishing her collection of rare tequilas, which she had specifically instructed be drunk at this moment. Older baby boomers—her generation—were in the majority at Sequoia's wake. But there were others in their thirties and a few kids; Greenfield is multigenerational now. I was dizzy with introductions to builders, writers, pot-growers, healers, scientists, even a winemaker.

A little bit of pot (the local cash crop) was being smoked on the smooth lawn outside the sole community building on the ranch, but mainly it was about drink and food this balmy October evening.

I showed up at mountainous Greenfield Ranch, in Mendocino County, too late to meet Sequoia. In her final e-mail, she had warned me to hurry; she'd had a lot to impart. She had wanted to tell me about the politics and the history and the fun of living off the grid in Northern California, outside the system, free of the Man, especially the Meter Man, Sequoia, like hundreds of thousands of others across America, had existed beyond the reach of the power cables and water lines that intersect and delineate the modern world—no peed for meter readings here.

* * *

In the hills edging Boone, North Carolina, a young man sits in a tepee. Outside steam is rising from the leafy forest floor—a combination of last night's rain and this morning's sun. He is an undergraduate at the nearby university. His father's company sells upholstery to airplane manufacturers, so the son could afford to live in a house. But he prefers the teepee, which is, at least, laid with incredibly hard-wearing aircraft carpet. He and his girlfriend own a large collection of guns, and he tells me that America would be a better, safer place if every household had to own a gun by law. As he cooks our breakfast on a tiny, homemade rocket stove, I nervously loose off a few rounds with his semi-automatic. It's the first time I've ever fired a gun, and each shot hits the bull's-eye.

* * *

The American Legion in Big Bend, Texas, is the only bar for forty miles in any direction. To the south is Terlingua and the Mexican border. At midday the doors open, seven days a week, and the local homesteaders gather in the wooden building for beer and gossip. The Legion is connected to the utilities, but none of its regular customers live in houses with power or water. There are several hundred homes scattered around the area— some of them holiday cabins for northeasterners. The majority are occupied by single guys: veterans, divorcees, desert-lovers, retired widowers, some alcoholics but not many—it's too tough out here for heavy drinkers. Fewer women than men want to adjust to the harsh climate and the desolate landscape. "There are mountains," says the woman behind the bar, a little too brightly. And it's true, there is a mountain range in this part of West Texas, and a national park. It's a place to come if you *want* to be lonely . . . and land is very inexpensive compared to most of the locations I visited.

These off-grid locations range from urban houseboats to suburban lots and gardens, from rural houses and communes to cabins, tree houses, converted shipping containers, and even tents and their ethnic variations, such as tepees and yurts. The people living this way—the off-gridders—might be middle-class environmentalists or right-wing survivalists, victims of foreclosure or long-term pot growers, international business travelers with their own islands or groups of friends who decided to start a community. They move around in buses and four-wheel drives, yachts and houseboats, caravans and Winnebagos, as well as more conventional vehicles.

The back-to-the-land movement was having its first flowering when Sequoia settled in Greenfield in 1972. The five-thousand-acre ranch is one of many that the original owners had clear-cut and then partitioned to sell piecemeal, back before solar panels had been invented and before land prices shot up dramatically. And it was harsh—no roads to speak of, no cell phones, no Internet. It was unthinkable.

Thousands moved in from San Francisco, New York, and everywhere in between—hippies and yippies, grad students and artists, dreamers, schemers, CIA spies, draft dodgers, and psychos. (Greenfield even spawned a mass murderer—Leonard Lake, who was ejected by his fellow residents in 1980, shortly before he began his killing spree.) They built homes from trees felled on the spot. They hauled in five-hundred-gallon tanks to catch the rainwater, powered a few lights with generators or car batteries, grew some pot, and tried to grow food. Anyone still here forty years later has a right to be considered among the most practical, self-sufficient, hardy, and ingenious Americans. The defining characteristics of this diverse off-grid population? A fierce resistance to convention and a pioneering spirit.

Mike Riddell, my guide at Greenfield, was newly divorced with no job and two young daughters in tow when he settled here. First he built a one-room structure, with a kitchen tucked into the corner, on his small plot of land. Once his children had a secure shelter over their heads, he started work on his own bedroom, and it's been going like this for almost forty years. Now he has one of the best and biggest spreads on Greenfield, having expanded through the purchase of additional lots completed on favorable terms as laid down in the ranch's bylaws.

Most of the lots are twenty or forty acres, he explained, and cannot be subdivided. Many owners, especially the unmarried ones, find themselves a "land partner" who may build an additional, semilegal dwelling on the same parcel. But Mike did not need a land partner. He remarried, and now here he was at Sequoia's wake, sixty-five years old, with his Mexican wife, Juanita Joy. He's fit and happy—or as happy as one can be at a wake—with a full head of gray ringlets; he looks like a retired rock star. But the rest of the band are beginning to die.

Are their children ready to take over the mantle? Mike thinks not. He has three daughters now, all living in the city, on the grid. "It's only my youngest who might possibly be interested," he told me as we stood in the kitchen of the rustic wooden clubhouse, "and she's too young to know what she wants."

The back-to-the-land movement is having its time again. A few hundred thousand elderly ex-hippies—or maybe enduring hippies—who went rural in the 1970s have now been joined by a younger generation, many of whom have abandoned the rat race in the past few years as economic conditions have worsened. Some were forced out. Others in secure jobs used the downturn to reappraise their values. They are sick of traffic, pollution, and the consumer-driven society. They have lost all trust in bankers and politicians. They are looking for a better way. Mike's youngest daughter is an urban environmentalist—the latest face of the back-to-the-land movement. She would take up her father's off-grid legacy, if at all, for the health of the planet. But going off the grid is only partly about living a greener life. It is also about freedom from the daily commute, mortgage-induced wage slavery, and corporate mass-marketing. True, people who survive without municipally supplied power and water are likely to reduce their carbon footprint—that esoteric calculation of the damage our every move is doing to the planet—but this makes them merely accidental environmentalists, assuming they use wind or solar power for electrical energy, capture rainwater for washing and drinking, and dispose of their own organic waste, perhaps with a composting toilet that replaces water with wood chips and allows the mix to mature for six months before returning it to the soil. With a certain design approach known as eco-architecture, warmth comes directly from the sun through big windows in the walls of the home. Solar thermal water heaters, wood-burning stoves, and ground-source heat pumps—which extract the heat from the ground—can also provide minimally harmful warmth.

Such is a life based on renewable energy and self-sufficiency. In my case, though, the ecological implications are secondary.

I went off the grid seeking freedom and more space between myself and the system. I also wanted to save money. I do not think everyone ought to live off grid. But I would like to make more people aware that living off the grid is an option.

As I crisscrossed America visiting the publicity-shy, off-grid population, I encountered an unsatisfied, pent-up demand to live off grid. Those who seek to live this way want to do so without obstacles like zoning, building permits, or social ostracism (all of which I encountered). I suspect most people consider using a composting toilet, for example, a fate worse than sleeping in their car. But for those on a limited budget, living off the grid appears to solve all sorts of problems, housing being the most immediate; there are no power or water bills, which reduces the amount of money one needs to live well. As long as one can afford the up-front payment for the equipment, one can live comfortably, use the latest gadgets, and avoid most of the hardships suffered by Sequoia's generation.

The main requirement is a change of mind-set. Americans are happy and proud to buy and use recycled toilet paper, but a composting toilet is another matter, a level most people won't even think about. Most Americans are taught, or at the very least encouraged to believe, that homes must be a certain way. Well before the invention of TV, marketers pushed "ideal lifestyle" scenarios that included fridges and washing machines and electric gadgets of all kinds. The power companies, of course, subsidized the development and marketing of these products, and intentionally or not, dependence on the grid became a fact of life in America. Living in homes that are the exceptions to this rule are hippies and traditional back woodsmen (and women).

The crunchy, granola off-gridders—environmentalists and other anti-capitalists—are just part of the story. The other big off-the-grid grouping is made up of right-wing survivalists, veterans, and traditional good ol' boys who were never on the grid in the first place.

Like many millions of Americans, they are losing faith in the ability of the state to fulfill its basic functions—to prevent the strong from oppressing the weak and to regulate the markets. The final straw was the triumph of the "banksters" (and insurers and hedge-fund managers) in keeping their jobs, barring a few layoffs. It was quite a trick the financial community pulled, scamming the world for billions of dollars through the real estate bubble, and then hanging on to the money while the rest of the world scrabbled around to keep them solvent. The anger is still palpable and off-grid real estate may be the only remaining answer for many. It sure beats impotently shaking your fist at the TV set.

I should point out that I am not an American. This collapse in trust, however, is global. With the global economy in danger, many believe that what's needed is a *glocal* (global and local) solution.

Over in Britain, where I come from, the breakdown of trust is as bad as in the United States. The government and most Members of Parliament are incompetent, self-serving scumbags. It's not me saying that—it is the verdict of the British voters, who express their disgust with the system at every opportunity. Legislators from every party were caught making fraudulent expense claims when their financial records were leaked in 2009. In elections that year, a fascist party won two seats for the first time since the 1930s, with a campaign featuring a "punish the pigs" poster, in which two pigs in suits are fighting over a pile of cash. The sums the politicians stole, it's worth noting, totaled perhaps one percent of the annual Goldman Sachs bonus pool, but it still stank to high heaven.

Global anger has increased as Goldman Sachs and the others keep paying the bonuses—with our tax money. That in itself has been enough to convince some to live off the grid, where the bankers' excesses cannot touch them. (And to convince the bankers themselves to apply for handgun licenses.) Over the last decade, billions of dollars in bonuses were paid on what were essentially falsely declared profits. If those bonuses were repaid, the taxpayers' burden of the bailout bill would be significantly lower.

I tried living off grid in Britain in a homemade RV—a converted white hospital bus—while touring a crowded, property-obsessed island the size of Kansas. It was liberating, even enchanting, but there were drawbacks. Finding an affordable piece of land is hard enough; then comes the really difficult part: being allowed to live on it. In all areas of the UK, one simply cannot get permission to so much as pull a trailer onto a lot, never mind to reside there full-time in it. There are two choices: Either live there in secret with the risk of exposure, or exploit loopholes in the system (i.e., lie). If the property is forested, for example, one might say, "This isn't a residence, it's my forestry office, necessary for managing the harvesting of the trees on my land."

In the United States, there are similar restrictions, although they vary widely from county to county. Living on agricultural or any sort of land other than residential is what planners call a "change of use." Residential land prices are kept artificially high by severely restricting change of use—and there are good reasons for that; officials don't want just anybody building whatever they want simply because they own the land. Yet the law is too strict. In places with high home prices, where someone might actually want to live, it is nearly impossible to find a homestead and build an affordable house. The people living in these expensive areas are delighted with this arrangement, of course. But it does not help the rest of the population.

JOINING THE FREEDOM MOVEMENT

I launched a Web site to help campaign for easier laws for what we in the UK call off-grid homes. (*Off grid* and *off the grid* are used interchangeably in what follows.) I urged the UK government to enact a new kind of building permission, allowing off-grid building in both rural and urban areas on land not previously zoned for residential use, but on one condition: that it remain forever off grid and therefore low carbon. The response to the site was far more positive in the United States than in the UK, which is peculiar, considering Britain's future electricity demand is predicted to exceed supply by up to twenty-five percent by 2020 (and thirty percent across Europe). So where will the extra power come from?

In the United States, vast new solar farms and wind farms are planned, with huge towers to carry the power to the population centers. Meanwhile, most grid-connected households that install renewable energy sources like wind or solar cut a poor deal from the local utility: They may sell back their surplus power into the grid, but are paid fully (i.e., at the same price as they are charged) only to the point at which they zero out their bill. Any excess energy is either "given" to the utility company gratis or paid for at about thirty percent of the retail rate. This is like a household tax, a contribution to the utility company shareholders' dividend. And the deal varies from one state to another, making it harder to calculate what your return will be before investing.

Via my Web site I receive a steady stream of e-mails and phone calls from Americans who want to live off the grid. Some are individuals just starting out; others have formed groups and pooled their money to buy some land. Some off-gridders and wannabe off-gridders are anti-capitalist in their outlook, but the majority are not anti anything—they are pro-market, pro-environment, and pro-freedom, and merely want to live a decent life, free of debt, free of utility bills, growing some of their own food, and making a living according to whatever skills they have.

The high level of interest from America led me to revisit Henry Thoreau's classic book *Walden*. I first read it years ago, as a philosophy student at Georgetown University, in Washington, D.C., and was immediately attracted to the idea of ridding myself of possessions and living simply in the woods in a ten-by-twelve-foot cabin—what the British would call a shed. The book's arrival in 1854 seems to have been anticlimactic. The *New York Times* at least noted its publication—Thoreau was already a known figure on the intellectual scene—and called the author an "erratic genius" but damned the book as "a contribution to the Comic Literature of America." I picked up a first edition, a plain brown hardback with gold lettering. The text is in a modest, almost unappealing typeface. A dowdy monochrome map of Walden Pond is included, but it feels like an afterthought. I came to enjoy its lack of showiness, and as I contemplated the timeless appeal of Thoreau's concept of disregarding the material world and drinking deep from nature, I realized anew that America is the home of off-grid philosophy. Rereading it, I saw that Thoreau was, like me, a part-time cabin dweller. He was not ashamed to bring his washing home to Mom and eat dinner while she took care of it.

It was then I decided to embark on a pilgrimage to the land of Thoreau and restless enterprise. I wanted to see whether the pioneering spirit is really still alive in America, what motivates it, and whether I could find my own off-grid dream along the way.

I have been visiting America all my adult life, first as a student and then as a journalist and documentary filmmaker. Whenever I want to know what the future might hold, I come to America, especially New York and California, home to many of the most important megatrends of the past forty years: the hippie movement, women's liberation, the IT industry, and the Internet. Now, at the dawn of the renewable-energy era, Silicon Valley has become Solar Valley and Fuel Cell Valley.

I began planning my American adventure. I had toured the UK in my RV, but that approach would not work in the United States if I wanted my journey to conclude within a finite period. I would be driving tens of thousands of miles—at ten miles to the gallon. The places I planned to visit also tended to be rather isolated, many of them down unmade roads, which was a further disincentive to travel in an RV. So it had to be, unfortunately, planes and rental cars.

Anyone considering the off-the-grid life might be interested to know how I carried a mobile office inside a small rucksack.

For communications I relied on my five-year-old Nokia 9600, one of the first flip-open models with a large screen and a keyboard. It was on the Vodafone network in the UK and Verizon Wireless in the United States, so I could make calls and check e-mail in most small towns in America. I also had a Vodafone wireless modem to plug into my laptop computer, an HP Pavilion with an extra battery. This gave me high-speed Internet in built-up areas and slower speeds elsewhere. Power was via a thirty-dollar in-car power inverter from the now-defunct Sharper Image. It plugs into the car cigarette lighter, converting 12-volt DC to 110-volt AC, allowing me to charge my computer, phone, and a Canon PowerShot G9 digital camera (though not all at the same time). These items, together with their respective chargers, all fit into the rucksack itself, a padded Tech Air.

If I ran out of signal range, I could rely on free Wi-Fi in the parking lots of motels and restaurants. I realized Americans would not want to call me using my British phone number, so I added a voice-mail service from Grasshopper, which for a hundred dollars a year provides a toll-free number, and for another twelve dollars I bought a prepaid Cingular account, with a basic Motorola phone and ten dollars' worth of free calls. The only other item of importance in the bag was a small cream-colored cloth rabbit belonging to my daughter, Caitlin. It is an elegant rabbit, about six inches high with a green velvet jacket.

Because I was visiting remote locations, I also experimented with a power-hungry Garmin GPS system. I quickly abandoned it. I am usually quite proficient with gadgetry, but I never really worked out how to use it, especially in outlying areas. It was one item too many that needed to be charged. I decided on Google Maps instead, accessed via the wireless modem.

So what was I looking for? What do I want in an off-the-grid home?

My first quest was for a community of like-minded souls who care about our society and want to make a difference. I was not looking to join a commune or cooperative—I don't want to cut myself off from society and I am not into cleaning schedules, interminable meetings, and the need to reach a consensus with others about every aspect of my life. I accepted, however, that I had plenty to learn from the off-grid commune dwellers—they are the foot soldiers of the eco-revolution. I am not looking to follow the example of the smattering of Hollywood A-listers who have quietly bought up their own private island as "bugout" locations. In 2004 Johnny Depp snapped up 45-acre Little Hall's Pond Cay in the Bahamas for $3.6 million and Mel Gibson (*Mad Max*) paid an over-the-top $19 million for Mago in the Fijis. However rich I was, being alone with my retinue on my own island would be of little consolation in the event of social or ecological breakdown. Leonardo DiCaprio at least says he will build an "eco-resort" on his 104-acre island in Belize, but that is hardly the sort of community I have in mind.

What I am interested in becoming part of is a society or group that has turned away from the hyper-consumption of the past thirty years, the pointless acquisitions, the hopeless material-ism, and the obsession with celebrity trivia. I want neighbors who solve their problems themselves instead of calling the po-lice or county commissioners about every little thing, and who solve them from within the present set of laws and culture that makes up the American way of life. I don't want to join a social experiment.

My second quest was for land—low-cost, mixed-use land, urban or rural, where I can live well, plant trees, generate power, and grow food, without falling heavily into debt.

As I mentioned earlier, some U.S. states and counties are as restricted as Britain in what can be built there—and, of course, the tightest rules are in places where land is most expensive. True, there are huge swaths of America where land is still dirt cheap and building codes are nonexistent, but this is because few people actually want to live there.

So as I traveled I took note of the best areas to live off the grid, and charted the rise of a new movement, aimed at off-the-grid land reform that would make it easier to homestead on wooded and agricultural land (and even industrial land).

Politicians like to deal in big numbers, and truthfully the number of off-gridders is not yet very impressive, although it has swelled recently. By 2007 there were approximately three hundred thousand off-the-grid households in the United States. I estimate that by 2010 there will be 520,000 homes and up to a million people living off the grid either legally or unofficially. (It's hard to say *illegally*, as living off the grid is not a breach of the criminal law.)

A spokeswoman from Backwoods Solar, one of the leading companies selling renewable-energy equipment specifically for off-the-grid situations, told me that the market is growing at ten to fifteen percent a year in dollar terms. Prices for items such as solar panels are falling even as I write this, so it is probably an underestimate to assume that the number of households without utilities is also growing at ten to fifteen percent annually (this includes second homes).

No individual or place I visited is representative of the entire off-grid universe—not the remote community in the Florida Keys battling over whether to connect to the grid, not the smattering of politically committed Texans living without municipal power or water, not the hardscrabble families living in New Mexico, where land is generally cheap.

I met unworldly writers eking out an existence in underpopulated woods and beaches; middle-class professionals who found that they were able to move into better neighborhoods if they were prepared to put up with minor inconveniences such as an outhouse or a battery bank; and billionaires who wanted remote ranches to add to their property portfolios. Taken together they create a kaleidoscope of a rapidly changing social movement.

As I traveled to different off-the-grid homes, meeting those who live in them, I categorized them according to the reason their owners gave me for making the choice to live this way. Some are largely within mainstream American culture and merely happen to be off the grid, almost incidentally. Others are actively developing an alternative way of living that sits on the outer fringes of civil society. The categories I describe below appear in order of most familiar to least.

The most familiar—to me, because this is the reason I was looking myself—are those whose off-grid properties are second or vacation homes, places to duck out from the stresses and ills of modern society: unhealthy lifestyles, fast food, commuter hell, urban violence, high rents, work deadlines, and uptight clients. The off-grid second home is a true escape from all that. The conventional second home is too often nothing more than a replica of the primary residence, an additional home simply situated in a different place that fosters the same habits from which one is trying to escape.

Then there are what might be called transitionalists or "off-grid-ready" residents. Their homes are their primary residences and are still connected to the grid, but they have solar or wind power and have reduced their energy and water consumption to the extent that they could if necessary live happily with just a few solar panels (or the equivalent) and a single rainwater tank. Traditionalists tend to believe that we are in the age of peak oil—meaning that the supply of affordable energy is dwindling. They are also motivated by ecological concerns.

Most of us feel the need to have flushing toilets and municipal power. Some people, for whatever reason, do not have that need. They are just the same as the rest of us, yet, unlikely as it may sound, they feel perfectly relaxed looking after their own power, water, and waste disposal. They spend their money on the things that are most important to them: With a limited budget, they are prepared to sacrifice the grid in return for a more desirable location or a larger house or a bigger yard. They have chosen to live off the grid in order to enjoy what they aspire to have on the grid.

The next category is unfamiliar but not unknown: people whose lives have become what many of us fear. They couldn't pay their rents or mortgages any more and their options were limited or undesirable: staying with friends or family, but perhaps only for a short time; or having no one to stay with at all. They are the dispossessed, the contemporary version of the characters in Steinbeck's novel *The Grapes of Wrath*. And so living off the grid, with cheap land and reduced costs, has become a viable solution, the difference between happiness and misery.

Most, however, actively chose to go off the grid, rather than being forced into it by debt or foreclosure. They still want to live comfortably, and are not trying to drop out of society altogether; they just want to minimize its role in their lives.

Even more distant from mainstream lifestyles, yet at the same time channeling one of America's most dearly held values, are those who acted out of an intense desire for freedom. They have no wish to be bound by the social rules of work, they feel deeply betrayed by current values, and they do not want to depend on American society for anything. They might do their own doctoring or schooling, make their own clothes, and grow their own food (up to a point). They want to disconnect as much as possible.

Although I do not want to live like that, I envy them because I find the challenge in modern life is to disconnect even a little—to turn off the TV and the phone and Internet; to stop rushing around doing things and buying stuff; to just *be.* Back in the sixties, there used to be a mantra, "Only Connect," to describe our need to communicate more clearly with one another. But the twenty-first-century challenge is how to take back the personal space that has been seized from us by cable TV, cell phones, and e-mail.

A subsection of the disconnected is the religious off-gridders. Some, like the Amish and the Mennonites, belong to sects that specifically order them off the electrical grid. Others simply see going off the grid as a way of being closer to God.

Then there is an altogether different meaning of living off the grid, which has nothing to do with power and water, nor stepping back from the system, and refers to elements of the surveillance society that we all resent as much as we accept it. There are people living with no ID cards, no bank accounts, no cell phones, and no Internet connection—all because they prefer to live away from the watchful eyes of various government and commercial entities. Some are homeless; others are criminals or civil libertarians.

The final off-grid type has fear as its primary motivation. Although they might call it something else, such as "preparedness," their actions are based on a conviction that the entire social system as we know it is about to disintegrate, or that a natural disaster could at any time sweep away the fragile order upon which our society rests. Some believe that peak oil, mentioned earlier, will have far harsher consequences than merely raising the cost of energy. Their sense of fear is one we all share to some degree, just as we would all like to jump off the treadmill and be free of the rat race at certain times—but we don't all act on it.

We humans are complex creatures; nobody has just one reason for doing anything. Everyone I met was acting on a combination of motives, falling into more than one of the above categories, so I have interpreted their primary motivations to try to make sense of them.

As I introduce the characters in the following chapters, I hope readers will recognize a little of themselves in each and, from time to time, think, "I could live like that. . . . I want to live like that!"

But before starting out on my journey I needed to learn more about the forces that shaped the modern grid, the ties that bind Americans to their current lives. I discovered that the existing structure of the power and water industries is the product of the historical conditions prevailing at the dawn of the twentieth century. Communities' needs and lifestyles have changed radically since, and if the grid did not exist, there would be no need now to invent it.

2 How the Grid Was Won

The grid silently and invisibly underpins modern society—until it goes wrong.

On August 14, 2003, I was in New York, making a documentary for PBS's *Frontline*. As I headed for the airport that day, I noticed bewildered groups standing at bus stops or walking in their business suits across the bridges. At first I was pleased with myself for finding a taxi. When I reached JFK it was total chaos. There was a power outage across the city, I learned, and the terminal might as well have been in Africa—no computers, no lights, no air-conditioning, just thousands of stranded passengers milling around. As it happened, my Virgin Atlantic flight was one of the few to take off—and without me on it. Because I did not have a printout of my ticket, my seat was given to someone else, presumably someone with a first-class seat on another airline.

Wearily I managed to find another taxi to take me back to

Manhattan. The outage was huge—I was one of fifty million affected across the northeastern part of the United States. With the hotels full or out of commission, I headed for the Chelsea home of my production assistant. By now, it had become clear what a mess the system was in and how long it would take to put it right (several days).

I assumed my assistant would react in the spirit of a national emergency and welcome me in. The documentary was about the battle among New York's elite over what would be built in the space once occupied by the Twin Towers. I had hired the young socialite to help with political connections in the city. Her father, a real estate titan, was known in the corridors of power as the "first buddy" because he had been George W. Bush's best friend during their college days. Eventually he would take legal action to try to prevent my documentary from being screened. (He failed.) For now, things were meant to be great between us all.

She opened her apartment door and looked at me as though I was a street bum who had somehow obtained unauthorized access to the building. In the end I had to stay somewhere else. Still, there I was in New York with a ringside seat for the biggest power outage in at least thirty years.

On day one of the blackout the electricity industry went into high gear to deal with the situation. At the headquarters of the Edison Electrical Institute, the industry's lobbying organization in Washington, D.C., executives realized immediately that they had a heaven-sent opportunity to set the terms of the debate. Tom Kuhn, president of EEI, went on *Larry King Live* within hours and demanded that Congress provide "additional incentives to build infrastructure investment."

The same day, David K. Owens, EEI's executive vice president, told the *Washington Post* that the "transmission infrastructure needs to be strengthened." The outage was due to the huge increase in the shipment of power across state lines, the *Post* reported. It failed to mention that this increase was one the EEI had lobbied for. The deregulation of the $400 billion-a-year industry had created phenomena such as Enron and also permitted non-utility companies to build power stations, but there was no corresponding incentive to beef up transmission lines. Strongly supported by EEI, Senator J. Bennett Johnston (D-LA) had coauthored the Energy Policy Act of 1992, weakening the law restraining utility companies from engaging in other forms of business. Newer companies had taken advantage of the 1992 act to increase power generation, and the industry had left the lines to look after themselves. Now the utilities were going to blame the government and demand more money.

Advocates of utilities deregulation had always intended the process to lead to price cuts, just as it had in the phone and airline industries. Nothing of the sort happened. Deregulation failed partly because the legislation was framed so that no entity was in charge of overseeing the maintenance of the grid. This situation suited the utilities rather well and led directly to the 2003 blackout.

The next morning Tom Kuhn was back on ABC's *Good Morning America* answering a question from Diane Sawyer about possible terrorist attacks. "The best, the best defense against cyberterrorism or terrorism in general is to have a robust transmission system," the EEI president solemnly assured her. "A lot of people have mentioned how important it is for us to enhance the transmission system. We have the most reliable system in the world, but I think additional investment, [as] I've testified many times, is greatly needed."

Investment by the government, that is, rather than power-company shareholders.

Simultaneously, another EEI spokesman, Bill Brier, was putting out a more conciliatory line, one that would eventually prevail in legislation. The Institute recognized the utility companies' obligation to keep the electricity flowing, he told the *Boston Globe*, and "still favors deregulation, but does support legislation that impose[s] mandatory rules on power companies to fulfill their obligations on the energy grid." These reliability rules were enacted in 2005, and with million-dollar fines looming over them, the utility companies are now improving the reliability of the network.

But they want us to pay for it. And the basic problems are still there. Of the energy used to generate electricity (in fossil fuel or nuclear power plants), only thirty-one percent actually makes it all the way to homes, offices, and factories. Part is lost in the process of producing the electricity, and the rest as it whizzes around the country along the power lines. When this loss of power is added to the inefficiencies of older appliances and factories that consume electricity, usable energy can drop to as low as twelve percent. The fact that we now have a hugely inefficient production and distribution process, not to mention grotesque rates of energy consumption, suggests that this ramshackle system probably should never have been invented in the first place.

Two days after the blackout, as normal service was gradually restored, the EEI was telling the *New York Times*, "Right now we have a highway to transmit power. We need a superhighway."

Yet another EEI spinner, Jim Owen, went on NPR radio. "We've been saying for some time that we do need to expand and upgrade our transmission capacity in most parts of the country," he told them, "basically to meet what is an ever-increasing demand for electric power."

Why should there be an "ever-increasing demand"? What rule of nature dictates that electricity use can only ever go up, especially during a recession? And what is this demand anyway? How has it grown so large? Never mind all the environmental issues—surely on economic grounds alone more could have been done to make our lives more energy efficient.

It took me months to find anyone who was questioning the grid in the ways I was. Eventually I happened across a Web site for a lawyer in the Midwest, Carol Overland, who specializes in opposing the utilities' proposals to build towers across beauty spots or increase power generation in nature reserves. "Transmission lines have become transmission lies," she told me when

I finally intercepted her on the phone between utility commission appearances.

Her deep knowledge of the industry made her sure of one thing: The industry does not want to increase transmission capacity in order to better serve the public. Rather, it is there to facilitate the burgeoning long-distance trade in wholesale electricity *between the power companies themselves.*

But the regulators and the U.S. Energy Secretary will not pay for better, smarter power lines merely to help the utility traders. "Investments must be 'reasonable and prudent.' Opportunity to play the market is not reasonable and prudent," said Overland, "so it's not a reason to build a transmission line." That is why the representations are made to the regulators in terms of "peak load," i.e., ever-growing demand. "Planning for peak load is a transmission lie," said Overland. "Utilities have incentive to overstate need when they build for peaks. The higher the peak they build for (with peaks occurring only several times annually), the deeper the off-peak valley and the more electricity they can sell on the market when generation is available but not 'needed.' Conservation and peak shaving is against their interest because it lowers peak and lessens the valley of market sales."

Overland claimed that "overloading the lines with bulk power transfers at off-peak times" caused the 2003 outage.

In the 2005 legislation, as part of the response to the 2003 blackout, the Federal Energy Regulatory Commission (FERC) was given limited powers over transmission lines, and an industry organization called North American Electric Reliability Corporation (NERC) was handed the job of reporting to FERC on reliability issues. Overland's point of view received some supporting evidence when a NERC spokeswoman told me the organization was unable to issue comparative reports on the reliability of the eight regions that make up the U.S. grid. Indeed, NERC does not offer any data about reliability or electricity usage on its Web site, although it does sell this information, which seems inappropriate for a federally mandated organization, as it inhibits monitoring of its own effectiveness. NERC, it appears, is just a creature of the electricity industry, funded by the utility companies and its board stuffed with retired utility- and power-industry fat cats, not a single one of whom represents the consumer. The whole setup feels to me like the industry's covering up its dirty secrets.

As I watched TV and read the papers and waited for a plane to take me back to London, nobody else was questioning the grid, asking whether it made sense to organize things this way. Sure, the event served to indicate how fragile is this electrical edifice that we all take for granted every day, yet not once did anyone suggest that perhaps we should not have a grid. Well . . . I did, but the first buddy's daughter was not listening.

DAWN OF THE GRID

Yes, it's convenient. We come in, flip a switch, and there is light; we turn a handle and water comes out of the tap. And I understand that for most of us, most of the time, the grid is welcoming. It bestows a sense of security; we know that someone is looking out for our power and water.

But today, all those things are available without the grid. The latest inverters, renewable energy sources, and rainwater-capture systems can provide for our needs. As the country prepares to spend hundreds of billions to upgrade the grid and transform it into the "smart grid," it is worth reminding ourselves how we came to build the grid in the first place.

The idea of power and water utilities as models of probity is one that, of course, they have steadily projected over the years. The power companies have a privileged monopoly position, and with that kind of a license to print money, the assumption has been that they would have no reason to abuse it. Yet they do abuse it and they always have.

For example, some random instances culled from newspaper archives:

■ In Staten Island in 1899, the New York and Staten Island Electric Company sent "gangs of men" into its customers' houses to rip out the wiring of anyone who refused to sign a new, disadvantageous contract within twenty-four hours of receiving it. This was at the dawn of the electric age, when local utilities were laying cable into homes street by street, the wealthier ones first, and then ensuring that householders wired up their homes to maximize their potential use of power.

■ The *Los Angeles Times* reported in 1902 that the local electric company was being sued by residents of the San Gabriel Valley for entering the area, cutting trails, and seizing land and water used by "irrigators" (i.e., farmers).

■ The Citizens' Electric Illuminating Company was featured in the *New York Times* in 1904, when it was caught stealing sixty-six million gallons of water from the city of Brooklyn annually, by the simple means of having its own workers connect a pipe to the DeKalb Avenue main line.

Absurd though they were, these random acts of subterfuge formed part of a larger pattern, foreshadowing the rise of the corporation in American life.

The growth of General Electric, and to a lesser extent Westinghouse, is a profound case study in the changing ways of American business, an early example of what economic historians call "managerial capitalism" superseding traditional "family capitalism," exemplified by the businesses run by the Rockefellers and the Morgans. The new-style corporations were run by managers who were not significant shareholders in the business, and companies such as GE were both vertically and horizontally integrated—i.e., they controlled every aspect of production, distribution, sale, and aftercare of the product, all the way from raw materials (in this case electricity and the machinery needed to produce it) to the use of the appliance in the customer's house.

The idea that they were building a corporate America was very deliberate in the minds of GE's senior management. One of the most powerful men at GE, Charles Proteus Steinmetz, sincerely believed that corporate functionaries should replace America's elected national government. Cigar-chomping Steinmetz, who kept six alligators as pets at his home in Schenectady, thought that re-organizing America along the lines of a corporation would rid us of illogical politicians.

It must have seemed like a brave new world at the time, a meritocracy being established and a new rational order replacing the semifeudal era of robber barons such as the Rockefellers. Not only was GE organized along the inhuman lines satirized in *Metropolis*, Fritz Lang's film about the drudgery of life in a mechanized city; the product it created—electricity—enabled other megacorporations to do the same.

Historian David Nye, in his book *Electrifying America*, says that managerial capitalism was possible only "in a large integrated market which allowed one company to produce in quantity at a few efficient sites and to sell the product to a large market." There in a nutshell is the rationale and the justification for the grid. It was not to help the consumer, nor to give communities more control over their own lives, nor necessarily to guarantee a more reliable flow of energy—that was a by-product. The grid came into existence to optimize efficiency (and hence profitability) for the producer. Society has organized itself around this approach to business, and in doing so, I believe, has tied itself in knots.

In the early days of electricity, as in the early days of the auto and other industries, there were many competing standards. Hundreds of equipment manufacturers and thousands of small utilities operated on a myriad of voltages and delivery systems, and this was highly irrational and inefficient, meaning it ran contrary the spirit of the age.

The battle between alternating current (AC) and direct current (DC) was just the best known of the many battles fought over standards in the early days of electric power. After sponsoring a series of lectures in which animals were electrocuted in an attempt to prove DC was somehow less humane, George Westinghouse famously delivered the knockout blow when he and his fellow AC proponents arranged for DC (advocated by Thomas Edison's General Electric) to be used to carry out the first execution by electric chair. This association was literally the death of DC, and it is significant to this story because AC power was at the time better suited to the long-distance transmission of electricity—i.e., the grid. To be fair, it was in the interests of both producers and consumers to eliminate the many differences in voltages and frequencies of electricity, and to agree on standards that were safe and reliable and that allowed manufacturers to produce fewer models of equipment—everything from radios to fridges—in larger quantities at a cheaper price.

The key event in the early history of the grid was the day that Thomas Edison installed the first electricity meter. His first central generator had gone into action on Pearl Street in Manhattan in 1882, and Edison began by charging his customers on Wall Street according to the number of lights in their buildings. That meant he was highly incentivised to make his system as efficient as possible in its consumption of both fuel and electricity. No matter that his incandescent lamp turned only ten percent of the electricity into light, with ninety percent wasted as heat. This inefficiency would have been solved were it not for the introduction of the electricity meter. Once he changed his business model, introduced meters, and charged for the electricity rather than the light, Edison had no reason to develop more efficient bulbs. And unnoticed, the metered supply became the standard way of delivering electricity around the Western world.

Agreement on standards did not inevitably lead to an industry dominated by one or two very large companies. This happened, of course, but commercial factors were what decided it, as best exemplified by the rise of GE.

Once GE established its control over the utilities industry through its dominance of the market in power generation, it turned to controlling the electric lightbulb market, which it did largely through overtly manipulative practices. I find this particularly revealing because GE is very proud of its illustrious past, referring to it all the time. In a July 2009 speech launching its smart-grid strategy, the president of the lighting and appliance division told his audience of journalists, by way of introduction, "In the first half of the twentieth century, [GE] produced one of the world's best home-appliance businesses."

The mechanisms by which GE developed this world-beating business model illustrate neatly how the growth of the grid and the growth of the amoral corporation went hand in hand.

Most homeowners were not interested in the many fancy appliances on view in the futuristic showrooms set up by the power companies from 1910 onward. But there was one thing they all wanted: electric light. And that was motivation enough to have power lines brought into their homes. The company selling most of the lightbulbs was GE, which owned the patents thanks to the company's founder, Thomas Edison.

By 1911, GE controlled seventy percent of the U.S. lightbulb market—a much higher figure than the number that officially established it as a monopoly under the Sherman Antitrust Act of 1890. How did the company achieve this? Simple: It secretly owned another company called National Electric Lamp Company, and through National it bought up its eighteen largest competitors. To keep up the pretense GE even sued National in 1904, for patent infringement. It was all a sham; GE was suing itself. And yet, even when this sham was discovered, GE managed to hold on to its two hundred lightbulb patents and, thus, control of the market.

In the great economic slump of the 1930s, GE's sales declined along with everyone else's, but its control of the lightbulb market saw it through the Depression just fine. Even in its worst year, 1933, the lightbulb division made a small profit. Electric light had become the one thing nobody wanted to be without. There was genuine demand for lightbulbs, which can't be said of the appliances on offer.

Its lightbulb business is just a small-scale representation of the way GE conducted itself through the first few decades of electrification. There were fifteen sizable electric companies in the early 1880s, according to Nye. By 1893 there were just two—GE and Westinghouse—and it was GE that went on to shape America.

The first step in building a company like GE or Westinghouse, after pooling patents to better control the market and to avoid costly legal battles over similar patents, is to acquire any smaller regional companies in order to reduce competition and create larger, homogenous markets for greater economies of scale.

From the dawn of the age of electricity, both GE and Westinghouse manufactured the expensive generating equipment that enabled local utility companies to produce power. GE was often paid in stock by these utility companies, and so ended up owning strategic stakes in most of them. Eventually GE created a holding company, the Electric Bond and Share Company, that would control the generating companies. By June 1929, the utility companies were the hottest category of sticks, i.e., among the most overpriced, and the holding company's president, S. Z. Mitchell, was known as the "world's richest man—on paper." (He lost almost all of it in the stock market crash of 1929, in which utility holding companies were major losers.)

After the First World War, GE's position as the industry's leader was unassailable, and throughout the 1920s, the company had a new strategic objective: "The creation and fostering throughout America of a positive electrical consciousness." In that single decade, GE, working with and through a trade association called the National Electric Light Association (NELA, the forerunner of the Edison Electric Institute), transformed

America. The headquarters of GE Lighting is still at Nela Park, East Cleveland, Ohio.

The annual meeting of NELA in 1923 was the venue for the launch of the proposed national grid. "One vast power system for whole country projected," declared the *New York Times* on July 17, 1923, in a breathless preamble to a front-page report from the conference by none other than the chairman of Westinghouse, Brigadier General Guy Tripp. There were two competing schemes at the time—the utilities favored one called Super Power; their opponents, largely municipalities, were pushing Giant Power, which would limit the influence of the utilities. Both factions agreed, however, that a national grid was needed. "The only reason for the existence of such a system," wrote Tripp, "is that it will increase the welfare of the people served by it."

In retrospect it would have been right to be cynical about this claim. Although the decision to create a pro-electric culture in America was a very conscious one, nobody realized quite how conscious until the late 1920s, when a Federal Trade Commission inquiry into NELA revealed the exact level of manipulation and the large propaganda budget devoted to persuading households to go on the grid.

Spending up to a million dollars a year through the 1920s, NELA secretly funded news agencies, sponsored research, held conferences, endowed scholarship funds, organized letter-writing campaigns, and even encouraged the rewriting of school textbooks. In 1925, for example, the chairman of the NELA PR committee, M. S. Sloan, of the Brooklyn Edison Company, addressed a group of employees at an internal meeting: "Schoolbooks in wide use all over the country have recently been analyzed. Many of them contain startling misstatements about public utilities. The pupil studying such material, hearing it discussed in the classroom, starts life with a warped and biased point of view regarding public utilities, and . . . is only too likely to remain unsympathetic and antagonistic through all future years."

This must be what happened to me.

As another example, in Illinois, a release was regularly sent to the nine hundred newspapers in the state, about 150 of them dailies. Speakers' bulletins were issued to employees, containing "ample material to any intelligent person for sound talks on each subject."

NELA also acted as a booking agency for its propagandists. According to an internal memo, "A bureau is operated to find engagements, before clubs, civic associations and so on. More than 800 Illinois high schools are regularly furnished informative literature for classroom theme work, and debating-society use."

In the slump of the thirties, with sales of everything else falling, electrification of homes and businesses continued to grow. There are echoes of this now, with the multi-corporation propaganda campaigns promoting the creation of a smart grid in the middle of the worst economic downturn in twenty years.

In 1935 (the only year for which I could find figures), light-bulbs were still by far the biggest power user in the domestic setting. Of the 20 million households wired to the grid by then, 13.5 million used electricity for lighting and small appliances, such as radios, while only 5 million had a refrigerator, and about 1.5 million had electric stoves.

Since the early stages of the grid, GE had been working hard to increase their sales of products other than lightbulbs. Merely running a few lights per household did not require the huge central generators that GE was building, nor did it require the elaborate power grid that was being planned. Things could have proceeded differently. Just as today the smart grid is hardly inevitable and not necessarily in the consumers' interests, back then the grid was not the only logical conclusion and not the best solution for the market. "It could have been a much less centralized system, even balkanized," David Nye told me. If the opposition had been better organized, or the pro-electricity lobby had not been so well funded, or if a man named Bruce Fairchild Barton had not come along when he did, the grid might never have formed.

Barton's advertising agency was hired in 1922 by GE. The young adman's assignment was to raise the "electrical consciousness" of the average housewife, who made the purchasing decisions about refrigerators, stoves, and washing machines.

For the first twenty-five years of Barton's life, his father had been pastor of the First Congregational Church of Oak Park, Illinois. The standard biography recounts that at the age of nine Barton had marketed his uncle's homemade maple syrup so successfully that the man was forced to buy extra supplies from neighbors in order to meet demand.

Barton graduated from Amherst College in 1907, and was voted most likely to succeed in his class. He did not, however, succeed much at first. He was hired to edit a succession of magazines, but they all suffered under his leadership. One was *Housekeeper*, a publication targeted at what were by then called housewives. So by the time he entered advertising, Barton was a deeply conventional—and religious—man who thoroughly understood housewives, and he felt that salesmanship was his calling.

Years later, he wrote a book about Jesus, *The Man Nobody Knows*. It made the argument that Jesus was "the world's greatest salesman." He also wrote hundreds of articles for popular magazines, offering readers advice and inspiration for pursuing the American dream. Barton may have even seen himself as a modern Jesus figure, with electricity in the same miraculous role as the loaves of bread and fish, destined to feed, warm, and clothe so many for so little.

Barton's pro-electricity campaigns were relentless. During the 1920s, GE's annual advertising budget increased from two million to twelve million dollars a year, and Barton ensured that each family would see two hundred ads per year, mainly in magazines. One typical campaign used the slogan "Make your house a home," a phrase that has survived to this day. (Barton once said, "We build of imperishable materials, we who work with words.") The campaign advocated wiring of the entire house, and the ads showed a series of tableaux of happy American families sitting together, surrounded by electrical devices. Barton is also credited with placing the GE logo, with its scroll lettering, at the center of the marketing strategy, ensuring it was used so often that housewives thought of it as the "initials of a friend."

Historian Stuart Ewen spotted that GE's advertising copywriters employed the rhetoric of women's emancipation to sex up appeals for domestic consumption: vacuum cleaners gave women "new life"; toasters made them "free." Rural housewives were a special target because they were the marketing route into the electrification of farms, which was stubbornly resisted for decades.

Most of the media went along with GE, not least to get a share of the advertising revenue. But there were a few voices raised against these tactics. The editor of *Woman's Home Companion*, Gertrude Battles Lane, who built the magazine's circulation up from 750,000 when she took over in 1912 to more than 3.5 million, feared that individual labor-saving devices were fragmenting communities. She ran a long campaign for "cooperative housework," arguing that the effect of the washing machine in the home (for the minority who could afford it) was to make the housewife more of a drudge than before. One article, "The Revolt of Mother," argued that "apart from the fact that millions of us are not able to command them, the washing machine won't collect and sort the laundry, or hang out the clothes; the mangle won't iron complicated articles; the dishwasher won't collect, scrape, and stack the dishes; the vacuum cleaner won't mop the floor or clean up and put away." Howes stressed the importance of the local community and the employment of domestic staff.

Of course this was a middle-class war, about middle-class

marketers working for the newly emerging corporations trying to capture the hearts and minds of middle-class consumers, and through them the entire population.

By the end of the twenties, *WHC* had accepted defeat on the issue of labor-saving appliances. GE, along with other advertisers, had been telling a story America wanted to hear, and had spent millions to make sure everyone heard it.

"Electricity permitted the intensification of individualism," Nye writes in *Electrifying America*. Centralized communal services such as washerwomen and community laundries were rejected in favor of less efficient but autonomous appliances that allowed for personal control of the weekly family wash, at a price. Nye offers Danish communities as a contrast: Most have cogeneration community power that is generated locally and shared among the houses of the community.

Another element of the electricity-consciousness campaign was the creation of "home-service departments" by local utility companies. Following the example of sewing-machine manufacturers that had hired women to demonstrate them from 1850 onward, the utility companies' home-service departments were groups of women who had been trained to instruct others in the use of household appliances.

In 1922, the People's Gas Light and Coke Company of Chicago launched one of the first home-service departments. The marketing leaflet described the service as one "that will make housework easier, show [housewives] how to feed their families for less money and tickle 'hubby's' palate so that he will never be late for dinner. Yes, all this without a cent of charge."

Between 1925 and 1930, the number of home-service departments in utility companies rose from fifty to four hundred. In 1925, the Chicago company estimated that its home service had contact with more than two hundred thousand customers by phone, mail, or demonstrations.

As early as 1931, the triumph of GE (and the electricity industry as a whole) was assured. An example of the way the company had burrowed into the national psyche is provided by syndicated comic strip *Gasoline Alley*. In the comic, an urban husband tries to persuade his wife that they should buy an off-the-grid second home, or as he puts it, "a summer place I have found in the country." His wife rejects the idea. "Without electricity we would have to use kerosene lamps. And we couldn't have an electric refrigerator. Think of the bother trying to get ice."

Thanks to GE, the American housewife, as portrayed in advertisements of this period, was a pitiable creature—isolated in her home, demanding evermore electrical goods while her husband went off to work. No wonder that by the early 1970s, as the back-to-the-land movement gathered pace, many educated American women no longer wished to be one.

DOWN-HOME ELECTRIC CO-OPS

While much of America was being transformed into an electric culture in the twenties, many millions were left out because the areas in which they lived were not considered profitable enough. The country was divided into electricity haves and have-nots.

The battle to ensure that rural communities also received power became the force that prevented total domination by the big utility companies. The GE-owned businesses would try to snap up the market in the wealthiest rural communities, building so-called snake lines—power cables that weaved from one wealthy pocket to another—while ignoring the less profitable areas in between. So rural electrical cooperatives were set up by the customers themselves, farms, and local townships, despite stiff opposition from utility companies that funded campaigns to warn farmers against them. The local utility franchises went through easement applications and found out where the rural electrical cooperatives were being planned, and in many cases they reacted by building "spite lines"—a few miles of cable to the wealthiest homes in an area they would have ignored but for the arrival of the co-ops.

Some places that were overlooked took matters into their own hands. In one of the poorer areas of rural Pennsylvania, 174 households formed the Morrison's Cove Light and Power Company, raising twenty thousand dollars to bring lines to their homes. Nye reports that the state public-service commission required the Penn Central Light and Power Company, the private power company with a franchise to this area, to sell electricity to the new company at wholesale rates. It did so, reluctantly of course, and the new venture was so successful that eighteen months later, in 1927, Penn Central bought out the 174 investors for fifty thousand dollars—a 150 percent return on their original investment.

By now several other minicooperatives had sprung up, building their own lines that stretched from Morrison's Cove to more outlying areas. Penn Central, however, did not want to assume responsibility for providing the service—not even if they were given the lines for free. So those customers were left without power.

In the late 1930s, the rural power co-ops, fostered under Roosevelt's New Deal, had a million customers. GE then turned its attention to these consumers. It marketed special economy packs of lights and other fittings that encouraged the farmers and farmworkers to switch from being independent producers of food and fuel (such as vegetable oil and wood) to dependent consumers of power.

Ultimately, electricity and its associated corporate mind-set toward efficiency ravaged the farming and rural populations. More than a third of Americans were still living in farming communities in the 1930s. That has fallen to one percent today. The utilities could hardly be accused of having sole responsibility for the change—the rural population had been decreasing for a hundred years—but they played a role. Over time electric farming implements vastly improved productivity, reducing the number of agricultural workers needed. Hence the remorseless logic of the electrified corporation was pushing agricultural prices down. The result, as Nye puts it, was that "farm communities that electrified, dispersed." To paraphrase, electrification increased productivity, so fewer people were needed per acre of production.

Today it's possible to reverse this trend, thanks in part to the improvements in energy technology. Millions of city dwellers would like to move to the countryside but do not because they fear they won't be able to continue to make a living. But they could, thanks to the Internet, mobile phones, local food production, and off-the-grid power.

Although I will not deal with them in what follows, it is worth mentioning that rural electric co-ops like Morrison's Cove could be a model for future microgrids, which offer the opportunity to separate ourselves from the big utility companies without then establishing a power station for each home. Microgrids are, as the name suggests, small self-sufficient grids. They run using local fuels—sun, wind, wood, or oil—but can be connected to the larger national grid. If they produce more power than the area needs, that power can be sold to the national grid or to the neighboring town. Microgrids are modular, so if one fails others will stay in service, reducing the chance of large outages. If the regional grid fails, each microgrid can continue to function.

I found no examples of microgrids in America today, and there is just one in the UK. In 2002, the Woking Borough Council enacted a climate-change strategy for its municipal buildings and replaced the national grid with a local one, using combined heat and power, fuel cells, renewable energy, and private wire systems. In 2006, carbon dioxide emissions had been reduced by eighty-one percent in the Council's chamber building, with a twenty-one percent reduction borough-wide. By 2009, the Council was operating more than twenty different combined heat-and-power (CHP) and photovoltaic projects, and was offering the service to private residents. Electricity consumption was down nearly fifty percent in areas covered by the microgrid.

THE EDISON ELECTRIC INSTITUTE

The devastating FTC investigation into the activities of NELA took years to complete. It was not until 1933 that the utility companies responded to demands that they clean up their act. On January 13 of that year, the *New York Times* reported that a new trade body had been formed, with a name that sounded as if it was a research foundation of some sort: the Edison Electric Institute. But propaganda remained important to the industry, and this was merely a new name for an organization that intended to employ the same old tricks. At the third annual meeting of the EEI in Atlantic City, the discussions focused on how to use the "electric kitchen" to increase power consumption. "Utilities must concentrate on inducing their consumers to use more stoves, refrigerators, and other heavy-current appliances," said the head of one utility company. The president of General Electric's appliance division delivered a lecture on selling "complete kitchens" instead of individual appliances, suggesting that this would increase sales of electricity by up to eight hundred percent, according to a June 1935 issue of the *New York Times.* (The seeds of the mighty GE Finance were sown in layaway plans for refrigerators.)

Nearly two decades later, in June 1952, President Harry S. Truman attacked the nation's power and light industry for their "vicious" propaganda opposing municipal power projects. The *New York Times* devoted a column on its front page to the EEI's denials of his charge that they were spending millions of dollars on their campaign. One utility boss called it "pure hokum," while another said that they were "defending the freedom of all industry." A third said that "the federal government has as its end the absolute monopoly of electrical power."

This wasn't some paranoid conspiracy theorist they were denouncing. This was the President of the United States, the democratically elected leader. At the time the electrical-power industry had annual sales of twenty-three billion dollars. The message they were sending out was as emphatic as it was shocking: "Don't mess with us, little man."

So things went on as they had. On June 27, 1977, the *Los Angeles Times* reported that the EEI was distributing "educational" materials in schools, except instead of opposing public power, they were now opposing environmental activists.

In 1990 the *Washington Post* reported that Senator J. Bennett Johnston, coauthor of the Energy Policy Act of 1992, had benefited from an EEI fund-raiser, receiving the "biggest single contribution from an energy PAC." Out of a total of $235,000 Johnston received from the energy industry that year (the biggest contribution to any senator from a specific industry sector), thirty-five thousand came from EEI. Senator Johnston, incidentally, was the longtime chairman of the Senate Appropriations Subcommittee on Energy and Water Development at the time, and it appears he first began work on the 1992 legislation just shortly after those donations were made.

In December 2000, the year the EEI spent, according to the *New York Times*, twelve million dollars on lobbying, President-elect George W. Bush offered Johnston the post of Energy Secretary. Johnston, by then no longer a senator, had no time to reply before Senator Harry Reid (D-NV, now the Senate majority leader) announced he would block Johnston's confirmation. "If [Bush] is appointing Bennett Johnston, we should all be afraid," Reid told reporters. This was in recognition of Johnston's long years of service to big energy, especially his role as author of the 1987 "screw Nevada" bill, which designated Yucca Mountain as America's site for long-term nuclear-waste storage. "I told [Johnston], 'I'm going to do everything I can to prevent you from getting this job.'" Two days later, sixty-nine-year-old Johnston announced he would not be pursuing the opportunity. "I decided it would be unfair to ask my dear wife, Mary, who spent many years being a political widow, to be asked once again to put aside her wishes for my political career. She would've said yes, had I insisted."

Today, fifty-seven years after President Truman's remarks

about the "vicious" electricity industry prompted uniform deri-
sion, the EEI has another man in its sights. Steven Chu is a
dedicated public servant who moved from the upper echelons
of academia to the post of Energy Secretary in Obama's cabinet.
The question is: Does the Nobel Prize–winning physicist have
what it takes to stand up to the energy lobby? Or is he a deer in
its headlights?

As I sat talking to Mike Riddell about Greenfield Ranch, Chu
was a hundred miles away in San Francisco, giving a speech
to the EEI to inform them of the billions they would shortly be
receiving—a big fat chunk of the stimulus funds, at least $3.4
billion, was going directly to the utility companies to pay for
the smart grid. It wasn't going to benefit Greenfield Ranch, because they are not on the grid, but their tax dollars would still
contribute.

And why should American tax dollars pay for the upgrading
of the grid at all, when that money could be devoted to, say, the
widespread and urgent installation of solar panels, or energy-
efficiency measures in every building? And where is the debate
about the smart grid? Are we just going to believe what GE and
the EEI tell us? Who can actually prove that the smart grid is
going to be all that smart, or that it is even going to work? And
who has thought through the implications? Privacy will be com-
promised when an IT worker at Florida Power and Light, for example, can see on a screen every time Mrs. Tuttle of Miami turns
on a light. One thing is for sure: The EEI and its members are
right behind it. That ought to tell us something. Based on their
track record, the smart grid is not in the country's best interest,
nor are they concerned with Secretary Chu's carbon-reduction
targets when they enthuse about rolling out the smart grid. They
are concerned with market dominance and profits. Incidentally,
because the new "smart" devices will communicate directly with
the utility-company computers, the need for meter readers and
billing-related call centers will come to an end, saving the utility
companies billions of dollars per year. How much of that will be
passed back in lower prices?

Imagine for a moment that the smart grid does work, that in the future the entire U.S. grid will consist of power switching this way and that as sensors convey usage information to central computers, the price varying depending on demand. Who is going to decide who will get that last extra unit of energy on a sweltering day when everyone is using the air-conditioning? Will it be the steel mill in Pittsburgh? Or the little old lady short of breath in the heart of Georgia? It will be decided by a pricing mechanism of some sort, and rather like airline tickets, electricity will be relatively cheap when nobody wants it, and jaw-droppingly expensive when demand is at its peak. For the big corporations with their managerial approach, this is perfect. What about everyone else?

Brigadier General Tripp neatly illustrated the parallel between the push for today's smart grid and that for the Super Power system of 1923 when he said in the *New York Times*, "a few years ago such a demand would have been hardly possible, but the economic troubles experienced by everyone during the past few years clearly demonstrate that some effective step must be taken if our civilization is to progress or even maintain its present level."

According to the Brattle Group, a $1.5 trillion investment will be required between 2010 and 2030 to pay for the new electricity infrastructure. Might there possibly be another way?

CENTRAL WATER AND CONFLICT

In March 2008, the Associated Press uncovered a scandal over pharmaceuticals in the nation's drinking water. In the course of a five-month inquiry, the AP discovered drugs in the drinking water of twenty-four major metropolitan areas, from Southern California to Northern New Jersey, from Detroit to Louisville, Kentucky. A vast array of pharmaceuticals, including antibiotics, anticonvulsants, mood stabilizers, and sex hormones, were found in the drinking water supplies of "at least 41 million Americans." In truth the figure is probably far higher, but this is all the AP was able to prove.

It is inconceivable that the world's leading drug companies were unaware of the extent of the problem, which is caused because certain prescription drugs pass through the bodies of patients and then through sewage-treatment plants unadulterated, and these particular drugs are not filtered out by the water companies.

True, the concentrations of these pharmaceuticals are tiny, measured in quantities of parts per billion or trillion—far below the levels of a medical dose. Thus the water companies insist that their water is safe. Yet critics contend that the presence of so many prescription drugs—and over-the-counter medicines such as acetaminophen and ibuprofen—in so much of our drinking water is likely to have long-term consequences on human health.

So how did this state of affairs come about? Why are these drugs routinely tolerated in the nation's drinking water?

Many of the same conflicts and principles that drove the expansion of the electricity business also drove the water-supply industry in the early twentieth century. The push for size obscured arguments about the public interest; scale was everything. Businessmen and bureaucrats agreed on this assessment. Population growth, especially in the Western states, was only part of the reason. Industrial processes needed more water, and the water industry itself preferred big projects.

But there is one crucial difference between water and electricity: Water is essential for life; power, while highly desirable and life-enhancing, is non-essential.

The initial demand for pure water delivered under pressure came from firefighters and from the health industry, especially as the germ theory of disease spread from the UK to America. As cities grew they needed more water, so battles began between those who wanted to bring it to the cities and those (mainly farmers and other property owners with water rights) who wanted to leave it where it was.

The pattern was established. Tension between municipal authorities and private water companies led, in many cases, to the municipalization of the water companies. Once they were brought under government control, they became tools of the politicians, and were used to line individual pockets, to promote population policy, and, in particular, to promote the growth of metropolitan areas. The political parties preferred to focus on urban initiatives because it was easier to bring out the vote in densely populated cities.

The story of how New York City first dealt with its long-term water-supply issue is instructive. In New York, the annual waterborne-disease epidemics were becoming more intense each year, and in 1798, when two thousand of its sixty thousand inhabitants died of yellow fever, the City decided to act.

The City of New York determined that it could pipe water into Manhattan from Brooklyn, and established a public company to do so. Unfortunately, the City was diverted from its intentions by a man named Aaron Burr, who went to great lengths to recruit prominent citizens to the board of his private water company, by appealing to their greed. He promised that the City would have a large stake in the company, a shareholding that was quickly and quietly "watered down."

He eventually succeeded in winning widespread support for the Manhattan Company, and as he shepherded its legislation (titled "An Act for Supplying the City of New York with Pure and Wholesome Water") through the state assembly, Burr slipped an extra clause deep in the heart of the legislation, where few noticed it: "And be it further enacted," the clause read, "that it shall and may be lawful for the said company to employ all such surplus capital as may belong or accrue to the said company in the purchase of public or other stock, or in any other moneyed transactions not inconsistent with the constitution and laws of this state or of the United States, for the sole benefit of the said Company." The bill was passed into law in 1801, and only then did it become apparent that Burr had taken the high-minded intention of ensuring New Yorkers a decent water supply and turned it into a bank that he controlled. This bank became Chase Manhattan Bank in 1955, and J.P. Morgan Chase in 2000. Meanwhile, the City of New York was condemned to another thirty years of disease, foul wells, and unreliable supplies. Those in charge of the water supply continued to ignore their duty to place the provision of their life-giving product ahead of all other priorities in the way they did business.

Water is a very old technology compared to electricity—the first water pipes were used in Crete around 1500 B.C. This means there's been no real technology race as there was with electricity in the early twentieth century, though there were certainly technology advances, particularly improvements in pumping, which led to modern centrifugal pumps displacing all others.

So the battles in the United States have largely been between the privately owned water companies and local governments. After attempting to regulate them, the government has often been forced to take the companies into public ownership (at a handsome profit to the investors, who were, lest we forget, only supplying us with what was ours to start with).

The water industry matured well head of the power industry and, despite considerable consolidation, has remained in local hands. In 1880 there were six hundred water companies in the United States. By 1900 there were thirty-three hundred, and around half were publicly owned. And by 1945 there were more than fifteen thousand companies, each supplying water to two hundred households or more, showing how local water companies had entered almost every community in America.

Nineteenth-century water development focused on the eastern half of the United States, while twentieth-century water development tended to focus on the West. Once most eastern cities established a water-supply system, it usually became an uncontested local-government entity, most of which still exist today. Meanwhile, the West was so underpopulated before the twentieth century that water scarcity wasn't an issue. Once the region began to develop large cities and consequently needed water, however, financial scandal and human tragedy quickly developed. The most notorious story is of the Owens River corruption scandal, in Los Angeles, an incident that left five hundred dead and shattered thousands of lives. It was symptomatic of the way that water projects were used to line businessmen's pockets right under the noses of elected politicians, some of whom must have been involved.

William Mulholland, who began his lengthy engineering career as a ditch cleaner, was head of the Los Angeles Department of Water and Power, a position he would occupy until 1928. As water shortages loomed for fast-growing Los Angeles, Mulholland identified the Owens River (more than two hundred miles away) as a promising water source. Residents of Owens Valley had plans for "their" water. Those who raised crops and ranched were expecting to get rich once the irrigation megaproject overbid their preexisting irrigation schemes. Mulholland realized that to acquire the Owens River for Los Angeles, he would have to put an end to the current irrigation uses, and he proved successful. He presented the Owens River project to politicians as a matter of life and death for Los Angeles. In reality, however, much of the water would be diverted to the nearby San Fernando Valley, where a private syndicate, personal friends of Mulholland, had been buying up land. This theme is explored in the movie *Chinatown*.

In 1913, the Los Angeles Aqueduct was completed, and as campaigners had predicted, most of the water was not needed in Los Angeles. The San Fernando Valley received the water while, according to a PBS report, Mulholland connived to "drain the farms of the Owens Valley to make the lands owned by his financial backers bloom." Protests included dynamite attacks on the L.A. Aqueduct and seizure of an aqueduct gate in 1924.

The City of Los Angeles reacted by creating a series of reservoirs to regulate the flow of water, which meant the construction of the Mulholland and St. Francis dams, completed in 1924 and 1926, respectively. Less than two years after it was built, the St. Francis Dam collapsed, releasing a fifteen-billion-gallon flood that was one of the greatest civil disasters in American history. The water began as a seventy-five-foot-high wave and scoured a path to the sea two miles wide and seventy miles long. In its wake much of Ventura County was left under yards of muck. The final death toll was nearly five hundred; weeks later, bodies continued to wash up on beaches as far away as San Diego.

In the early years of water supply in the West, dams were an endless source of intrigue and corruption. In 1890, the year Yosemite National Park was created, the mayor of San Francisco proposed a reservoir in the Hetch Hetchy Valley. Applications to the U.S. Interior Department were repeatedly denied over the ensuing two decades. But in 1913, San Francisco finally convinced Congress to allow the city to create the reservoir, and the O'Shaughnessy Dam was completed in 1923. To this day, San Francisco sells the water and electricity generated at Hetch Hetchy to Pacific Gas and Electric Company (PG&E), which then sells it to consumers at a significant markup, despite the fact that this sort of sale was arguably prohibited by the spirit, if not also the letter, of the initial congressional legislation that authorized the flooding of the valley.

In most cases, the battles for control of water were between powerless locals, who regarded the water as inherently their own and vehemently opposed its diversion, and big-city politicians; or, in cases in which the water source crosses borders, between states, with one believing it was getting screwed for the benefit of another state. The scale of the projects and the fact that they often crossed jurisdictional lines meant that they were overseen by the government, on some level, from the beginning.

City governments were most directly affected by fire hydrant rental rates, and disagreement over hydrant rentals was the major source of friction between cities and private companies. The problem was usually the conflicting goals of short-run profit maximization on the part of the water company and of adequate supply for household consumption and fire protection on the part of the municipality. Typically, the private companies concentrated on the most profitable areas of a city, ignoring its outlying districts and poorer sections.

For a long time the health-related arguments for centralized, carefully monitored water have prevailed. But the belief that water is healthier when it is centralized has now reversed, and in many cases the water is now healthier when it is not centralized. It still needs to be treated and filtered, and that can now be done locally. The point of collection can be the same as the point of consumption, and that means greater predictability and control for the end user. In the same way that energy from a solar panel on the roof will not diminish traveling down the wire, water sourced on site does not go through a transmission system and so cannot be contaminated.

As I researched this chapter my interest in the off-grid life as a solution turned to anger at the deceptions that have been practiced on the American people for the past century. A great deal of deceit was clearly employed to persuade American families to increase their use of electricity, and the ideal lifestyle put forward as part of the marketing has now moved from the advertisers' fantasy and become the conventional mode of living. But we are beginning to realize we do not need many of these things—that they do not make our lives better, do not make us happier.

One crucial aspect of the grid has changed as a result of new technology: the factors that made the grid necessary in the last century do not apply in this century. New technology and low-energy appliances mean that we can generate our own power safely and cheaply, at the community or household level. The same applies to gathering water and dealing with sewage. But you do not need to believe that the power grid (and to a lesser extent the water grid) were created to satisfy corporations rather than customers to summon motivation. The notion of going off the grid is valid with or without this context. Its real justifications are the benefits you may find as an individual or family or community.

3

My Other Place Is on the Grid

"One generation abandons the enterprises of another like stranded vessels."

Henry David Thoreau, *Walden*

Later chapters describe off-gridders who have little or nothing beyond their homes and a few possessions, but this chapter is about off-the-grid living for middle- and upper-class pleasure. Numbers for off-grid second homes are hard to come by. I estimate that half of off-grid houses are used as part-time or vacation residences, either by tenants or by the owners themselves. Sometimes the residents are former full-timers who grew old, or whose circumstances changed because of work or family issues. Other times—and this describes my situation—they are downshifting city dwellers who want a refuge in a tranquil spot but do not want to wait until they can afford their dream getaway.

The survivalists use the term *bugout location* to indicate the place you plan to flee to when society collapses. You also need a bugout vehicle (such as a motorbike) to get you there and a bugout bag full of goodies for the journey, including water, bandages, dried food, and guns. I wouldn't personally want to go to that extent. It smacks of self-imprisonment rather than personal security, but I sure would like a bugout location of my own.

The history lesson, however, is not quite over. I must tell the story of a man whose off-the-grid second home is a small part of recent off-the-grid history.

In her final e-mail, Sequoia told me how she had powered her home in the early days. "I started by installing a plug in the front of my vehicle," she wrote. "I could plug it into a line on my porch to run a few lights." That was the way most off-gridders managed things in the mid-seventies.

Dave Katz founded a business empire on the same simple idea. AEE Solar now has two hundred million dollars in sales per year, and is the largest solar wholesaler in America. The company is based in Redway, California, which is where Dave built what is now his second home. It was originally his only home, when he joined the first wave of back-to-the-land settlers and hung with the pot growers. "[Pot growing] was just starting up then," he told me.

Dave, a laid-back, humorous guy, who is still president of the company he founded, came west from New York, where he'd worked for the Department of Defense. His father had been a Jewish sweatshop tailor, and, he says, the entrepreneurial spirit had been passed on. In keeping with the fashions of the time, Dave stopped cutting his hair in 1969 and has kept a beard and long locks ever since. Because of the pot he seems more like a hippie than the shrewd businessman he clearly is—but first you have to get to know him. He showed me his old Department of Defense ID card, "for civilians who accompany the armed forces," with a photo of the archetypal hairy-faced rebel. "How I got my job," he told me in a tough East Coast accent that hadn't softened any in thirty-five years, "was by accident."

Dave was an electrical engineer in electronic warfare for the U.S. Navy in 1973, and he intercepted a call from the DoD that had been meant for someone else. "Would I take a job in one week in California? The guy, my boss, needed three more people in his department or it was gonna get closed down. So he got three degenerates—I mean, there's not a lot of people who would take a job without knowing what it was," Dave cackled. "But the money was good. It was back in the day of the five-hundred-dollar hammer, just after Vietnam. No wonder we lost that one." The job consisted of spending the DoD's money—lots of it. Dave went around the world for the next three years with a minimum budget he had to blow each month.

Earlier I had met Dave's much younger wife, Annie, at Intersolar, the annual jamboree of the solar industry in San Diego. Governor Arnold Schwarzenegger had just delivered a toe-curling speech, praising this relatively new industry as an important addition to the list of taxpaying Californian enterprises. "I want a solar Hummer," he growled, to huge applause.

By the time I caught up with Dave, it was back at his main home—the one on the grid—in Arcata, a classic California small town, perched on the northeast edge of Humboldt Bay, just near enough to the ocean to have a surf shop.

Prior to my arrival, he and Annie had offered to take me to a Halloween party in the Emerald Triangle, the pot-growing capital of America. It was harvest time and I was driving up Highway 101 from Ukiah. At the turnoff for Holmes, I passed a road sign sponsored by NORML (the National Organization for the Reform of Marijuana Laws). At Eureka I stopped at a thrift store in hopes of buying a Halloween costume. There was nothing suitable, but I met two guys reeking of pot who were buying work boots. They both had very short crew cuts and checkered work shirts, and they slurred their words as they mumbled their request to the counter clerk. I asked them whether just anybody could work on the harvest. "Go to Laytonville, man" one of them wheezed, as though he was still drawing on a joint. "Just stand out on the street, and make like this." He made a scissors gesture with his fingers, hand down by his side. "That's the sign, man," he said with a throaty snigger. Back in the car and a few hundred yards down the road I realized I could have gone to the party as a pot grower; I just needed a checkered shirt and some pot. Too late.

Dave and Annie live in a big, comfortable house on a tree-lined street. Dave answered the door wearing a bear costume, or maybe it was a rabbit costume. The white, fluffy tail was a bit indeterminate. There was another guy there, dressed as Robin Hood. Annie lent me a cape and some eyeliner, which was all my costume amounted to.

It was a long drive out to the party, so Dave told me his life story. In 1980, he still had his little VW-parts business on the side, operating out of a grocery store. He had started it from his electronic-warfare office back East, and diversified into off-the-grid supplies after he came West. He decided to quit his job.

"Land was four hundred dollars an acre," Dave told me as Annie drove, "so it was an opportunity to quit and build a house, outside Redway, in the hills—Briceland, actually. People were just starting to grow pot—they all had these hand-built houses in the hills. Dark, with kerosene lamps. And we would sit around and smoke pot. We were doing things like running lights and stereos off the car battery. Then I thought, Why don't I put two batteries in the car? Then I can always have one battery charged at home when I need it, even if the car isn't there. I designed a little setup and you pushed the switch and disconnected the car battery and charged the extra battery. Then the neighbors wanted it and I was doing it for people."

It was then that Dave got really lucky; he was the right guy in the right place at the right time—what Malcolm Gladwell would call an "outlier." Dave liked to go to the consumer-electronics show in Las Vegas. This same year, 1980, he spotted something called a solar panel. It was an ARCO 33-watt panel, sitting in a booth full of solar toys. "I asked him about it," said Dave, "and he said, 'Oh, nobody wants those.' I bought a hundred of them and sold them in a couple of weeks, and people would pay cash." The word went out among the back-to-the-landers, and Dave was besieged. "I bought a bunch more and sold them in one week."

When he rang ARCO for more supplies, they were intrigued and insisted on sending a salesman "to find out what was going on in this little grocery store." The guy from ARCO sat there for days as scores of pot growers passed through, paying cash for the panels. What Dave and the salesman were witnessing was the birth of the solar industry in order to serve the pot growers of the Emerald Triangle.

Up until then it had been a real hassle to keep all those batteries charged up, and it was expensive on gas for the generator. Solar panels transformed the economics of pot growing. Freed from the need to buy gas, the growers not only saved money, they made fewer risky journeys into town during the harvest season. "Most of the people who buy solar panels, and inverters and batteries use them to cool greenhouses," Dave explained. "A lot of the pot farms are very small—mom-and-pop in a ten-by-ten [greenhouse] because it's legal to do that." It is now; it wasn't then. "I sold [solar panels] only, no installations," Dave was careful to stress to me. If he went up into the hills, you could be sure it was just to *smoke* pot, not to help grow it.

"There were so many people who lived on the land who wanted electricity," he said. He had a guaranteed market. "Everybody else was happy with playing guitars and [using] candles. I probably ruined all that. Pot growers definitely helped the solar-panel industry. If you look at the major distributors—SunWize, Solar Depot, and AEE, all between Petaluma and Redway—that was where the big start was. All the companies that sold to the pot growers are still there." This doesn't mean that there would be no solar industry without the pot growers; it just means that it might have become a very different industry.

Dave's business masterstroke came in 2002, when his revenue was still only a few million a year. He learned that the big utility companies paid only a fraction of the three percent or more that other businesses were charged on credit-card transactions. "The card companies were always calling me, looking for my business. I said, 'Look, we're a utility; we provide power to all these houses in the hills.' The guy said he'd ask his boss, and he came back and he said, 'Yeah, OK.'" With wafer-thin margins on wholesale items such as solar panels, adding an extra couple of percentage points to the bottom line meant Dave's profits almost doubled overnight.

In talking to Dave, I had been talking to a utility-company boss. I could hardly accuse him of selling out; he's proudly been a card-carrying capitalist from the start. I was pleased he was beating them at their own game. No wonder he had moved back onto the grid.

"The smart grid is years away," he said as we parted, "but it's the utilities controlling the way we use power. It's like, We'll give you a better rate, but we can turn you off when we want."

FOR THE MAN WHO HAS EVERYTHING

I never managed to visit Dave in his off-the-grid home. Still, I did get to another off-the-grid second home, owned by a multi-millionaire, Bill Bieber, who runs a huge metal company. Bill was not there at the time, and we never met in person; we only spoke on the phone. Dealing with these multimillionaires is like herding cats.

Bill was running his family-owned Minnesota metal company when he first fell for Colorado. He bought a ranch seventy miles from Aspen, and although he loved the remoteness, he wanted somewhere even more remote. So in 1990 he acquired a bigger ranch, near Creede, and moved his summer retreat to the new property.

Of all the places in the United States to go off the grid, Colorado is near the top of my list. I am hardly the first to say that the mountains soar, that they hang like castles in the air and delight the eye. They are both stunning and grandiose. Land is not cheap, but you can't deny that you get what you pay for.

The front door of Bill's Creede home is four miles from the nearest road, and six from the nearest neighbor. Had I not been guided in by a local, I would have turned back several times, convinced that the Forest Service's work road was going nowhere. I met the caretaker, Caleb, and he showed me around the two outsize homes made from outsize logs.

Bill is easing off the business reins a little now, and he and his second wife, a Minnesota Supreme Court justice, plan to spend three months a year on the high-mountain ranch, 12,500 feet above sea level.

"I've been working on my business all my life long," said Bill, age sixty-seven. Now his eldest daughter is CEO, and he is chairman of a group with $160 million in annual revenue. Among other things, his company makes aluminum castings for jet engines and medical products. One of its largest customers is Harley-Davidson.

"[Colorado] is a simpler way of life," he told me. "A chance for our family to connect and focus on the things I always thought were important, to be with nature and be away from the hustle and bustle of the city and urban life, which I've never really cared for. It refreshes me, cleanses my soul."

There is no hardship involved in Bill Bieber's lifestyle. In addition to erecting two houses and a number of workshops and garages, he built a state-of-the-art hydroelectric plant to power the ranch as soon as he moved in. "Our hydro system is extremely dependable. The only problem we really had was lightning strikes on the inverters." Inverters are boxes that take the renewable energy and turn it into 110 volts. In addition, Bill rejoiced, he has "a wonderful spring, good water pressure, a wood-burning stove, a propane heater, refrigerator, lights . . . the only thing we don't have is a hair dryer and a TV."

Not that he needs them. It's spiritual rather than material comfort that Bill takes from the place. "There is a spiritual aspect to being in [that] environment. I feel closer to a supreme being when I'm there. It's easier to cultivate your soul being surrounded by the majesty, the size, the scope; it kind of overwhelms you. I feel part of something much bigger."

It took Bill years to find the ideal property and nothing was left to chance. The process began when he "sat down and profiled" what he thought was the perfect ranch. "It had to do with a live creek, trout fishing, a lake. It had to be in the heavy timber of dark spruce, be a wildlife sanctuary, and be remote." Although remoteness was a key factor, the property also had to be near an airport. "I had an airplane at that point," said Bill, modestly omitting the fact that he had a local airline company and a small airport to go with it.

Bill made a deal for the land in which the sellers would obtain permits for a bridge—which he built at a cost of thirty thousand dollars—and a road. "The lady I bought [it] from was the matriarch of the valley. She had a lot of political connections," he said, explaining how he was able to sort out the permits. It cost Bill $130,000 to lay gravel on the Forest Service's track.

Bill's is one of the few top-tier off-the-grid homes I visited. Most of the wealthy off-gridders I contacted were unwilling to cooperate with my research, although they seem perfectly happy to pander to media coverage when they are trying to promote something. John Doerr, for example, is co-owner of one of the mightiest Silicon Valley venture-capital companies, Kleiner Perkins Caufield and Byers. He was plastered all over the media in February 2010 when he fronted the launch of the Bloom Box, a fridge-sized fuel cell in which he had invested and which he touted as the future of off-grid energy. The fuel cell industry agreed that although the new device was impressive, the only truly remarkable thing about it was the level of hype that surrounded the launch. I happened upon his two-thousand-acre California ranch, near Half Moon Bay, while visiting one of his neighbors. Doerr, whose interests, according to his Web site, include "the next big thing," refused to discuss his second home, other than to deny local gossip that it was built in preparation for the coming social collapse. "Please respect my privacy" was his only other comment, via e-mail, when I asked why he had bought his off-the-grid estate.

NO NAME KEY

Sadly, an important part of the off-the-grid story is the opposition to it. This is often driven by considerations of property values and how to protect them, masquerading as concern for the environment. Wealthier homeowners consistently oppose off-grid homes or communities nearby because they think these might reduce their wealth. Whether they are trying to prevent new properties springing up off the grid, or force existing off-grid arrangements to be abandoned, the results are the same. Sometimes entire off-grid communities are dominated by second-home owners, as is the case on the island of No Name Key, in Florida. The Keys are the southernmost point in the United States, ending only eighty miles from Cuba, the proximity of which I was reminded of most forcefully by one of the part-time residents, Bob Reynolds, an insurance broker from Miami. Bob, a relative newcomer, had inserted himself firmly into the center of the torrid conflict I encountered there.

An intense, bitter, and personal battle is being fought between those who want to keep No Name off the grid and those who want to bring in municipal power. The island, with its forty-three homes, was once a model off-grid community. By the time I breezed into the Keys in 2009, its residents felt themselves under siege from the media and rent asunder by vicious factional politics. The split has set neighbor against neighbor, and caused old friends to ignore each other.

My challenge was to meet as many members of the warring factions as I could and somehow divine the rights and wrongs of the situation. Local papers had been covering the struggle for years, and now the big-city boys were becoming interested. The Associated Press had recently sent the temperature soaring with a half-amusing, half-serious piece about the battle. The appearance of yet another writer (me) was met with suspicion by most, and with warmth by a few of the residents. All of them, from both sides of the argument, told me the man I should talk to is Bob Reynolds.

I drove to No Name Key in the company of Solar George, a solar-panel salesman from neighboring Big Pine Key who was working his way through a messy divorce at the time. He had offered to make a few introductions for me one sunny afternoon. As we crossed the long bridge from Big Pine to No Name (a bridge allegedly built at the behest of Bebe Rebozo, Richard Nixon's bagman, who had been a major property owner in the area), we encountered a shaven-headed figure riding imperiously toward us on a Segway. Perhaps it was the angle at which the machine forces the rider to stand on its platform gripping the handlebars, or perhaps it was the personality of this particular rider, but it appeared as though he'd planted himself on the device as if he was addressing a crowd.

The man is Frank Atwell, a tall, heavyset fellow well past retirement age. He was on his way to the local grocery, a journey of some twelve miles that would take about thirty minutes on the vehicle. His Segway, he told me, is solar powered; it's the only kind of power he has at home. He would have to recharge at the grocery store for the return journey. We agreed I would visit his house the next day to talk about the electrification battle. "You should try to speak with Bob Reynolds," he added as he sped off.

Until Reynolds had appeared, the minority who wanted to stay off the grid were easily winning the fight, largely because of the immense cost and organizational effort required to change things. Once the insurance broker had bought his $1.3 million home, the most expensive property in the history of the island, he told his new neighbors, the balance of power had suddenly and irreversibly shifted.

Solar George and I drove out to Bahia Shores Road to check out the Reynolds mansion. It's a beautiful home, a gleaming white box with 180-degree views across the bay, split-level living and dining areas, and a place to moor the yacht at the bottom of the yard. It's located at the end of the most expensive street on the island (although there are only six streets). Bob had plunked down his money at the height of the housing boom, a sign that, although he thinks himself a rather shrewd businessman, perhaps he had in fact been a little naive.

Having viewed Bob's home from the outside, I was ready to meet the owner himself. He runs the insurance brokerage, which he inherited from his father, from just outside of Miami, and it was there that he chose to invite me. I drove straight up from No Name Key.

Retirees who move to the Keys are buying into the proximity to the water and the international airport; the land itself is flat and featureless, a series of low-lying islands connected by spectacular bridges. The vegetation is less luxuriant than I expected given the year-round warmth, which turns humid and sultry in the summer months. A 1903 *New York Times* article about the Keys reveals that "the islands are changing constantly, and new ones are appearing until it is difficult to maintain accurate charts." Who can say whether in a decade or two global warming will evaporate so much water that the Keys stretch all the way to Cuba? Or perhaps the reverse will happen and the bitter battle over the grid will be rendered obsolete by rising sea levels.

What puzzled me during my drive to Bob's office was this: he (and the other twenty-five or so homeowners now fighting for municipal power, water, and sewage) knew from the start that No Name is not on the grid. It's up to each of the households on No Name to generate its own power, pipe its own water, and deal with its own waste, usually in the form of a septic tank buried deep in the yard.

Only after he had bought the land was a new federal waste-water code imposed, one that was quickly picked up by pro-gridders as grounds for a renewed fight. This is the point at which Bob joined in. "The charm of this island has nothing to do with the lack of power, water, or central sewer," he told a local paper. "We came here in spite of these things. The charm is the lack of people and the nature." Now, why come to a place that is unique mainly because of its isolation; a place whose charm lies in the inky blackness of its night skies; whose minimalist approach to all forms of modern convenience including heating, cooling, and electric appliances has kept the population explosion at bay; whose carbon footprint could hardly be any lower—why come to a place like that and then systematically set about making it just like every other subdivision in America?

Others shared my doubts. Steve Estes, owner and editor of the local paper, the *News-Barometer*, is fairly sure the answer has to do with economics. "Some of [the pro-grid faction] moved here in the past two years," he told me. "My guess would be this whole thing is driven by property values. No Name Key properties sold, on average during the housing boom, pretty much for what Big Pine sold for. But those folk are sitting on big losses now."

Whatever the truth of the matter, there is no doubt that the battle for electrification has taken a surprising twist. The new federal mandate states that by 2010 Keys wastewater has to conform to stringent new standards preventing its effluent from leeching into the surrounding coastal waters. So the argument about electrification has morphed into an argument about sewers, or alternatively, the argument about power is now being fought through the argument about sewage. The forty-three families, their lawyers, engineering consultants, and all the politicians of Monroe County are now locked in an obscure technical discussion over whether or not the large, expensive central sewer system Bob Reynolds is demanding is really necessary to deal with the effluent from these forty-three homes, most of which are occupied only part-time.

The Morris and Reynolds Web site proudly states that Bob is the third Reynolds to run the one hundred percent family-owned company. The site pays tribute to Bob's grandfather, founder of the family firm and, for forty years, a senior officer with the utility company Florida Power and Light. Is it here, in his family's past, that I have found the root of Bob's obsession with electricity?

I parked my rental car on the South Dixie Highway outside the Morris and Reynolds Insurance building, situated next to Party City, a chain retailer of party paraphernalia, the window stacked with balloons and Halloween costumes. There was no partying at Bob's office. His is an unflashy low-rise building, tidy and well organized, exactly what clients love to see: evidence that their fees are not being wasted. A peek through the tinted glass windows reveals that all the doors are brown and all the walls are white, unless they have bookshelves on them, which are wood, like the doors. There is a framed letter from a client every fifteen feet, and a photographer with a zoom lens would be able to confirm that each praises the company's dedication to client service. The staff are shoehorned into cubicles, and the atmosphere is stilted and over-formal.

Conceivably it is indicative of the boss's tendency toward hyperbole that the Web site for this fifty-person company calls it "one of the most dominant and dynamic insurance organizations in America." Elsewhere on the Web, a cursory search reveals only one reference to Bob in an insurance capacity (as opposed to Bob in his aggrieved No Name Key–resident capacity). In a speech at a 2006 insurance convention he revealed fears that his customers think he is "ripping them off."

The Web site inaccurately reports that the family has been in insurance since 1910. In fact, Bob's grandfather E. H. Reynolds joined Florida Power and Light in 1910, and held a series of positions from treasurer to risk assessor. In 1950 he founded the insurance company that he eventually passed on to Bob's father. While Grandfather Reynolds was supposedly doing such fine work for the people of Miami, the Florida Power and Light Company in actuality had as bitter and rancorous a relationship with its customer base as any I found in my research.

FPL was created in 1925 by the Electric Bond and Share Company (which, as previously mentioned, was part of GE) to sell power to 115,000 citizens at a whopping twelve cents per kilowatt hour (compared with a relatively modest 3.2 cents in 1950). FPL also owned Miami's water system and operated the municipally owned streetcars and buses with a city guarantee against operating deficits. The Depression caused a rethink of the relationship, and in 1932 city elders demanded to know why Miami citizens were paying "about three times the [electric] rate" that other U.S. cities paid. Their question unanswered, the following year the city cut electricity rates by one-third, and suspended payments to FPL for streetlights and hydrants. The war was on. The utility stopped paying its taxes and went to court to reverse the rate cut. The city appealed, and won in 1935.

FPL appealed and the case continued for more than two years. Then the FPL president, Bryan C. Hanks, stunned the public with a boldfaced three-column ad in local newspapers titled "I Won't Pay a Bribe." In it he alleged that an unnamed Miami city staffer had informed him that a settlement "would only be effective on the secret payment of $250,000," to be divided among certain city figures. A grand-jury probe ended with indictments of the city's rate consultant, Thomas E. Grady, the mayor, and two city commissioners on bribery and conspiracy charges. On November 18, 1938, a jury took exactly eight minutes to acquit the defendants, who immediately announced they would sue FPL for $2.5 million in libel damages. There is no record of the suit.

Seventy years later, FPL is still at it, with plans to build huge power lines (more than three hundred towers, according to protesters) in the Everglades National Park.

It was with all this in mind that I entered the portal of Morris and Reynolds. I had taken a character reference from another local reporter, who asked not be named. "He's a pretty cagey guy, if you notice. Wealthy, drives a nice Porsche. We hear that quite a bit he accuses people of lying to him. He's very confrontational."

Bob appeared. No expensive designer clothes for him; he wore a plain blue shirt, open at the neck; and a blue V-necked sweater with the company logo on the breast pocket. His thinning ginger hair had been arranged carefully across his head. Only the heavy bags under his eyes and a tightly wound air of stress give away the truth behind the veneer of order and frugality.

Unfortunately I am not allowed to report the exact contents of our conversation because Bob wrote a letter asking that I not use his interview in this book. Like many of the letters sent to those who have the temerity to disagree with him, it was full of bitter personal vituperation and allegations of un-Americanism. It's here that the comparison with Cuba comes in.

As it happens, there is so much material already on the record that Bob's basic position can be reconstructed from public sources. What Bob would want you to remember at all times is that he "loves and cherishes" No Name Key, that in campaigning for electricity to be brought to the island, he is campaigning not for himself but for his children, so they can enjoy the unique environment.

Steve Estes sees it differently. "His line all along is, 'I don't make bad investments. I am going to make sure it's worth what I paid for it.' He said that to several folks," Steve told me. "The whole fight is economically driven."

Nevertheless, the pro-grid faction insist that the battle is one hundred percent about sewage, and in particular their selfless campaign to prevent any pollution from their toilets reaching out into the wider world. The option of a composting toilet, which does not require any electricity, however, has been eloquently rejected. Bob Reynolds and his wife had experienced a violently negative reaction a year earlier, when they viewed the workings of the only composting toilet on the island. Bob wrote the following e-mail to one of the county commissioners:

Last Friday, I visited the one person on No Name that has a composting toilet and it nearly made me *sick* (and it did make my wife cry).

It's basically an *outhouse* system, George, where you put mulch into the toilet chute every time you use it plus the fact it's [sic] receptacle box basically must be located right under the toilet. The box was filled with roaches and maggots the likes of which you've never seen when we looked inside. The dumpster at your business is cleaner than her black water storage box and this gal keeps her home in lovely condition. The lady who owns the house *hates* the compost toilet and is passionate about wanting to connect to the main line ASAP.

Based on this one example, Bob was able to conclusively advise his correspondent, George Neugent, then the mayor of Monroe County, to dismiss composting toilets as a possibility. The e-mail continues:

All of this leads me to know that expect [sic] for those few folks that think they are *camping* out on No Name that composting will not work, it's like using a bucket for a bathroom.

Interesting to note is that the homeowner, a single mom and long time full time resident explained that she has only been able to have one party there over the years given the reaction her guests had (they were, she said, "grossed out") when they used the head, that she can't have a boyfriend over as they too can't understand/stand it, and that she can't sell her home (every single possible buyer has balked over the place upon seeing the toilet and she's dropped the price over the last three years nearly in ½). She's first in line in wanting a central connection.

Then Bob moves in for the kill:

George I know or suspect that a *small* handful of folks will be against a sewer line but the vast majority of homeowners are very serious about making this happen.... I am confident that we can, in time, find the money and that the few who are against it will, also in time, see the light. Things on No Name have changed in recent years in many good ways and will continue to evolve and although no one favors new building (I surely do not) the *vast* majority of homeowners want basic services that others receive. We plan to do all needed before the next Commission meeting, be there in a unified voice as you long ago suggested and continue to seek what is fair no matter how long it takes or how hard it becomes.

Your help and guidance is appreciated more than I can say or write.

Thank you.

Robert D. Reynolds, CIC, CPIA, AAM, AIS, AU

Still pondering the Bob Reynolds phenomenon, I returned to my HQ in the area. Long Hair Ranch, just a few miles away on Big Pine Key, is an eccentric place, solar-powered, and part-time home to a colony of East Coast artists, photographers, and writers who winter there. It is the full-time home of Bob Morrow, a retired master sweetsman, as candy-makers are sometimes called. (At least I assume they are, because that is how Bob refers to himself.)

Bright and early the next morning I was heading back across the long Bebe Rebozo–inspired road bridge to No Name Key, and down Bahia Shores Road. Each of the houses to the east sits on the edge of a wide canal, and the opposite side of the canal has another set of identical yards stretching toward another row of medium-size detached homes. The canal is wide enough to accommodate a double row of moored yachts with enough space for a yacht to sail between them. I stopped outside Frank Atwell's place.

I noticed a young woman sunning herself on the deck of a boat at the end of Frank's yard, so I introduced myself to his mooring guest, who is living there full-time. She works for the local nature conservancy council, and as a result of her unconventional situation was unable to give me her name. However, she lost no time in telling me her opinion of the "lowlife" who wants to bring municipal power to the island.

She went below decks to change for work, and I knocked on Frank's door, to be met by his beaming Japanese wife, Miki. Delighted to see a new face, Miki floated around making me green tea and recalling her days as a Fulbright scholar. Frank finally returned and dismissed her with an imperious wave of his hand that made me realize it's not just the Segway that gives him a regal air.

Frank, a retired IBM consultant, is one of the island's firmest supporters of solar power. He has a large home designed to withstand hurricanes, with plenty of cross breezes through open windows. A small air-conditioning unit in the bedroom is run by solar panels. He originally moved to the area because of his love of yachting, but has since become bored with the sea, and is becalmed with his wife, whom he clearly finds intensely irritating, and the neighbors, who no longer speak to him because of his anti-grid views, and his empty mooring, though he has at least found a use for that in the form of his guest.

For those who favor bringing municipal power to the island, Frank Atwell is a mere sideshow, an old fellow to be tolerated and humored. The real villain—by which they mean the Devil incarnate, the beast haunting the dreams of all those on the island who want municipal power—is a woman who first settled there nearly two decades earlier precisely because it was off the grid. Alicia Putney had been living elsewhere on the Keys and was forced out by the rapid pace of development. So she was determined that her next home would not succumb to the same fate.

I was received by the Putneys with considerable suspicion, the same suspicion that would characterize my reception by the pro-grid faction. Giving the couple my business card with the

Off-Grid.net Web address emblazoned upon it did little to lighten the atmosphere. Alicia disappeared back to her office, and it was left to her husband, Mick, a stooping retired sociology professor dressed in blue jeans and a white shirt, with thinning gray hair tied back in a ponytail and a courteous manner, to conduct the screening interview that would decide whether I was fit to be allowed a conversation with Alicia herself.

Mick did his best to keep our chat on a theoretical level. We discussed the modern phenomenon of home improvement, the effects of peer pressure, and the nature of fragmented society without actually getting on to the matter at hand.

Having evidently decided that I was to have an audience with Alicia, Mick first ushered me upstairs for a tour of the small house. It was built with fossilized coral mined in Key Largo, with red-ash wood for floors and stairs. The central atrium conducts the hot air up and out, eliminating the need for air-conditioning in the sultry months of the Florida summer. The rooftop holds the solar panels and solar water heaters—and over there, as the eye stretches just beyond the water heaters, is the $1.3 million home of Bob Reynolds, whose arrival had galvanized the pro-grid faction into decisive yet so far impotent action. "The house of Reynolds," as Mick called it with a hint of irony, has a fine northerly view over the water that leads eventually to Biscayne Bay, where FPL had for years been dumping heated waste from its power plant, until it was sued for thermal pollution by the EPA.

The final flourish of the tour was the couple's three-room bedroom—the first room with just a double bed, then a combination study and changing room for him, and another for her. And there at last was Alicia in her lair, with as many bookshelves as possible squeezed against the walls, all piled to the max with papers and folders. I assume these are the records of her constant legal battle to keep NNK off the grid.

Alicia is a tubby woman, about five feet three inches tall and fifty-five years old, with her hair pulled back in a bun. She wore blue shorts and a pink top that concealed an ample bosom. She rose up to her maximum height and introduced herself thus: "Hi, here I am, loved by many and loathed by some." She then began reciting the allegations made against her. "They have demonized me. They believe I have manipulated the system to write the statutes and somehow inputted a 1988 statute." She showed me what she had been working on, yet another court case in the long battle she has been fighting since moving here in 1991.

"We moved to Key Largo and after four years it wasn't the same. We picked this place because it was inside a refuge, targeted for acquisition by the federal government and the state government. We found this place had no utilities and we thought, Who would want to live out here, other than like-thinking people?

"The first battle, in '98 and '99," she continued, "the other side came in saying they were promised power, and the county said, 'No, you were never promised power.' We all thought that after we won the last time public perception of solar had moved to acceptance." This was the first time I had heard the phrase "the other side." Each side uses it to describe their opponents; it is the shared language of war. "I really thought that by the year 2000, the whole concept of living within your footprint would be more widespread," she said.

It transpired that she has already won the battle against the grid many times over, yet, as in the movie *Groundhog Day*, she is forced to repeat it ad infinitum. "In 1999 the planning commission listed the reasons for their decisions [to keep NNK off the grid]. They talked about the people who have become accustomed to living here without commercially supplied power, who took pride in their lifestyle. It changes the community character if you are off grid or on grid—it isn't just something I made up," she said, and I did not doubt her. "The Monroe County land-use plan is one of three to protect the area in the case of hurricane, and also protect the uniqueness and environment." It seems on the surface that Bob and Alicia are agreed on at least one thing: Neither of them wants development on No Name Key.

I felt that Alicia was sincere, but I wasn't entirely convinced that Bob would fight to his dying breath to stop one more house being built on the island.

When it came to my main question—Why would the residents want to bring power to this unique off-the-grid community?—the one thing that Bob stressed constantly in e-mails and speeches is that his campaign has nothing to do with real estate development. It is, he said, quite out of the question that a single new house will ever be built on No Name Key. How can he be so sure of this? America is littered with ugly developments in beautiful areas, once designated as no-build zones—until policy changed, or some wily developers created a loophole around the rules.

As I dug deeper into the bitter feud, I met many of the pro-grid campaigners, each of whom later wrote to me withdrawing permission for their interviews to be used. Mary Bakke, the group's lawyer, was the first to do so; the letter arrived shortly after we met. My guess is that she did some research and discovered my long record of campaigning in favor of off-the-grid living. I had in actuality approached this particular battle with an open mind, but there was no way the pro-grid faction was going to believe me.

The online video archive provided by the Monroe County Board of County Commissioners is a record of each of their public meetings. On July 23, 2008, there was a well-attended formal hearing, at which the pro-gridders attempted to persuade the board of commissioners to rescind an earlier decision to prevent power from coming to No Name.

There, in the video, is Bob, sitting on the left side of the hall, his back to the camera, his trademark ginger comb-over shining out. He is in the front row next to Beth Vickry, a very thin peroxide-blond neighbor on No Name Key. Her father has been involved in Florida politics for donkey's years. Her brother Rick is undersheriff of Monroe County. And now Bob is marching up to the lectern to take the county commissioners through his PowerPoint presentation about why it would be un-American to oppose electrification of the island.

Alicia Putney walks across the screen, now wearing a lawyerly black suit and a white shirt. As she surveys her possible seating choices from the front of the hall, she reminds me of Mr. Toad in *The Wind in the Willows*. She opts for a chair on the opposite side of the room from Bob.

Beth, wearing culottes and beach shoes, hands out a thick folder to each of the commissioners as Bob opens his presentation. "I want to thank you personally on behalf of my family," he tells the commissioners, who've granted him this opportunity to address the meeting. His wife and two children are not to be found in the meeting hall. I have a sneaking suspicion he is referring to his grandfather, the old man of Florida Power and Light. In a nod to the formality of the occasion, Bob sports a navy blue blazer with a pocket handkerchief, the same French blue as his shirt.

"My home is at 2160 Bahia Shores," he announces by way of introduction. Of course, that is not his home—it's his *second* home. Nobody seems to notice this discrepancy, the first of several to go unremarked.

Bob continues by stating that he and his family "love and cherish" No Name Key. Having spent many months, by the time I watched this video, studying and thinking about Bob Reynolds, I rather doubted he loves and cherishes anything other than Bob Reynolds. Second on the list of things Bob loves and cherishes is, I suspect, money. Bob would probably not accept this characterization, though he admits as much when he says during his presentation: "those of us who own property there and have homes there believe we've got a serious commitment of time and money."

At the center of any attempt to make sense of Bob Reynolds's investment in the island is one fact: the nearly $1.3 million Bob shelled out in 2005 was the largest amount ever paid to purchase a house in the history of the island. Now, according to Zillow. com, the property is worth barely a million. The drop in value must be galling for a man who expects everything in his life to work out as he wants. Indeed, "I want" is one of his favorite phrases; in the course of the forty-minute address he treats the board to, Bob manages to use it twenty-two times, along with "I also want" and "I just want."

Back at the lectern, Bob is now saying he speaks for "the vast majority" of residents. Since there are forty-three homes on the Key and at least thirteen of them are members of the pro-solar group, *vast* is a relative term. Moving along, Bob asserts "one hundred percent of the people on No Name Key have requested the Board of County Commissioners allow us to connect to the central sewers of the Monroe County wastewater sewer system: that's indisputable." This is false. It is not the case that the solar community has accepted the idea of a central sewer, Alicia informed me. They want a "modified septic tank" that will meet the 2010 standards. This would be the cheapest solution, Alicia said, costing about twenty-five thousand dollars per household.

Bob then proceeds to deny that he has any malice toward anyone on the island, a sign that he is about to say something malicious. "It is time to stop the misinformation and perhaps even madness that the residents have been subjected to." I suppose this means he disagrees with some of the statements made by Alicia Putney and her anti-grid supporters.

And so it continues, until these stirring words: "This is not the country we live in. It is not the country I am raising my children in. And this is wrong." Bob has concluded—much to my relief.

By the time I was watching this footage, the battle seemed to me to come down to a fight between a minority of long-standing, full-time residents and a majority of more recent arrivals, some of them part-timers. Each household has the same rights and status, whether they are living there full-time or not. (Although, according to Alicia Putney, several part-timers declare their No Name home as their primary residence for a variety of tax-related reasons.)

Jim Newton, a full-timer and relatively recent arrival, is next up at the meeting, and there to support the grid. Newton and his wife retired to the Key six years earlier, without the sort of income most of the second-home owners enjoy. According to neighbors, he makes himself useful by looking after boats and homes while their owners are away. Jim would happily prattle on about effluent, wastewater, drainage systems, and anaerobic composting toilet bowls until the cows come home, but the subject of electrical power really gets his juices going. His brother-in-law works for Florida Power and Light, coincidentally running the department that installs connections for new customers.

A retired teacher with thirty-two years of experience, Jim has a deep, gravelly voice, in contrast to Bob's metallic, reedy voice. It should sound imposing and attractive, but somehow it is tedious to the point of insanity. I'm curious how many wretched students he has lulled into a miserable sleep with his awful drone. Jim has hardly begun speaking when he is stopped short by the mayor on some procedural issue; he curtly ends his presentation by telling the commissioners, "I fear for the future of our island if we do not have central wastewater."

At this point I should apologize to the reader for returning to the issue raised so eloquently by Bob Reynolds in his letter to the mayor: toilets.

It's a big subject when you are off the grid—possibly the biggest. Everyone who lives off the grid has lost count of the number of times they are asked in a coy, slightly amused way, "So what do you do about, you know, going to the bathroom?" And now the entire drama unfolding on No Name Key has come down to toilets and the acceptability of the forty-two septic tanks and one composting toilet currently dealing with the human waste from the forty-three mainly part-time small family dwellings on the island with its aging population of retirees and second-home owners.

There are just four alternatives that would satisfy the new federal rules designed to prevent the leaching of chemicals and other noxious materials into the soil of No Name Key and then into the water table. Sticking with the status quo is not one of them.

The first is to build a full-scale commercial sewage system to service the forty-three homes. It would require a grid-scale power supply, and once installed it would be able to service a near-infinite increase in the amount of human waste in the small community.

The second option is known as a "thin-pipe" sewage system. It would be operated by electric pumps situated on or under the Bebe Rebozo bridge, but powered from the mainland.

The third is the alternative favored by Alicia: a modified version of the septic tank that would meet the new standards.

The fourth and final alternative is the composting toilet. This is a well-understood technology that, if correctly managed, produces a harmless material, very similar to rich soil, and can be used to grow organic vegetables. The solar-power faction had tentatively proposed a composter at one point, but had been howled down by the other side.

The one functioning composting toilet on the island is built by Clivus Multrum, a market leader in composting toilets. Although the owner, a postal worker, was out of town when I visited the island, Jim Newton took me to the home because he wanted to show me the huge object, conveniently stored under the raised first floor of the house, which like many on the island rested on stilts in order to reduce potential damage in case of floods. This design creates a covered area under the house—a basement at ground level, so to speak. As I walked around to the basement entrance, I passed a huge array of solar panels perched on a wooden pedestal, and a set of four Rolls batteries—the Rolls-Royce of solar batteries. They are known to have a far longer life and to be three times as heavy and four times as expensive as normal deep-cycle batteries. Next to the batteries, a white tank holds the gray water from the house. *Gray water* is the term for water from sinks, showers, dishwashers, and the like. Once used for washing, it can be used to flush a toilet or water a garden.

While most composting toilets are simple, functional, and inexpensive, the Clivus Multrum is the Hummer of composting toilets, a vast and intricate object. The unit in the bathroom is a normal toilet bowl, and a basement of some sort is required because a long, wide pipe travels down from the toilet to an ugly, green-ribbed plastic container. This container stands as tall as a man and takes up fifteen to twenty square feet of floor space, with several doors for different functions. One is used to put in worms; another is used to remove the compost once it has transformed into an earthlike substance. The process can take many months. This is the reason for the large size of the contraption.

"The effluent drops down through this tube"—my escort indicated the green tube entering the composter—"from the potty upstairs." Jim walked ahead of me toward the silent, brooding object. Once I had raised my video camera, he turned to me gravely and said, "Are you ready? This is not going to be a pretty sight." He gripped the handle of the smallest door. "Are you ready for this?" he asked again. I nodded. "Now, I'll lift the lid, but I won't hold it open for a long time," he said. The cover came back and hundreds of cockroaches ran for the darkness across a black, tarlike substance that was, presumably, the effluent. I instinctively looked away, and by the time my eyes returned a second later, Jim had slammed shut the door. How the cockroaches had got there I cannot imagine, as the whole system is sealed. Could it have been via the toilet bowl upstairs?

One other pipe, a narrower one painted white, exited the composter, snaking its way around the basement before disappearing up into the house. I asked what this was for. "It's an air vent," Jim told me. "It allows gases to escape, all the way up to the roof. In any system—my own septic tank—gases are produced." Jim's whole body sagged at the thought of the gases being produced. "So instead of letting them out around your home on the ground level, the gases are transported through the pipe to the very uppermost area so they can escape into the atmosphere."

"What if the wind is blowing the wrong way?" I asked.

"Yup," he said, looking grim.

By then I had met at least ten of the leading actors in this drama, and although I doubted the sincerity of some of the witnesses, I was still unsure about the detailed rights and wrongs of the matter.

But I knew where to go for an answer. There was one household in the pro-grid faction who had agreed to talk to me and did not later withdraw their permission. Bob and Petronella Benton are the very picture of a peacefully retired Florida couple. Their house, just next to the Reynolds mansion, is approached through a high wooden fence, and I was lucky enough to find them at home, because they, too, had become part-timers since the trouble began. I walked past a tasteful sculpture and up two flights of wooden steps to the front door. Bob Benton, a former real estate agent, greeted me and ushered me in. He was tanned, with precisely combed gray hair and an ironed shirt.

Simon and Garfunkel was playing loudly on a stereo as I walked into the large, airy sitting room. How appropriate, I thought, in the context of the pro- and anti- grid factions. Another pair who aren't talking to each other. I felt like I had stepped into an orderly, cosseted world, a bit like an expensive cruise ship.

It was no surprise to learn the Bentons had settled here for the sailing. They are well informed about the ecology, the waterways, and the politics of No Name Key, and I felt they were as close as I could get to the truth.

I accepted a glass of wine and we sat down for a chat. Bob and Petronella each took up their positions on parallel lounge chairs, looking out toward the sunset. I was on the sofa, facing them. "Some of our best friends have moved off the island because of the animosity. I don't want it when I go for a walk—we want to live in harmony," was Bob's opening gambit. "But we get along with most of them."

I mentioned the Board of County Commissioners meetings, where the debate is being fought out. "At the meetings," Bob said, "they divide us up on opposite sides—it's a sad commentary." I recalled seeing this in the video. All the pro-grid campaigners sit on the left side of the room; all the anti-gridders on the right.

As "Bridge Over Troubled Water" swelled to a climax, awful smells began to waft into the room, which in every other way is a perfectly controlled environment. There are no composting toilets here, so where did the stench come from? My nostrils must have twitched, because Bob explained before I could ask. "It's the illegal east-facing canal. Washes the green grass in, then it rots."

I couldn't really see what difference the toilet arrangements of forty-three law-abiding households, most of them part-time, were going to make if this was the current status of the local ecology. And I doubted Bob Reynolds had been aware of the odor problem when he parted with $1.3 million to buy his home.

As if reading my mind, Bob Benton recounted a conversation with his neighbor on the separate, equally horrendous matter of the feces that were gathering in the canal. Reynolds had been very upset. "I paid $1.3 million," he told Benton, "and I can't rent it anymore because of the feces." Benton sympathized—after all, he had worked in real estate. He understood that not being able to rent a property is a very serious matter. Reynolds had been convinced that this was human waste, but Benton disagreed. "In fact, it was the alligators," he told me authoritatively.

Bob and Petronella began to talk about the new sewer system. "We have our property values to consider. If we have self-composting toilets then it's not . . . well, I don't want to live in a place like that," said Bob.

Petronella added, "We don't build our own road. We shouldn't have to build our own sewage system individually."

I mumbled a note of sympathy as Bob moved on to the issue of electricity. "Need a hardwired fifteen-kilowatt generator for the AC," he said. "Need a toaster oven, and a hair dryer."

"Room would be more attractive if we didn't have the propane gas heaters," said Petronella.

Bob walked me over to a nautical map hanging on the far wall, and pointed at a tiny speck just off No Name Key, which was itself minute. "Cook's Island—there's the place for them to go," he said. Alicia had mentioned to me earlier that the pro-grid faction wanted to banish her to this godforsaken outcrop.

"The Sound of Silence" was playing as I bade them good night. Bob politely showed me to the door. After I left, I assume he would refill Petronella's glass, then his own, and then settle back down in the lounge chair to watch the rest of the sunset.

To me the essential tragedy of the part-time residents of No Name Key is that in their apparent rush to shore up their property values in this peaceful spot, most of them have forgotten what brought them to the Keys in the first place: solitude and a chance to escape the concerns of their daily lives.

NO MATH ISLAND

These same desires are what motivated Denise de la Cerda, a tattoo artist with a studio in Manhattan, to flee the city. Her off-the-grid home is her primary residence, where she goes to spend the money she makes in the city. She charges about $150 an hour for her tattooing services, with a three-hundred-dollar minimum. Her second home is a tiny studio on the Lower East Side, scarcely larger than her single bed. Her off-grid property is the first "real" home she has had since she walked out on her parents when she was sixteen.

Denise is a little over five feet tall with masses of dark hair, sultry Latin good looks, and appealing freckles. Her back, arms, and shoulders are covered with tattoos. When we first met she had almost finished paying off the real estate loan on her breathtakingly beautiful spot in Connecticut, barely a four-hour drive from Manhattan.

As soon as she bought the land in 2000, she had a little house built near the end of the path: two high-ceilinged rooms and a platform bed. From there it's a few minutes' walk down to the river, through spruce, fir, and birch trees. The river itself is exactly what you would want from a recreational waterway: wide, yet not too wide, about thirty feet across; a nice amount of white water; and no more than ten feet deep in the places where I looked. She also owns the land on the other side of the river, about five hundred yards of river frontage in all. Once you're there, the rest of the world might as well not exist.

Some of the locals swim off her property when she is away in the summer. She sees this as a positive, her contribution to the community. The real estate company that sold her this haven, and owns much of the land around her, took a loss on the deal. Denise thinks they wanted out, their thoughts dwelling on the liability implications of a potential drowning, or the security costs of preventing anyone from swimming in the first place. It was cheaper to sell at a loss.

"I always wanted to own an island when I was a kid," she told me as we stood facing each other on an islet a hundred yards long, the white water of the river frothing gently around us. She had named the little spit of land where we were standing No Math Island. She elaborated on her childhood fantasy. "I would set the laws and as I was really bad at math, just couldn't get it at all, I always swore the only law would be that there is no math on the island. Any equations of any sort, any arithmetic, any algebraic calculations are verboten on the island. OK?"

The math in my mind at the time had to do with the finances and security of her investment. The ten acres had cost her fifty-two thousand dollars several years earlier, the house another thirty thousand or more. She had already learned about some of the problems of landownership. One of her first acts after buying the plot was to try to clear some trees. She came to a deal with a pair of unlicensed loggers, who felled several hundred trees as agreed and took away the trunks. But they exploited her inexperience, and instead of removing the branches or chopping them for firewood, they left them lying around everywhere, obstructing paths and access to other trees. It had been a useful lesson.

For a while this was her only home, and she slept on friends' couches when she came to the city to work. That didn't last. Denise is an attractive single woman, and couch surfing was bound to be problematic. Her sleeping arrangements became complicated, with her benefactors constantly turning into would-be suitors. Her other friends, like most ordinary New Yorkers, lived in places far too small to share on any but the most irregular basis.

Just before we met, Denise had found a cheap lodging house on the Lower East Side, where she had taken a permanent room with just enough space for a monkish single bed and a small side table big enough for an electric kettle and a radio. Between this arrangement and her basement tattoo shop on Macdougal Street, she is all set.

It was election day 2008 as I set off by train to meet Denise. She picked me up at the station, in a small, "shit-colored" car with her dog in the backseat, and drove us to her house. The original plan was to travel together to the home of another off-gridder, Steve Spence, who lives several hours north, near Potsdam, New York. Steve is a survivalist who spends huge amounts of time in Internet chat rooms dispensing free advice on how to set up your solar panels, dig an ice chamber, or build a wind turbine with your bare hands. Steve is a right-wing-libertarian kind of survivalist, and although we had corresponded for years via e-mail, we had never met. It was by then obvious Obama would sweep to victory, and I wanted to spend the night with Steve and some of his McCain-supporting off-grid friends and watch them weep into their whiskey as the results came in over the radio. He had kindly consented to host both Denise and me.

But it was not to be.

I had rung Steve the previous day to confirm our plan, and all he would say was that he was in a car with his son, racing to the hospital, and the meeting was off. It was left to a mutual friend to break the news: Steve had accidentally shot his son, Steve junior, in the hand. At first it seemed almost comical that a survivalist would mess up in this way. Then I learned Steve junior would have to spend some time in the hospital for reconstructive surgery on his hand. Not so funny. To top it all off, Obama did win by a landslide, so it was gloom all around the Spence household that night.

Denise was elated by the Obama win, but she still felt the need for her bugout location, a place to run to when the whole system looks like it's about to collapse. Yet for Denise this house is much more. As mentioned earlier, it is the first real home she's lived in since she left her parents' house. When she was sixteen, her older sister died suddenly, and Denise found she could preserve the intimacy of their lost relationship by talking to her as though she were still alive. That changed her attitude to Catholicism in ways her parents found unacceptable, and there were heated arguments. Denise left. She has seen her family only rarely since then.

Her father has been to visit her once in ten years; her remaining sister and brother have not. "We're not terribly close; it's modern life. People don't have time for closeness and family anymore," she said. I found this strange, especially because she had just explained to me, at great length, how intimate the relationship between a tattoo artist and a client is. In a way, her clients have become her family.

Denise became a street person after she left home, and was then offered shelter in a big house in a suburb of New York City by an elderly man who lived in squalor. When Denise began tidying up he objected and asked her to leave.

"I had no money, so I went to a welfare office and found that with no home address I couldn't get welfare, and with no money I couldn't get a home address. I ended up in a skid-row-type single-room-occupancy hotel where the landlord was familiar with this catch-22 situation, and he allowed people to move in on the grounds that you would hand your welfare check to him when it arrived. So I did that for about a month. I was really depressed, and after that I did get a job and slowly got myself on my feet."

A few years later she moved to New York, went to art school, dropped out of art school in 1988, then drove taxis at night for a few years. She would sit in cafés doodling designs, and some of the other drivers told her she should start turning her sketches into tattoos. Now she's one of the best tattoo artists in the city.

Denise has firm ideas about her work. She won't do "small, cutesy things" anymore. "No cartoon characters. I want to do fine art on people." The motivation behind the tattoo interests her more than the content. "It can help you define your direction and your intent, the most important thing to you. Marking your body indelibly . . . all of a sudden you stop with the nonsense, you stop playing around, you get serious. That's why I say no to something somebody saw on a movie star or in a magazine."

What I learned about Denise is interesting—intriguing,

even—but it doesn't really explain why this savvy and success-ful woman is opting for off-the-grid existence. I asked her the question as we trudged contentedly through the dry leaves near the river on a cold fall morning."Freedom," she sighed, tousling her hair as she conducted an internal interrogation to find out what her real motives are. "Privacy." And then a pause. "I want as little government involvement in my life as possible, and that sounds like a really Republican thing to say, but it's not. I've been trying to make a life where I can disengage from corpo-rate and government serfdom as much as possible. I'm not com-pletely free of it, but I am trying. This corporate-government structure seems to always be thinking of new ways to curtail our freedom, and keep us thinking that we should be chained to the treadmill.

"One of the most effective ways for them to do that is to sell us products that we don't really need, and persuade us to com-mit to yet another monthly bill. At least if you are off grid you don't have to sign on for monthly bills.

"We're forced to live beyond our means because the basic ne-cessities of living are beyond our means—most importantly, the ground we stand on, light to see with, clean water to drink. These basic needs have been hijacked by the wealthy in collu-sion with governments, starting with claiming large tracts of land, which then are parceled and rented out."

These are among the most political statements I heard during my journey around the states. But Denise is no activist, and outside of work she prefers her own company.

She has friends come out to visit her "once in a while." She added, "I want to be alone some of the time—it seems like the wrong place for social activity to me. It's for being alone, and heavy concentration and artmaking and meditating, but not a place I want to socialize."

As she spoke we were approaching a big tree house in a clear-ing not far from the main house. We broke off to examine it.

It's a very fine example of its kind, bigger than Denise's room on the Lower East Side. It was erected by a client who traded "a lot of tattoos" for this sturdy plywood building with telephone-pole supports, a long ladder to climb up, a nice wooden railing from which to survey her realm, and a purple velvet curtain covering the entrance and partially hiding a pack of parquet flooring from "Home Despot."

The tree house doesn't raise her property tax because it's considered a temporary structure, and it gives her what she wants: a meditation retreat by day, and a summer guest room by night. She plans to build more of them.

We returned to the question: Why here, why off the grid? "I'm just drawn to here," was her answer. "It's the place I feel I need to be. It's close enough to New York City. I can keep going there and I can harvest some money there and bring it back here. I mean, a lot of people come from other countries to do exactly that."

Denise and I met once again, when I was passing through Manhattan. She was celebrating because she had paid off her real estate loan that week. We met in a bar, though she doesn't drink anymore. "It wasn't an addiction, but I couldn't control it," she told me as I toasted her success. I had been worrying about her since she had told me about the real estate loan. They are risky because a single late payment can mean losing the property. Nevertheless, Denise's gamble had paid off. For less than a hundred thousand dollars all told, she had a ten-acre estate under a half day's drive from Manhattan. On a river.

She had been afraid of being tied down by a conventional house, and her low-maintenance cabin is far from conventional. She can travel the world and take any risk, knowing her home is there waiting for her.

The idea of living off the grid part of the time may strike some ardent off-gridders as cheating, or at least as lacking seriousness. Personally, as a part-timer myself, I don't care. I am not one of the legions of authors who treat all this as a game, setting

out to reduce my carbon footprint for *a year,* or becoming a survivalist for *a year,* or doing whatever else the latest "immersive"
stunt may be. I am trying to find an off-the-grid sanctuary for
myself somewhere in America.

Initially, I intend to use it only part of the time, although
who knows what the future may hold? I still love the big city,
and I still love the rest of the planet, but I can easily imagine
spending the rest of my days (visa status permitting) in one of
the beautiful and inspiring places I visited during my travels.

4 Stepping Away

"Asleep in their drowsy villas, sheltered by benevolent shopping malls, they wait patiently for the nightmares that will wake them into a more passionate world."

J. G. Ballard, *Kingdom Come*

Living off the grid part of the time is all I aspire to at the moment. I might end my days living this way all the time, but at the moment that feels too extreme. Although intermittent experience off the grid does make the full-time prospect less menacing.

There is an in-between approach, softer than the full-fledged experience. In my travels I met many people who live on the grid yet possess everything necessary to allow them to be independent of municipal power and water if they ever need to be. This is what I mean by "off-grid ready." It might be just a solar panel charging a couple of batteries in the spare room, or something as complex as a full-blown renewable-energy system.

Zeke Yewdall's place, outside Boulder, Colorado, falls into the second category.

Boulder calls itself the greenest town in America. My visit convinced me that it is at least the smuggest town in America.

Well-heeled government workers and their families stroll the store-lined streets looking for opportunities to spend their money as if the recession never existed. These are environmentalists who will be as green as you like, so long as it doesn't affect their home heating, TV viewing, or car driving—all regarded as inalienable rights. For them, being green means buying organic veggies and recycling the wine bottles.

Driving out of Boulder and up the steep mountain pass to the east, one could easily miss the small town of Wade, in a box canyon down to the right. A few roofs peek over the top of the valley, one with a rainbow-colored wind turbine that catches the eye. A passerby might observe a cluster of Subarus grouped around the strange-looking house; masses of solar panels on the roof and another windmill lying on its side. Around back he would find a beautiful old bus that appears to be inhabited. That is Zeke's guesthouse. "My father was a hippie," he said, as if that somehow explains everything. He and his huge, lumbering dog, Borealis, give the impression of being amiable and rather vague, but the truth is that at least one very sharp brain is constantly at work.

Zeke, thirty-four, is chief engineer for a renewable-energy company. He has tricked his house out as a permanent test market for next-generation developments in renewable energy. He can sell unused energy back to the power company, but once he has zeroed out his energy bill, he says, "they don't pay the excess at the same cost as retail—usually a third to a quarter, so it's really not worth it." For Zeke it made sense anyway, as it's an inherent part of his business. The laws covering this situation vary depending on where you are, changing dramatically from state to state.

With the idea of net metering (as this deal is known) taking an increasing hold, and grants for off-grid solar panels now overtaken by the money available for panels that are "grid-tied," off-grid-ready living has become a bigger trend than the pure off-the-grid lifestyle.

Not that you need renewable energy in order to be off-grid

ready. A generator and a rainwater-harvesting kit will do just as well. It's a state of mind as much as it's a physical existence.

WRITER IN THE WOODS

I visited one woman—a writer whose latest novel had just been published as I began my journey—whose mental state is entirely off-grid ready. The meeting with Carolyn Chute was carefully planned; she doesn't have many new visitors to her remote Maine hideout. Her phone does not ring, so it was not possible to speak to her directly before we met. All calls go straight to voice mail, and since she has little money, each of my messages to her was answered by one of hers to my toll-free Grasshopper voice-mail service, giving gradually more and more detailed directions to her home, near Porter, Maine. She eventually described every significant landmark on the final twenty miles of the journey along Highway 160 and then the various and twisting side roads, right up to the long, heavily wooded driveway with its handwritten chalk signs every few yards, with warnings such as, WHOA, SLOW DOWN and SECURITY.

The road ends in a clearing with trees all around. There are two main buildings, and several cars and items of machinery are dotted about. Carolyn emerged to greet me. "We are hermits, kind of, but we are sociable, though," she said, explaining their isolated, cluttered home. "I like to be with people when I am with them, then be by myself."

My conversation with Carolyn started in the yard, then moved to her husband Michael's big, crowded, two-story wooden cabin. This is his studio and also serves as the guest bedroom. There are boxes, tools, and artist's materials everywhere. A couple of elderly rifles with elegant wooden stocks lean upright against a table next to the French windows. Art paraphernalia from paints to frames and nameless things are stacked up neatly. Little pieces of art and decorations cover every available shelf and tabletop.

Michael's line drawings are stuck to walls and to the individual panes of the Georgian-style sash windows he happened to salvage when building the cabin himself, without power tools, fifteen years ago. The drawings, all on squares of cheap paper of different colors, are illuminated by the light coming in—a sort of poor man's stained glass.

On the other side of the cabin is a series of windows looking out onto acres of woodland. It seems idyllic, and I talked of taking a walk around their land. The suggestion was met with peculiar silence by Carolyn and Michael. I never made the walk because even in April the blackflies are out in menacing force, and remain so until October. Step outside and they leave you alone for a few minutes before gathering in increasing numbers to drive you back indoors. It has become steadily worse over the years, I am told—one consequence, supposedly, of global warming.

Michael can work outside only if he's wearing a beekeeper's hat and mask, and gloves; otherwise the flies "crawl into your ears and up your nose." It has become much worse, he said— "wicked bad." He uses the word *wicked* in every other sentence.

In a full-page report on his own visit at the time Carolyn's latest novel was published, a *New York Times* correspondent describes Michael as having a beard like those of the members of the band ZZ Top and looking like "a nineteenth-century hunting guide." He isn't wrong. The long white beard and black eyebrows were topped off with a battered, round-brimmed, black felt hat pulled low over the eyes, and he wore blue jeans, work boots, and a red checkered shirt layered over a light-colored shirt and a T-shirt. (It was spring in Maine and still chilly.)

Carolyn wore big brown climbing boots and a blue dress over blue tights. Her legs were swollen and, I later discovered, she is in near-constant pain from a leg injury in a car accident a few years ago. She also wore a matching blue headscarf, tied gypsy-style, a blue T-shirt under an armless cardigan, and big plastic-rimmed glasses. She is a fast-talking, jocular sixty-two-year-old who has had a tough life. Her health is poor, and she has been

on various kinds of pills for decades, at first for a heart condition; the number has increased since the accident. Despite all of
this, her spirits are high, and it is impossible not to like her.

She sat on the blanketed daybed (later to become my night
bed). Two black Scottish terriers, Mary and Edward (named
after her grandparents), bounced around on top of the furniture
until Michael uttered a high-pitched "cue cue cue cue" and they
ran outside, seemingly undisturbed by the blackflies. Michael
was carrying a silver coffee pot in one hand as he held the door
open with the other, still singing his strange call.

I am not sure how it came up, but before we had even sat
down, I learned of the stillbirth of their only child, twenty-five
years earlier. I immediately thought of Carolyn's latest novel,
The School on Heart's Content Road, which has drawn huge praise
from critics. One of its subplots concerns a poor Maine family
who cannot afford the painkillers for their dying two-year-old.
They own the house they live in, making them ineligible for
state-funded MaineCare. "In this household there is no money
today. No money. No money. No money," Carolyn writes. "Out
there in the world are whole bins of pain pills unreachable as
clouds. The key to painlessness is money. Money is everything."

The media coverage I read before my visit did not prepare me
for the poverty Carolyn and Michael are facing. The articles
make it sound like they are playing a rather amusing game of
living like poor people. Now I realized the seriousness of their
situation. Carolyn and Michael are truly poor, and with the
exception of an occasional celebration, such as the day Carolyn
received a royalty check, they have been all their lives.

Carolyn had not been able to afford proper medical care during her pregnancy, and to this day she is sure that her child died
because she was not allowed into the hospital when she presented herself, saying she was going into labor. She was literally
turned away and treated like a simpleton. The heart pills she was
taking, she now realizes, prevented her from properly going into
labor, and this is a point she made repeatedly to the doctors,

who ignored her—this silly, kindly, humble, brilliant woman.
They ignored her, told her to go home, and then were horrible to
her when the child was stillborn.

Michael showed me a large, heart-rending black-and-white
close-up photo of the little boy's face lying on a pillow as if he's
sleeping. He hangs it at every art show he does (which is only a
few over the years), and clearly not a day goes by that they do
not think of their lost son.

"Yeah, we decided not to have another one, because it's a
mean world," Carolyn chuckled in her rough Down East accent.
"[My treatment by the hospital] was pretty mean, pretty low, and
we decided we didn't want to bring another child into . . ." she
trailed off. I guess she meant "into this world." I don't know if
that awful death is the wellspring for all Carolyn's work, and I
wasn't about to ask her such a crass question, but if I were in her
place, it would have been so for me.

In the silence following her unfinished sentence, I pondered
the collapse of trust that is leading many off the grid, and wondered if the stillbirth on its own had led Carolyn to withdraw
her faith in the system, or if instead it had been shattered from
many different directions.

One hand on her right hip, the other fist pushing down into
the bed she was sitting on, to relieve the pressure on her left
hip, Carolyn explained that the following year her first grand-
child had been born to her daughter from a previous marriage.
"And I thought, Let *her* have them. And we just fussed over him,
and he's twenty-five now, and she's had two more, so . . ." She
shrugged. I was reminded of one of the characters in *Heart's
Content Road*, who says, "Life isn't a great gift. It is shit."

The activists Carolyn works with, she said casually, are now the
age her son would have been. "So we've adopted them, the JED
kids." JED stands for Justice, Environment, Democracy, a group
of friendly middle-class anarchists who live in a commune a hundred miles away. We agreed that I should visit them next, and
arrangements were made.

Carolyn said that as she and Michael get older, their thoughts are turning toward having a couple of the anarchists live on their land, neighbors they would have something in common with. Why not the locals, I wondered. They are, she said, "pretty incurious." This is a disappointment to me, because the media have made so much of the armed group 2nd Maine Militia, founded by Carolyn. She called it a "no-wing organization . . . very right, very left, and very shy." But it turns out the Maine Militia, while by no means a figment of the imagination, is more celebrated in the pages of the *New York Times* than it is in Maine.

Because the locals are incurious, she added, "their opinions, which flow constantly—as we all do; we all like to have an opinion and talk about ideas—their opinions are uninformed." At first I was surprised at this elitist remark from such a staunch defender of the dignity of the rural poor, but as the conversation unfolded and I learned what a truly remarkable woman she is, I realized what she meant by "uninformed," because Carolyn is extraordinarily well informed.

She does not have the Internet, and writes her books on the kind of IBM golf-ball electric typewriter I gratefully jettisoned when I was given my first computer. She reads voraciously; before I departed the next day she had forced several books on me (including *The Long Emergency*, by James Howard Kunstler, and *The Shock Doctrine*, by Naomi Klein). She had also shown me a pricey subscription-only newsletter from Washington, D.C., with information that I would see regurgitated in newspaper headlines weeks later. (For example, the newsletter reported that the "stress tests" then being conducted on America's banks had in fact set deliberately low hurdles for the banks to clear, using as their most far-out scenarios liquidity ratios that pertained in some of the banks already.) Complex stuff for a simple rural militiawoman from Maine.

The locals, she said, are either older right-wing survivalist types, set in their ways, or "extreme Democrats" who "had to get a big-screen TV when Obama was elected, and, you know, celebrate." She punctuated it with a dismissive shrug. "So they don't dig too deep." The anarchist kids, however, do measure up to the standards of Carolyn and Michael.

At this point Michael came back in from some chore outside the cabin. We all sat out on the porch for a few minutes and he and I indulged in the political act of smoking a cigarette, but the blackflies soon found us and we dove back inside for more conversation.

I noticed all of the curtains in the main house were drawn, even though there was still plenty of daylight, and asked Carolyn why. "Because of the CIA spy satellites," she said, half amused at her own naïveté. "I say to myself, This is silly, why am I doing this here in the middle of the woods? Still I do it."

I had brought food and wine, and Carolyn had prepared soup, so we were able to go on talking and drinking, interspersing a few smoke breaks, until after dark. I was treated to a range of Carolyn's opinions, from the lack of vision among right-wing militiamen to the predictability of left-wing activists. "The CIA is always infiltrating things, so why don't the good guys infiltrate things, use what [the CIA] use against us? And I say this to people and they just go, 'Oh no, we'll just do our little lectures and have healthy snacks and sit in little circles.' That's the professional middle classes. The working-class guys, they form a militia and then just sit around in the kitchen and complain. They weren't into doing anything, right?" She looked to Michael for confirmation. "Just sit there with their guns and say, 'Nobody better bother us,' right?"

Carolyn's first book came out in 1984, and earned them just enough money to buy the land and build the main house, so they started with no power. Water is from a shallow well.

They had moved from an apartment in town. "There'd be fighting in the next room, banging around. Ooh, yuck. It would get me so upset. Or if *you* wanted to have a good fight you couldn't." She laughed her good-natured belly laugh.

I ran the gauntlet of blackflies in order to use the outhouse. By the time I returned, Carolyn had remembered a visit from a "big-city journalist" who left the outhouse "filthy . . . yuck." This in turn reminded her of the *New York Times* article, and she insisted on taking me through it, line by line, pointing out a dozen alleged inaccuracies, perhaps as some kind of warning to me.

Before I went to sleep, Michael brought me a big pitcher of water from the well. The next day, as I woke at first light to make some notes, I wished I was not leaving so soon. The blackflies give an edge to the summer there, but there are not two sweeter souls on this earth than Michael and Carolyn, and it would be hard to tear myself away.

I visited the main house for breakfast, and it's even more crowded and chaotic than the cabin. There is more artwork, and funny little decorations—such as a cardboard TV with the words *Damn Lies* written on the screen—all crammed even more closely together. Pride of place is given to a huge photocopier, one of the reasons Carolyn had electricity brought in more than a decade earlier. She uses it to correct drafts of her novels, and also to turn out copies of the anarchist cartoon tracts she and Michael produce. She writes the words, he does the drawings, and the cartoons sell for a quarter each at local fairs.

When they first moved there more than two decades earlier, the couple lived without any power, just using the truck engine for sawing wood and the car stereo for playing music. That habit has lasted until this day. Michael said he wanted me to hear a song, and we went and sat together in his truck and smoked a last cigarette while he played me a sad Irish rebel tune about a soldier who died in the war. Michael also wanted to tell me his reason for living an isolated life. He said that things like county fairs used to be for everybody. Now, he said, it "costs big bucks to get in, and if you see something you like, it's expensive. I guess the corporation has really taken over."

No corporation has taken over at Carolyn and Michael's house, though. The tin-roofed outhouse, the old fireplaces,

Michael's hunting rifles, and a few candles are all the couple needs to survive. They don't even have solar panels. In the event of a brownout, Carolyn's electric typewriter and photocopier would not work, but her neighbors would still bring food around, her logs would still burn in the fire, and she would probably continue to write with a manual typewriter or pen on paper, just as she did before the power line was laid.

"The electricity going off is something we think about a lot because of the peak-oil situation," said Carolyn. "In fact we got ourselves a hand pump that we're installing in the well because it comes up to about eight feet from the top, so we can run it alongside the electric pump." So they would have water. Michael has a bucksaw, and they have stocked up on blades, so their access to firewood is secure. They have some dry food in jars. Everything else involves money, which they don't have. Even the hand pump needs a pump house built over it.

This talk of outages and heating and lighting and toilet arrangements, however, leaves out the human element. Their house may be off-grid ready, and Carolyn's spirit may be ready, but Carolyn herself is not off-grid ready. Quite the opposite: This brave and big-hearted woman is teetering on the brink, grappling with pain, poverty, and unspent grief. She needs help—they both do. Luckily, help is at hand.

For years they have been discussing with the anarchists some kind of equitable arrangement in which a couple of the kids would live at their place, and quite simply help look after them in their old age. The idea is that this magical spot that Carolyn and Mike have created will never turn threatening and lonely, and will, after their deaths, become the home of the new couple, on the condition that it cannot be sold or squandered, and will have to be passed on in the same way in another two generations.

It's a great idea, but the mechanisms to make it run smoothly are still being worked out and depend at this stage entirely on goodwill and trust between the parties. This is not traditionally a sound basis for land transactions. Would the vexed question of passing on and parceling out the ultimate asset, American land, ever be allowed to become part of such an idealistic and ideologically laden enterprise?

I was about to find out.

THE POLITE ANARCHISTS

I said good-bye and promised to return, then set out for JED to meet the kids who might be about to save the day, not only for Carolyn and Michael, but for many others of their generation.

After a few minutes on the road, I received a call asking me to delay my arrival. "We have another meeting," a female voice told me, "to work out our constitution and do some planning." The slight delay was no problem, but I must confess my heart sank at the thought of the planning meetings and the idea of a constitution. Much as we may all rail against the impersonal State, to which we hand over so much of our individual power, the alternative requires that we exercise that power ourselves, and in a responsible way. This is what JED, and groups like it, grapple with on a daily basis. I don't want to overemphasize the tedium and potential for personal conflict from this way of organizing one's life. I have to say that it is certainly enough to put me off the idea.

I took the scenic route toward Greene, seventy miles to the northeast, via Poland Spring. On the way, to pass some time while JED deliberated on their constitution, I stopped at the end of Bayou Road, looking out over Sebago Lake. I passed some big houses on the way to the edge of the lake, but nobody bothered me, and I could probably have stayed there for a few days.

I found the JED headquarters easily enough. It's one of a small cluster of conventional homesteads, each with its own land stretching behind it and, as is often the case in rural America, built close to each other for neighborliness, security, and the pooling of resources—such as the electricity supply. This way they need only to bring the wire to one location rather than trail it around the valley between their neighbors' little McMansions.

The houses are modern colonial. JED's communal home, originally designed as the barn for the machinery run by the farm across the smooth green lawn, is a wood construction covered with brown asbestos siding. The farm itself is inhabited by an old couple who recently sold JED its first big plot of land. A couple hundred thousand dollars is due to change hands on fairly generous credit terms.

The JED collective building is the most unkempt of the four or five homes in the cluster, and the most romantic. It has a porch and a big communal eating area. Thirteen of the anarchists live there full-time, about half in the house and half in the cabins around the estate, Vanessa, from Quebec, told me as she showed me around.

The thirty-acre estate leads from the house across a field, down through a woodland, and to the lake, where a boathouse and two other small cabins are available for guests or interns or any of the full-time residents who fancy an overnight stay.

Most of the cabins are completely off the grid. One resident was about to move into an octagonal tree house he had nearly completed, with windows and outside treetop benches. The main house "benefits from municipal power," as the real estate agents would say, and water is from a spring. Wastewater goes into a septic tank. The JED collective had already installed a bunch of solar panels that are feeding back into the grid, and their aim is to become one hundred percent independent, although at this point any spare money they have is going to pay back the loan on the property.

Next-door-neighbor Jim, the eighty-eight-year-old ex-hippie who sold them the land, had formed the Clark Mountain Sanctuary (CMS) as a way of holding on to the nearly three hundred and fifty acres he owns. There is an informal understanding that the collective will help the old couple as they become infirm, but it would be misleading to call it merely an agreement. "It's more like we've come to see Jim as a grandfather figure in our lives," one of them told me. "He's our neighbor and our wise elder, and we will behave accordingly when the need arises."

The deeds for the remaining 315 acres will go to CMS, a non-profit. Jim wants JED to manage CMS by having a majority of seats on the board. At the time of writing, these arrangements have yet to be finalized, which might lead to occasional sleepless nights for JED members.

At dinner I met Ethan Miller, who has been a JED resident longer than anyone else. He forged the initial relationship with Jim, and he also had the original vision to see that what he is trying to achieve on a small, local scale has wider national and international implications. Ethan, age thirty-two, is a specialist in alternative economic structures. His mother is a Catholic and his father has "a strong critical perspective on the current power structure," so mealtimes were rowdy in the Miller household when he was growing up, in eastern Pennsylvania. He has had all kinds of "random odd jobs." As well as designing the financial structure of JED, he picks blueberries and is working with others on an idea for a land trust, an entity modeled on Evergreen Housing, an affordable-housing developer in Seattle. The land trust will, if it succeeds, take over the land from idealistic owners such as Sequoia or Carolyn Chute and ensure it remains undeveloped.

Here, it seems, is a possible solution to the problem Sequoia had of how to protect land from exploitation. This is a way to hold land in a trust and help two very different groups within the off-grid community. It could assist the elderly by providing reliable companions, and the young by allowing them to take over land without paying inheritance tax as the existing owners die off.

In some cases land will have to be sold to pay medical bills or because the children want the money. Other owners are childless, and even friendless, and trading a comfortable, secure old age in the company of like-minded youngsters for all or some of their property (some properties cannot be subdivided, but many can) might be considered a fair exchange. Ethan's vision is of an organization that acts as an impartial clearinghouse for all such arrangements, holding or owning the land, managing it, and assigning it to suitable recipients. The unstated premise of the JED land-stewardship initiative is that the young, these days, cannot get their hands on land where they could live off the grid. It is too expensive, too hedged in with building restrictions, and, as the population grows ever larger, likely to remain forever out of reach.

VIRTUAL SPRINGFIELD

There is, of course, a minority of privileged folks who can afford outrageous prices for a few acres of land. And there is a larger, less privileged minority who can afford to buy a cheap home on a bad street in a small town, repay the mortgage over relatively few years, and then live an off-grid-ready life on a low income.

Daniel Staub and Kristin Brennan fall into the latter category. One of the JED members put me in touch with them, and I was fascinated by their story. They live about two hundred miles south of JED, at the end of a quiet, pleasant street in a low-income neighborhood in Springfield, Massachusetts. When they moved in, there was a crack house next door (which is why they paid only $110,000). It's gone now.

I never visited the house because Daniel had made it a condition of our meeting that I would travel to him by public transport, so as to reduce the carbon cost of the journey. At the time I was in his area, I had my budget airplane ticket already booked, so I wasn't able to oblige. But I did even better (from the perspective of saving energy) by looking around the Staub-Brennan house with Google's "street-view" software. I checked out the neighbors, admired the front yard, with its bushy hedges along the perimeter, and spotted a mass of unkempt vegetation around the immaculate-looking blue house. Then I spoke to Daniel at length by phone.

They still owe sixty-five thousand dollars on the house and make payments of six hundred dollars a month, two hundred of which, at the time of writing, is interest and building insurance. They sell honey, and Kristin works part-time to earn enough to pay the mortgage (along with its compulsory building insurance of eight hundred dollars a year). Daniel supplements that by giving a few piano lessons in their home each week. The piano also provides free entertainment in the evenings, when most American families are watching TV.

Daniel starts his day by milking their two dwarf goats. "Then we'll have our homemade granola, with fresh goat's milk and fresh fruit," he said. He his wife, and their two kids, who are homeschooled, grow strawberries in June; raspberries, blueberries, and peaches in midsummer; and apples and pears in the fall.

The family have withdrawn from conventional society as much as possible. They don't have health insurance, insurance for the contents of their house, life insurance, or a pension plan. "We don't own, and rarely ride in, cars. We don't watch television. We shop extremely rarely but still have sumptuous meals seven days a week."

Because of their purposely low income, Daniel and Kristin know they will never put their kids through college. They have thought it through and are happy they are not subscribing to that particular con. Daniel says his image of the American college student is "of a babbling drunk." In their teaching methods, he and his wife subscribe to the principle that "real learning comes when a young person is directly engaged with an older person in a meaningful activity." They have taught their four-year-old daughter and six-year-old son to change a bicycle tire, speak Spanish, and play the piano. "[Our daughter] learns how to make a recipe and then how to double it," so math is incorporated as well.

As part of their reduced dependence on municipal energy, the Staub-Brennans light most of the house with candles, and heat it with wood they are given by neighbors or that they scavenge. Much of the time in winter is spent "chopping, sawing, stacking, bringing in, loading, and hauling wood, and taking out the ashes. Sometimes in winter it seems like we live to heat rather than heat to live," Daniel said. He has a way with words.

Their neighbors haven't complained about the goats in their yard and are, in fact, "from the Caribbean and used to that sort of thing." The guy from next door often drops by with fish he has caught in one of the town's ponds, and leaves with some of the fruit and vegetables that Daniel and Kristin grow in the two-thirds-acre double lot behind a conventional-looking, two-story three-bedroom home.

Daniel had no particular skills when they embarked on this way of life. I wondered why fate had singled him out. Of all the boys and girls in class at school, what had led him to live this way? His father is a social psychologist, so on one level this could be a social experiment. On the more practical plane, Daniel and Kristin have learned gardening, food preservation, bike mechanics, animal husbandry, wood splitting, cooking, and some carpentry. But Daniel said he is still "totally clueless" about other skills, such as soapmaking, knitting, and concocting herbal remedies.

Daniel doesn't think there is anything special in what they do. "[It's] ridiculous to me that providing for your family's basic needs from the land that surrounds you and the people who live on it is somehow new," he said. In this relatively low-income town, the seeds of small-scale economic exchange and neighborly interdependence have already been sown, yet Daniel is forced to accept that several years into their experiment, and despite prolonged national TV exposure, there is not another soul in Springfield living the way he does, although there are quite a few nationally. "My dream would be to make these ideas, and the practice of living them, so ordinary that you would have nothing to write about," he told me. I am not holding my breath.

Many "urban homesteaders" have opted out of the normal ways of city life. If they have a yard, they probably grow vegetables rather than flowers. Many are, if not vegetarians, then at least locavores, as Daniel is, eating mostly produce grown in the immediate area. They might be "freegans," who scavenge in grocery dumpsters for some of their food. Daniel, however, disapproves of the practice known as dumpster diving. "I don't really regard hand-me-downs, thrift stores, or dumpster diving as a legitimate part of the answer. They're sort of an intermediate step—a way of refusing to consent to our global economy without actually providing an alternative."

This kind of purity is a difficult argument to sustain, and I am not sure if I agree with his logic, because if you take it all the way, if Daniel is seriously committed to severing his dependence on the global economy, shouldn't he have built a house himself rather than buying a preexisting house on a preexisting street? Or shouldn't he have started a whole new community, however impractical and over the top that may be? I certainly would never do it myself, and it is hard to draw the line in Daniel's experiment. It seems wherever you do go is an arbitrary decision, and that makes me question the point of it all. Even worse, after many years of living like this, Daniel confirms that not one Springfield resident has followed his example.

There are all sorts of ways to be off-grid ready, from a trailer powered by the municipal supply to a houseboat in Sausalito. In each case the test of whether someone is off-grid ready or not is partly practical and partly related to his or her state of mind.

The Staub-Brennans are highly off-grid ready, and they come at it from a very positive place. They are affirmative and generous in their approach, where some are acting with a survivalist's bunker mentality, a defensiveness that is basically selfish. After *Walden* was published in 1854, the *New York Times* sharpened its criticism of Thoreau and moved from merely dismissing the book to accusing him of precisely that negative approach to the subject, saying that he lived in "cold and selfish isolation from human cares and interests." I prefer to believe that Thoreau was motivated by his search for "a life of simplicity, independence, magnanimity, and trust," as he expressed it. And he did continue that search at all times for the rest of his life.

My communications with Daniel Staub took place over several weeks, after I had visited JED. Having spent the night with the "anarchist kids," I realized with a start that I had a choice—either junk my ticket and visit Daniel, or go to Boston airport and on the way treat myself to a brief visit to Walden Pond, home of Thoreau's epoch-making experiment in self-reliance.

A WALDEN WEDDING

As readers will have discerned, I have a soft spot for Thoreau. He was, like me, a part-time off-gridder. Whereas I flit between city life and rural, off-grid seclusion, Thoreau walked home to his mother in Concord, Massachusetts, with his washing, and depended on her goody bags while he thought great thoughts in the forest. I also approve of Thoreau's disdain for work—he called it the "spending of the best part of one's life earning money in order to enjoy a questionable liberty during the least valuable part of it." I try to spend as much of my life as possible being idle.

Such were the great thoughts passing through my own head as I pulled into the Walden Pond parking lot that Sunday morning. These days it's a thriving recreational area, and although there were visitors on the Thoreau pilgrimage, many more were there to run, swim, kayak, or simply enjoy the view. It did not affect my enjoyment in the least to learn that every year six hundred thousand people come for the sight of the pure water and to wander among the oak and pine. Thoreau, after all, celebrated Walden as a piece of nature, not a church.

However, to my delight I did find a semireligious event taking place as I wandered around Walden in "companionable solitude." It was a wedding, no less, in a little-used section of the park, far from the major attractions of the lake and Thoreau's cabin. The bride was wearing a white shawl over a red dress, and clutching a bright bouquet of humble flowers—daffodils, irises, and pansies. The groom had on a brand-new suit several sizes too large for him, with a badly creased red-and-white-striped extra-wide tie and a five-dollar haircut. They had eloped the previous day. The rest of the wedding party consisted of just two other couples. I return to them in Chapter 8.

5 Reinventing the American Dream

"Every generation laughs at the old fashions but follows religiously the new."

Henry David Thoreau, *Walden*

Everyone I've profiled to this point has been white and middle or upper-middle class. There are a number of reasons for this. First, I am white and middle class, and tend to meet people like myself. I won't apologize for that. Second, rural America, with several glaring geographic exceptions, tends to be white. To be Hispanic or dark-skinned in Texas or Kentucky is to be discriminated against and disadvantaged, a situation that's less than ideal. We're talking about the rural areas; the big cities are slightly more likely to be places of equal opportunity. Finally, the previous two chapters were about the semi-off-grid life, which is closely related to the middle-class comfort zone.

There are off-gridders who aspire to live the conventional middle-class life but whose aspirations are not matched by the size of their wallet. When it comes to the house you live in, there is only one way you can go when money is limited: Shift your desires to something you can afford—an apartment in the city center instead of a house in the suburbs, or one on a bad street instead of a good street. If you are toward the bottom of the pile, the options shrink and fade into insignificance, especially when the question is whether you should move in next to a crack house or live in your car.

THE WILD, WILD WEST

Carlos Proffit just wanted a home, somewhere he could call his own—"a toehold," he said, "a place no one could run me off of."

He had not exactly chosen where to place his paltry savings. His land just happened along. And equally by chance the area he bought into was, and remains, a criminal neighborhood, even though he is a man who likes to live by the rules.

He was working as a mechanic at a trucking company about twenty years ago. A coworker owned five acres on a tract in the desert on the edge of Albuquerque, New Mexico. Although most of rural America is white, New Mexico is one of the exceptions. For obvious cultural reasons, Hispanics are on a more equal footing with whites. The FBI has cited New Mexico as one of the most corrupt states in the union, but its Wild West mentality works in favor of going off the grid if you have the stomach to defend yourself when the cops won't get involved and the stamina to survive the harsh, unforgiving terrain.

Carlos was eighteen. He needed a home and he needed his freedom. He began by buying one acre, paying it off at $150 a month. When he had paid for the first acre, he bought the next acre, and when he had paid for that, both buyer and seller went to see a lawyer about splitting the land into two parcels. It wasn't possible for zoning reasons, so Carlos bought the remaining three acres.

"It was the only thing I could do," he told me as we drove out to his home. "I have never been in the position where I could get any kind of a loan or financing. It was a real estate contract—the most expensive way to buy any kind of land." He proceeded to build a house with his own hands; the first room was the kitchen.

"I was working seven days a week," he said. "I didn't have any of the nice equipment I got now. But from not paying rent I was able to buy it eventually." He is forty-five now, still with jet-black hair. He is not hugely ambitious. He just wants to live with dignity.

We were about twenty minutes from the center of Albuquerque, driving into the empty desert along a perfectly straight county road, toward Pajarito Mesa—as close to downtown Albuquerque as the city's other suburbs, yet utterly different. As we neared Carlos's home, I commented on the vast amount of garbage on the side of the dusty road—plastic bags, sofas, building supplies, fridges, children's toys. "Yeah, and a lot of stolen vehicles being left," Carlos informed me, due to the area's proximity to the county landfill.

Pajarito Mesa is a former land grant awarded by the King of Spain to a loyal courtier. It comprises thirty square miles of mountain, forest, river, and desert, plus sagebrush, four-wing saltbush, a bit of yucca, and a lot of rodents, which Carlos hates because they eat his vegetables. Carlos's section is sparse desert, with the county road running through it. Some tracks lead off that road to the scattered homesteads. There are three hundred families, mainly Hispanic, living in the area off the grid.

Shortly after Carlos began building his home, the county opened a landfill a few miles from him. The problem is that dozens of vehicles—carrying builders, private householders, professional dumpers—arrive every week with their garbage and find that the dump is closed or that there is a fee for dumping, so they just drive on past and dump on the mesa. The stuff is everywhere; it's as if the streets are paved with mattresses. Paper and light-weight garbage flies around in the breeze. The heavier stuff just stays where it was dumped. Dead bodies are an occasional occurrence, according to Carlos. They are often the result of Mexican cartel executions, but also ordinary murders by ordinary killers who need somewhere to dump an ordinary body. Twelve miles away, the Denny's at Interstate 40 had been held up by armed men the previous weekend. They held a hundred people hostage for a few hours.

Carlos used to pick up as much garbage as he could in his truck and take it to the dump himself, thinking that somehow his good example would teach others to follow. He was a welder with a set of regular clients, and the landfill became one of his biggest, until a change of ownership a few years later. Then the new owners told him to stop and he didn't speak to them for a few years. Nor did he work for them. Now the landfill has changed hands yet again, and he is back doing regular welding for them. He doesn't bother to pick up the garbage anymore.

And he's a bit more careful about calling the cops on illegal dumpers. "[The cops] can't find their way out here—can you believe that?" he asked angrily. The police say they do not know where his street is, even though he has called them many times. At one point, he had called them out to arrest a couple of garbage dumpers, but while he waited for them he managed to persuade the dumpers to pick up their stuff. Then he went to the prearranged place to meet the cops. "I only needed to tell them not to worry." To his horror they started pushing and beating him, and then arrested five-foot-three-inch Carlos, for "resisting arrest."

"You have to hand it to these New Mexico cops—they at least have a sense of humor," he said. That was two years ago. Carlos was acquitted by a jury. The punch line isn't so funny, though: The not-guilty judgment has cost him twelve thousand dollars in lawyers' fees so far, and the cops have appealed.

As we neared Carlos's home, I could see a few trailers and a couple of houses on the horizon. Elsewhere in the subdivision there are fancier places. The electricity towers stop on this side of the hill, just as they did twenty-five years earlier, when he bought the land. Carlos's home is on the other side.

When I looked it up on Google Maps later, I found that Pajarito Mesa isn't listed at all. Its roads are there, along with the little dots of the buildings, but there is no sign of the area itself. Carlos said it's because the county just does not want to service the area—or police it. He does not know his own zip code, even though he pays property taxes, or at least he did until the previous December, when he stopped on the grounds that the police refuse to go out to the area to keep order.

Water is an issue for those who do not have their own well (Carlos does). The county has, for years, been hounding the one semipublic source, an enterprising dealer who sells water to the community. "Without Dennis they have to go and get it from gas stations, or burger joints," said Carlos. Dennis is doing a useful job. He pumps the water up from his well using a generator, and offers an all-you-can-eat deal that gives the locals access to his water for thirty dollars a month, limited only by the inconvenience of driving to him and filling up containers to bring home again.

Carlos's five acres cost him ten thousand dollars, including all of the interest, and he built the house soon after taking over his second acre. The land there is worth "way more" now, due to the drug money being laundered through the area.

"It was always lawless," he told me as we pulled up outside his house. "But there was less crime. It's snowballed in the last five years. The criminals do stuff because they can get away with it. It's their livelihood." Carlos's own home was broken into every six months for the first twenty years. Once, his dogs were attacked with a claw hammer. Recently the crime has stopped, and he thinks it's because a new, well-armed neighbor moved in nearby.

We got out of the car, and the chained dogs barked a welcome.

Carlos's girlfriend, Dora, had recently moved in, after a long courtship, and given up her apartment in the city. The extra money is helpful to them both. She welcomed me in with the same quiet, humble friendliness as Carlos, and the same manners, intimate and courteous. She cooked us a meal—tacos, salad, enchiladas—as we sat in what had once been the only room.

Through a pair of glass doors is the winter greenhouse, facing a blank, garbage-strewn landscape to the east. The greenhouse, which doubles as a storeroom, is also the entrance area, which in Hispanic family houses is called the entrada. Carlos pointed out the floor tiles for solar gain (they absorb the sun's heat by day and release it by night), as well as the high windows, chimneys, wood-burning stoves, water heaters, and solar panels—the stuff off-gridders talk about.

He plans to build a walled garden next, for grapes and figs. He has a 575-foot-deep well with a cistern up on a hill. An air bubble in the tank stopped the water for a while. You won't find a more practical guy than Carlos, but that one had him foxed. He solved it in the end, like he solves just about everything else. Only twice has he had to call someone for help: once to pour the concrete base that his house sits on, and once to lift the solar thermal collectors into place on the roof.

The next morning we were up early. Carlos wanted to show me the local illegal horse-racing track before it started filling up for the regular Sunday races. It's a full-fledged track sitting next to a chop shop, with a grandstand, starting stalls, fences marking out the course, and the largest collection of solar panels in the entire Albuquerque area. At that point, it had been open for about a year, and a crowd of two or three thousand would gather there when the racing was on.

"This is not a six-furlong thoroughbred race meeting," Carlos said. Usually there are several two-horse races with the principal bet between the two owners at around twenty thousand dollars, and the spectators are all free to make whatever side bets they want with each other or the bookies.

As it happened there would be no race that day, nor for the next few weeks. Carlos learned later that a competitor had opened another racetrack just to the west of his house, and, as if by coincidence, "one of the owners of the old racetrack was kidnapped. Nobody knows where he is now—it's been two weeks. It's dangerous to be a wealthy Mexican around here."

"The new track is now operational," he told me when I phoned him a few weeks later on a Sunday morning. "They will all be there in their Sunday best with their big SUVs and processions of thirty-thousand-dollar three-horse trailers, each full of racehorses, showing everybody what they've got. Most of them are from the state of Chihuahua, but they live in town," he said. "It's another way of laundering drug money—gambling is what it's all about.

"We, the United States of America—we give people the benefit of the doubt," he added. "That's our system, but not to paint with too broad a brush, a lot of these guys, you give 'em an opening and they take it and they're gone. It's like the self-checkout section at Wal-Mart. They just say to themselves, 'stupid gringos, stupid gringos.'"

Both sets of Carlos's grandparents had been raised during the Great Depression, and he had learned his values from them as he grew up, had "learned to live without a Wal-Mart," he said. He finds great solace in the writings of Wendell Berry, the Kentucky farmer and writer who reminds us that man is part of nature, and that work is natural, something to be enjoyed.

The son of a Tex-Mex (mestizo) mother and a Scottish immigrant father from North Carolina, Carlos grew up with a modest amount of money but nothing lavish. "Always had a garden, always worked for Dad," he said softly. "I just never bought into the recreational lifestyle." He left home as soon as he could, and worked hard for a couple of years before he started paying for his patch of land.

His mother's family were U.S. citizens who had lost sons in World War II. She went to college, he proudly told me, which was almost unheard of at the time for men or women of her race and class. "She was virtually the first person from her community to do so." She pushed her way through the system with all the power of her five-foot frame.

Carlos is not tall either. He has mid-length hair parted on the side, a neat beard, and rimless glasses. He dresses cleanly in blue jeans and a red-and-white collared shirt, speaks perfect English with a slight Spanish accent, and is always respectful and correct in his manners. There are many others like him in the area—law-abiding and decent people who play by the rules and are shafted for it.

When I called him a few weeks later, there had been some developments. The local congressman and county commissioner had been out for their first visit in twenty years, probably ever since Carlos has lived on the mesa. It had lasted exactly an hour. They had barged into the regular community get-together at the request of the local Residents Association, which was, for some reason, being run by a grant-aided organization from Albuquerque. The politicians were there to meet the local community and persuade them not to vote the existing committee off. But Carlos and his friends went ahead anyway, and appointed their own representatives in a 40–0 vote that left them feeling more empowered than they had for a decade.

The old committee had been pushing for municipal power to be brought over the hill. Carlos and his friends feel that their independence is worth fighting for. "This is the unwashed and the unprepared," he said during my visit, speaking on behalf of himself and his neighbors, "and we have an opportunity here to show the world. If we can do it here under these conditions, then anyone can." When I first met him, the pressure had already started. "You bring in the cheap energy," he told me, "and then you create an addiction to it. We can live better and cheaper with the photovoltaics and the good thermal [mass] buildings. I would lose, financially, from the grid being here, even if my property values went up." He pointed to the solar panels. "This is the good investment."

I had a premonition that Carlos would one day end up in the minority, like Alicia Putney in Florida, defending a way of life that others would dismiss as pointless and outmoded. He had originally come to the mesa to build his home and live his life the way he saw fit. Unlike grumpy Alicia, Carlos has boundless charm and a laid-back manner. It might be what ensures that he keeps the majority on his side. Our next stop on the tour was a local religious service, held in the front room of the preacher's house. The congregation cannot afford to build a church, though there are plans. A dozen families squeezed in, the wealthier men wearing suits. A band of teenagers played gospel music on guitars and drums. The preacher, a big, chubby guy with the air of a businessman, greeted everyone at the door. It's an open-plan room with the kitchen off to one side, and as the service progressed several women began preparing a meal, whether for the entire congregation or just the family I was not to learn. We continued the tour.

I followed behind Carlos in my rental as he took us along the potholed track, past a massive AT&T control tower dominating the landscape, an emergency backup tower in the event of a major outage of the national communications system—one caused by a nuclear strike, for example. Undoubtedly there is a reason why this vital piece of the national communications jig-saw puzzle would be situated in such an exposed location, the only structure as far as the eye can see, with its own uninter-rupted power supply and three eight-hour shifts a day to man the communications controls.

A SAD TALE

Just beyond the red and white tower, a mile from the defunct illegal horse-racing stadium owned by the Mexican who disap-peared, Carlos took a sharp turn off the road and headed up a winding track toward what appeared to be a deserted trailer. "I just want to check up on a friend," he said. "He hasn't phoned for a week, and we keep an eye on each other."

Except for a jerry-built wooden corral holding six patient horses, the yard looked as if a posse of tinkerers had traded scrap metal there for a few years and then upped and left in the dead of night.

As we neared the trailer, a pack of slobbering, monstrous dogs ran toward the car, barking and hurling themselves against the hood. A tall, slim, gray-haired man appeared wearing cowboy boots, dark blue jeans, and a light blue denim shirt. He walked toward us with the gait of someone who has spent a long time sitting on horses. Once he had chained up the two largest hounds, I opened the car door to say hello.

The story of how David Derringer ended up in this out-of-the-way spot, living in a tiny trailer that deserves to be condemned, is one of the most abject I have ever heard.

His downfall was a legal dispute, he said, with the neighbor of his million-dollar ranch in the far west of New Mexico. The legal fees alone had finished him off, and he claimed he had been run off his ranch by men with guns.

His misfortune might have crushed a lesser man. David is still fighting for what he sees as justice denied. Tall and distinguished-looking, he has a voice like actor James Stewart's. Where once he had millions in assets, he now has an old car and no money. He is still fighting. He has been waiting for a date with the U.S. Supreme Court for more than two years.

On October 20, 1993, David says, he bought himself a ranch in Catron County, New Mexico, next to the Gila National Forest, 250 miles north of the Mexican border. He invested every cent he had in the four-hundred-acre ranch. When he said goodbye to Albuquerque, it was a big moment for the forty-seven-year-old, the great-grandson of Henry Deringer. (The spelling of the family surname changed over the years to reflect the widespread misspelling of his eponymous pistol.)

David has a knack for getting on with horses. The way he tells it, he could summon every single one of his hundred-stallion herd and they would each thunder toward him. He had assumed that his easy way with people and horses would allow him and his wife to run a fun, profitable outfitting business for the rest of their lives.

"The whole issue is to buy property with water," David told me. "We had eleven springs, septic tanks. Half the land was farmable. I had backup solar and wind generators. We were raising goats for milk, cheese, butter."

But he hadn't reckoned on his neighbor, a rival outfitter by the name of Mike Chapel. The battle was ostensibly about water, but David thinks it was about much more than that. He proceeded to tell me the story, all of which was later denied by Chapel.

"He terrorized us almost every night. When she was on her own, my wife used to hide in the middle of the house in a closet; she was so afraid. He attacked me the first day we bought the property, trying to drive me out. Instead of bringing brownies and saying, 'Welcome to the neighborhood,' he came over with ten thugs."

On the morning of Friday, February 28, 2003, David said, he saw a white helicopter with no markings appear from the south and go into a hover on the back west side of his neighbor's hill. David had seen many helicopters arrive, usually at night, and he alleges that they would drop a few duffel bags onto his neighbor's land, then leave. This one was different. To start with, this was during the day. Furthermore, the helicopter turned and hovered directly over David's home. And finally, it was a Chinook. "Very few of these helicopters are privately owned in the United States," he said. "This is a double-main, counter-rotating rotored helicopter of extreme size, with a payload capacity of twenty-one tons. [It costs] several million and about twelve hundred dollars per hour to fly."

David said the Drug Enforcement Administration confirmed this Chinook was of Mexican origin, and was one of several white Chinooks used in Mexico to transport cocaine and marijuana into the United States. He said he informed the DEA of his suspicions that his neighbor was dealing coke on a regular basis, and the DEA sent agents who spent time with him, watching his neighbor. But they never made an arrest.

At this point I began to doubt David's story. He explained the lack of an arrest warrant by virtue of the fact that Mike had a $250-an-hour lawyer, and a string of cops, judges, and border guards in his pay. I began to think that David sounded like a paranoid. I made to leave, and then, like an idiot, I locked the keys in the trunk of my rental car. Now I was stuck—I had no spare key, and the backseat of this particular model does not fold down.

David was magnificent. First he discovered that he could push his arm through the seat and into the trunk. Had the trunk been empty it would have been easy to retrieve the keys, but it was chock-full of my stuff, including a heavy suitcase. He managed to raise the suitcase up onto lumps of wood he fed into the trunk, then extend his long arm all the way to the back and find the keys. I was free to go, but now I owed David and I felt bad for doubting him. So I tried my best to confirm his story, or at least find some chink in the armor of the fearsome Mike Chapel.

Mike had, through the courts, established ownership of the water rights that David had thought he owned when he bought his ranch. And later a New Mexico court declared Mike also owned David's ranch.

As events unfolded, David's wife became more and more fearful and eventually left him. I asked him if I could phone her, for her corroboration. No, he replied; he is no longer in touch with her.

He gave me the phone number of a friend called Cheryl, who had stuck by him through the years. When we spoke she seemed confused and had not witnessed the key moments of David's story.

I phoned Janice Stevenson, the chief forest ranger at Gila National Forest, who must have watched the battle between David and Mike unfold. It took many calls until she eventually came on the line, with a hoarse, masculine, monotone voice—a cop's voice. She wouldn't talk. "I can only say that the whole relationship between the two was controversial locally. I worked with [David] in a professional capacity, and it would be unprofessional to say any more."

I thanked her and phoned Mike Chapel himself. A bold, confident baritone answered the phone and admitted that yes, this was Mike Chapel, and yes, he does own an outfitters in Quemado. "And a whole bunch of other businesses," he added with a mix of smugness and brash confidence. I didn't like him already.

"Oh, David Derringer," the deep voice boomed down the phone line. "A not-so-fond memory. We're glad he's gone." Mike laughed when I told him of David's claim that Mike had had him run off his own property.

"The wild, wild west is not that wild anymore," was his answer. He had answers ready for everything I asked him.

Yes, he did now own the former Derringer ranch. The battle had all been to do with water rights, and "when David broke the dam, the judge fined him a hundred dollars a day, and punitive damages, and a whole bunch of cumulative damages, and that mounted up, over time, to more than the property was worth." This would be Judge Cynthia Fry, whom David claimed he later sued.

Mike then volunteered the information as to how David had come by the property. "Oh. His estranged wife did own it with her mother, and when he agreed to marry her he was cut in for a third of it. The whole thing was over the water rights," he repeated, "and his reluctance to leave the water alone." Then he said he had another call coming in, and he was gone.

I feel sad when I recall poor David, sitting alone in his trailer with his wretched horses. He is now involved, he told me during a later phone call, in yet another lawsuit, this time with the Albuquerque animal authorities over his donkey, which they had, for some reason, confiscated. Soon he would be down to his last horse, his last dog, and then . . . nothing.

I celebrated, not for the first time, how lucky I am never to have become involved in a legal dispute with neighbors or anyone else. Better to walk away from your life savings than enter into a legal battle that sucks up your time and your energy, and leaves only the lawyers richer.

Having thanked David for rescuing my car keys, I headed north to Colorado, through Durango, and meandered up to Aspen, where I stayed a night with Wayne Poulsen, a sixty-year-old skiing ace who lives off the grid on the back side of Aspen Hill, in a self-built Swiss-style log chalet with a twenty-five-foot-high atrium and a view through large pines to the slopes opposite. He cooked dinner over a log fire, and as we ate the food and drank the red wine I had brought, I thought again of David Derringer sitting alone in his trailer and asked myself what would become of him. Wayne probably saw himself as living a fairly modest life compared with his father, who had founded one of America's first ski resorts (a fact I discovered later with no prompting from Wayne). Compared with David, he had everything. For a skier it was living the dream; for anyone else it was a bit of a pain, as his chalet could be reached only by snowmobile in the winter (and this was the middle of the winter).

ANTI-NUCLEAR FAMILY

My next destination was Ridgway, Colorado. I had an appointment with a local politician whose reasons for living off the grid have as much to do with saving money as with saving the planet.

Ridgway is small, quaint, and not especially historic. Its beauty is in its setting. The town is compact, with tree-lined streets. It is set among green fields enclosed by low mountains, which are themselves flanked by high, snowcapped peaks. Even for Colorado it is especially well situated.

I was instantly drawn in as I walked around the town (population 1,100). I wanted to enter every store, buy a drink in every bar (about eight of them), and eat a meal in every café (about a dozen of them). What I could see were citizens enjoying every aspect of their lives, without the excess and the greed I had sensed in Boulder and Aspen. Everything in Ridgway is to a high standard. Everybody, without exception, was friendly, and there is a real sense of community. I had been there a few hours when I decided I wanted to stay—or at least come back for a long time.

I headed for a second-story office in the center of town to meet Lynn Padgett, whom I had found on the Internet when she was running for the post of county commissioner for Ouray County. She had been "just" a single mother when we first spoke. A few months had passed, and now she was married and a serving Democratic commissioner—no longer a mere candidate.

I climbed a wooden outdoor staircase and knocked on a wooden door. The small office is crowded with wooden furniture. Lynn turned out to be a tall, pleasant, dark-haired woman in her late thirties. I guessed that her new husband, Jeff, is some years older. He quickly escaped to pick the kids up from school. (Lynn's daughter, Anza, is in second grade at Ridgway Elementary, and her son, Cutler, attends Ridgway Preschool.)

Lynn had lived in the Ridgway area for about eight years before she bought her home, way out of town on a forty-acre lot. Since then another eight years had passed. "I simply couldn't wait until my retirement years to live here," she said. I could relate to that.

"This is where I wanted to raise a family," she went on, "where neighbors are neighborly, and there is plenty of clean air, clean water." House prices, of course, are consequently high.

Lynn graduated with a degree in geology and began working as a wetland scientist and mapping expert for a local consulting

firm. She is, through her educational background, her professional expertise, and now her move into local politics, a committed environmentalist, so it is no surprise that part of her
reason for moving off the grid has to do with a desire to be closer
to the environment, to feel connected to the sun as it affects her
own family's warmth and daily routine. "The wind is coming in
at forty to a hundred miles an hour, and a snowstorm is closing
in, and we are very much into that wildness."

Once Jeff returned from the school run, we all went around
the corner to the local microbrewery to drink a few pitchers of
beer and eat a meal. We discussed the plight of the Lower San
Luis Valley, in southeastern Colorado, where big utility companies are planning to take power from the people. Huge solar
farms are being built, and towers will carry the electricity far
away, across mountains and through bird sanctuaries. The kids
were getting tired, so we agreed I would drive out before work
the next morning to visit the family at the house. It was a work-
day, so I would arrive early.

I decided to spend the night at Orvis Hot Springs, just on the
edge of town. It proved to be one of the best hot springs I have
visited in America. I arrived right at the evening deadline of
nine-thirty. All the rooms were full, so I would be sleeping in
my rented SUV—no great hardship, even though it was a freezing night. I had all-night access to the hot springs, to warm
myself at any time, use the kitchen to cook a meal, and generally make like a luxury guest without the inconvenience of having to remove my bags from the rental car.

I was tired, but the enchanted lighting, the big night sky, and
the thrill of being somewhere so civilized in the middle of the
desert were as refreshing as the water itself.

Sleeping in the SUV was almost luxurious. I could stretch out
fully, in a very warm sleeping bag, with a five-dollar bedroll and
a three-dollar pillow from the nearest dollar store. It was all I
needed. Later on, elsewhere in Colorado, I would receive a much
fuller education in car dwelling. (See Chapter 8.)

I stayed up late enjoying the bubbles, and the next morning

somehow managed to find my way to Lynn's house through a maze of private roads past a huge golf club and residential development, eleven miles out of Ridgway in the boondocks, between Ridgway and Telluride as the crow flies. It is a beautiful setting, with total privacy.

Although her place is down a bad road, it is grade-A real estate. Her neighbors are lawyers and doctors, horse owners, wealthy retirees, and even wealthier weekenders.

I wandered around the house admiring the views of the distant mountains from big windows designed to maximize sunlight, and felt the warmth emanating from stone walls that absorb the sun's heat. "You can ski out of the door in the winter," Lynn said. Ouray County is known as the Switzerland of America, with world-class ice climbing as another of its attractions.

It was a house she had been able to move straight into when she bought it. Apart from its off- grid modifications, it is a typical suburban home, complete with a large, messy, toy-filled room shared by the kids and another bedroom for Lynn and Jeff.

Lynn cooked eggs and waffles as she taught me off-grid home financing 101. She had found the house when she was sent out on a geological survey in the area. It has the proximity to a millionaire's setting, but at half the cost of the same house near Fairway Pines, the golf club I had passed on the way.

As she had searched through the late nineties, she watched prices moving inexorably upward. She paid $195,000 for the house in 2000. "You couldn't find anything in town for less than $250,000 at the time," she said, "and more like three hundred thousand where we are." Prior to the downturn it had been impossible to find a house in Ridgway for less than four hundred thousand dollars, which meant five to six hundred thousand in Lynn's area. (Her property was valued at $450,000 at peak. Prices have dropped twenty-five percent since.) The couple next door (two miles away) had to hand their keys back the previous year, after they ran into debt and divorced. They were one of just fourteen foreclosures in Ouray County in 2008.

There is a high percentage of second-home owners—thirty to fifty percent—in the Ridgway-Telluride area. Most are holding on to their properties, Lynn reported. "Realtors are saying property values are down about ten percent to fifteen percent here," she told me. "The resort communities are doing much better than in the cities."

Ironically, the off-grid second-home movement is driving up property values and feeding the problem faced by anyone who wants to go off the grid with limited funds, intensifying the very problem most off-gridders want to avoid.

Part of Lynn's motivation had been to buy into a better neighborhood than she could have afforded on the grid, I realized. She had not intended to live off grid, but she felt at ease with the life. While some would be scared by it, or even feel that it is a sign of failure, for Lynn the reverse is true. This difference of perception allowed her to buy a house at thirty to fifty thousand dollars less than its on-the-grid equivalent.

Being off the grid also has its financial downside. It is always an issue for the mortgage company, which makes obtaining the financing a major strain. Lynn was down to her last fifteen dollars when she finally landed a mortgage after being declined by a succession of banks, each further undermining her credit score.

I had a similar report from another couple, Ron and Angela Hague, an early-retired East Coast plumber and his wife in their fifties, who built an off-the-grid McMansion outside of Creede, Colorado. Their house is extraordinary, high on a hill overlooking the Creede landing strip, with castellated circular walls and split-level roof gardens. They had moved to prepare for the coming collapse, Ron said, which will be brought about by two factors: a hopelessly subservient media and over-exploitation of the planet's resources. "We've been sold a bill of goods," he said. "We don't think anymore—we are a bunch of sheep. Whatever they want us to know we know."

Although their place is completely off the grid, Ron and Angela designed and furnished it like a totally conventional home, with an all-American kitchen, three-piece suite, low occasional table—the works. It is completely inhabitable—indeed luxurious—yet several planned rooms remain unfinished due to a lack of finances. "We can't refinance the house because we're off the grid," Angela told me. They showed me a letter from their bank, saying they had been turned down specifically because "you are off the grid."

Ron continued, gloomily attacking the powers that be for his dilemma. "They tell you they want to go solar, but they're talking out of both sides of their mouth. If they really want to help people, to me it's put the money up," meaning guarantee him a loan, since he is perfectly capable of repaying it.

Back at Lynn's breakfast table I learned a few tricks that the Hagues and anyone else could find useful. Lynn did manage to refinance, without telling an untruth in any way, by simply failing to mention to the finance company that she lived off the grid. "If they don't ask, you don't need to tell, right?" She winked as I sat in on the family breakfast. She had ticked all the boxes truthfully, but there was no box asking her if she had access to municipal power and water. "It was a bit of a 'don't ask, don't tell' mortgage," she admitted. "I got it through a broker [this was in the pre-credit-crunch days, when mortgage companies were falling over themselves to lend], and I'm not sure how he did it." The lack of central heating was an issue for the lender, and when the appraiser came out Lynn needed to give a long technical discussion about passive solar heating to convince him. Some of her neighbors, she told me, had bought electric baseboard heaters from Home Depot, fitted them specially for the appraiser's visit, then took them back to the store afterward. This trick relies on the appraiser's ignorance regarding solar power, because panels alone could never power a house full of electric baseboard units.

On his visit to Lynn's residence, the appraiser failed to notice the flow of her well. It is only half a liter per minute. (Mortgage companies usually insist on at least a liter per minute and prefer five liters.) He could hardly miss, however, the low quality of the road, and Lynn's right of access had been grandfathered in by virtue of usage; there is no paper trail of deeds guaranteeing access.

In the end the lender accepted that her passive solar windows and walls, plus the solar panels and wood fires, make up for the absence of central heating, and was relaxed about the road issue. The final hurdle was a ratio lenders usually insist upon: The value of the land should be no more than thirty percent of the value of the entire purchase. "They did not want the land to be worth more than the structure," Lynn said. "Vacant lots here sell for $150,000, and mine was valued at $330,000 at the time." She just squeaked through. I doubt whether she would do so today.

Once she had her mortgage, Lynn made a very smart move. She went back to her lender and asked for (and received) an additional loan, which she justified on the grounds that she is off the grid and therefore does not have any monthly utility bills, so she can afford higher monthly payments than her salary would warrant if she lived on the grid.

RANCH STYLES OF THE RICH AND FAMOUS

Before I left the area I couldn't resist a visit to look at Daryl Hannah's home. Hannah is probably the world's most famous off-gridder. I had interviewed her for my Web site a few years earlier and the story of her off-grid home had gone viral. These days most media profiles mention her staging-post hideaway with its soft seat of moss-covered rock.

It's located a few miles back from the road connecting Ridgway with its richer and more ostentatious sister town of Telluride, not far from where the world's first alternating-current electricity plant was built, 120 years ago, for a local goldmine. Soon other mines were asking for power from the same source, and the Telluride Power Company was created to meet demand.

A decade later, in 1902, the area was one of those that suffered from "spite lines," mentioned in Chapter 2. The Telluride Power Company faced local opposition to erecting pylon towers, but a combination of court cases and propaganda efforts forced the lines through the local farming community in the end. Florida Power and Light also built a sixteen-mile spite line in nearby Delta County.

Together with my guide, I drove out of Ouray and into San Miguel County, past Ralph Lauren's twelve-thousand-acre ranch and its field of tepees, past neighboring Hastings Mesa, where a few years earlier a handful of wealthy landowners had moved in and forced the rest of the owners to pay for an extension of the grid. The "no-power people," as the residents were dismissively called by the *Denver Post* in frequent coverage of the dispute, had been happy that way since the late seventies. They used propane and wood for heat and light, and, similar to the dispute in the solar community on No Name Key, opposed the grid for fear that it would make the area just like all the other nearby ritzy enclaves.

Five years on, some are still angry that the will of the funky could be stilled by the power of the wealthy. "We thought with our social consciousness we could be a force strong enough to hold off people who want to come up here with power," said John Janus, whose home overlooks the site of the 4.75-mile underground electric line installed at a cost of three hundred thousand dollars. Behind him lies Old Elam Ranch, the only subdivision in Colorado (and possibly America) with a covenant requiring homeowners to derive power solely from solar panels.

San Miguel County planner Karen Henderson appeared to have little sympathy for the off-the-grid arguments. The off-grid holdouts were a "small outspoken group," she told the *Denver Post*. "Having the amenity of electricity makes a huge difference, especially with kids," she said. As you might expect, my sympathies lie with the holdouts.

Janus, in an interview with the *Denver Post*, said, "Here we are as a test bed, a research and development place for the world, an actual practical application of sustainability in a harsh environment." Echoing Carlos Profitt he added, "If we can do it here, it can be done anywhere."

A few miles farther toward Telluride (and therefore a few hundred thousand dollars more expensive), Brown Ranch, where Daryl Hannah bought her thousand-acre plot with its nineteenth-century staging post, had also suffered its share of local turf battles. The old stagecoach route had run through the ranch, which meant there was a right-of-way across this community of nature-loving millionaires, who had bought in so they could enjoy moose and elk and solitude. The owners had paid the County to build another nature trail somewhere else, and kept their privacy in return.

We drove into the ranch through the main gate, which was unlocked, past a giant letter *B*, several feet high, and into the steep and wooded "PJ country," as the piñon-and-juniper hillsides are known locally. A weather-beaten Sotheby's International FOR SALE sign suggested that even at the top end of the market, the credit crunch is biting.

Each of the thousand-acre lots has a utility box at the front gate—a big, square concrete tower of power. It is up to the individual householder to bring the power down from the road to their home. Daryl Hannah, I trust, has not connected her parcel to the grid.

Each plot is marked off with wildlife-friendly fencing, to prevent snagging the elk that roam freely and copiously in the area; they were everywhere I looked, outnumbered only by NO HUNTING signs.

We drove past a gateway with a small tower made of flat stones placed by hand, and a few hundred yards later my companion pointed down into the valley at an enormous house with a wraparound second-story deck towering over the land around it. Off to the side, partially obscured by trees, is a smaller building—the former staging post and bathhouse, according to the local showing me around.

With few exceptions, Colorado is a place of extraordinary privilege. Yet that privilege does not invalidate the off-grid dream. It in fact serves to show that life off the grid can be savored from the bottom to the top of society.

Neither Carlos Profitt nor Lynn Padgett would claim to have perfect lives, yet both have grasped their dreams. Carlos has lived through robberies and racially motivated police harassment to build good standing in his community and a place nobody can take from him. Lynn has gone through a divorce and scooped herself and her kids into a house where she can rear them pretty well, whatever fortune throws at her.

Lynn and Carlos both bought property in places with high real estate values, even post-crash. (Colorado's off-the-grid community is largely wealthy and privileged, while the prices on Pajarito Mesa are sustained by drug money.) For both of them, the larger economic collapse that some are forecasting requires only that enough of their debt has been paid down and overhead is kept low. Then if they lose their main source of income each will be able to cling to their dream home, whatever the fates throw at them.

6

Coping with the Crash

"Things do not change; we change."
Henry David Thoreau, *Walden*

Carlos and Lynn both chose to go off the grid. That makes them quite different from Melinda Secor. She didn't have a real choice, though of course one always has a choice unless one is utterly and completely homeless (see Chapter 10). But her choices were limited. She could claim welfare and risk having her kids taken away, or live in a car in the cold, rough Northeast—and run the same risk. So she felt she could only do what she did.

A BETTER LIFE

Melinda arrived in Big Bend, Texas, a year earlier with her three children, two dogs, two trailers, one brother, and no money. She and her brother had chosen their unpromising piece of real estate via the Internet, bought it online as if it was some pair of boots on eBay, and then, with their last few hundred dollars, drove down from Schenectady, New York, and moved onto the land. "It's the most impetuous decision I ever made," said Melinda. "And I'm the levelheaded one of the family. Everybody who knows me was quite stunned that I just dropped everyone—my house, my friends. Once we lost Mom, basically we just took the family we were close to and dragged them with us."

Back before the credit crunch, Melinda had had a well-paying nursing job. She cut back her hours when her mother fell ill and needed constant care. By the time her mother died, Melinda had fallen behind on the mortgage payments on her home, in Schenectady. It was not because of the shorter work hours so much as the fact that her hourly rate had been cut just after she switched to those hours. She spent some time working directly for clients, caring for the elderly and for disabled kids, which improved her income slightly.

Pretty soon, like millions of others, Melinda not only owed an impossible amount in back payments, but the house she had bought in 1997 was worth less than her debt. The closing fees had been close to three thousand dollars on a mortgage of $78,500. She had had to come up with a five-thousand-dollar deposit on the Schenectady property.

Over the next decade, her home became part of the mortgage derivatives merry-go-round leading up to the crash. "It was only a couple of years before they sold it. They sell all of their loans. Can't remember who it was after that. I can only remember I worked twenty-hour days for months to make the deposit."

It was then that she learned the true meaning of working for the Man. So, she dropped the keys in the mailbox and gave the house back to the mortgage company. At least, she thinks it went back to the mortgage company.

Melinda is tall and thin and elegant, with fine, swept-back shoulder-length hair, high cheekbones, and a mouthful of gawky teeth. An intelligent and well-read woman of about thirty-five, she wears little silver Maltese cross earrings and seems to favor long, flowing print dresses; she wore a different one on each of the three days we met. It was the middle of the Texas winter, so she wore a cardigan over the dresses.

I met her at her job, working behind the bar of the American Legion in Big Bend (not to be confused with Big Bend National Park, which is farther south, past Terlingua). That makes it sound like a local bar on a normal street. In fact the three hundred households of Big Bend are spread over maybe one hundred square miles. Everybody in the area lives off the grid, and the American Legion is the neighborhood club. There isn't anywhere else to go apart from a luncheonette wagon in a cluster of RVs a mile back from the highway.

The Legion is, to say the least, isolated. It sits on a long, straight road that runs due south. Driving back a few days later, with the Mexican border at least fifty miles behind me, I went through a DEA checkpoint. The locals hate the checkpoint, which is manned by burly, rude men and sniffer dogs. The pot smokers carry spray cans of Ozium, "the dealer's friend," to eliminate the telltale odors.

The Legion opens at midday, and the first of the locals usually drift in at ten after—mainly guys driving pickups and wearing baseball caps. It was late February, so the permanent population was swelled by retirees from the Northeast who own cabins and come for the winter. The weather was cold at night and baking during the day. The combination of sun and constant wind gave me a quick suntan and dried up my lips, which stayed cracked until someone gave me a piece of medicinal aloe vera.

The Legion does not seem to be the scene for particularly heavy drinking—at least, not when I was there—partly because the regulars have access to so much pot from over the border, in addition to any they happen to grow themselves. Melinda and her brother both work there, and if it weren't for the Legion, I doubt whether she would have survived financially during her first year in Big Bend.

I had driven a couple hundred miles to the bar just to meet Gary Dean, a leathery-faced, weather-beaten vet who scratches

out a living looking after vacationers' second homes. He gave
me a tour of a few other houses, all occupied by single men like
him. None of the (mostly divorced) guys seem lonely; there is a
good community in Big Bend. It's a culture of music, pot, and
DIY. There aren't many women.

One single guy Gary took me to see lives in a small, brown,
perfectly formed dome-shaped building, made of extruded
polystyrene by a company called Monolithic. He had bought it
from a guy who had built it as a weekend place. The original
owner had been really pleased with it, but when he went out to
the dome with his wife and daughter one weekend, he learned
for the first time that there is a tarantula season in Texas; the
place was infested. His wife never returned.

It was Melinda Secor's story that interested me most, however.
She invited me to spend a night at her trailer, and we rode out
in a convoy, a short fifteen-mile journey to their compound.
Her brother David drove her in their only car, as he always does
when she finishes a shift at the Legion. Shifts start at midday
and usually last about twelve hours. David is based at home,
building a water catchment and making sure food is on the
table for the kids.

It was one a.m. when we reached the trailer, and all I could
see in the dark outside was its outline. Melinda's two older children were still awake. They are homeschooled and their routine
includes a siesta so they can be with Mom after work.

"The father's in Tennessee," she explained over a final beer,
after the kids had gone to bed. "It's a shame for the kids they
don't see their dad. . . ." She shrugged.

I looked around the encampment myself the next morning.
That night we talked more about the life Melinda had escaped
than their future here in the desert. I listened as she described
Schenectady, once a leading community in New York—a bell-
wether town, along with Peoria, Illinois, and Muncie, Indiana—
now a leading example of Rust Belt decline. Fifty years ago it

was known as Electric City, but now General Electric has moved tens of thousands of jobs elsewhere, and ALCO locomotive works has been closed for decades.

"Everybody is moving out to the suburbs, except the poorest," Melinda said sadly. "Even low-income working-class folks are moving out nowadays. There is a lot of drugs, violence, absentee landlords, places just decaying," Melinda said. "When we moved there it was a nice little street and we knew everybody, but by the time we left there was a house selling heroin two doors down. There were several other drug houses on the street. The police were incredibly corrupt, more in the habit of tipping off the dealers if there was going to be a bust." The record shows the 166-strong Schenectady police force has a remarkably high proportion of drunk drivers, drug dealers, rapists, and out-and-out thieves. Maybe other crumbling Rust Belt cities have the same problem.

Even worse than the drugs and the cops in Schenectady are the sex offenders. "If you looked up my neighborhood, there were twenty names from the sex offender list within three blocks of us," said Melinda.

She didn't seem to be aware that the same can be true in any depressed neighborhood, or that the register creates strange statistical quirks. In Miami, for example, offenders on the register may not reside within two thousand feet of a school or playground. Under a freeway in the center of Miami, I visited a community of fifty men on the register who live there because it is literally the only place in the city that conforms to this rule. "Once I came home and there was a stranger talking to my daughter in the yard," Melinda recalled. "And that was when I said to David, 'OK, we're leaving now.' And we just found the land." I can understand Melinda's overreaction, because her seven-year-old daughter, Celia, has the looks to be a truly world-class child model.

"Aside from that, the atmosphere in society today was another reason we wanted to get the kids out of the city. All the kids have to have a six-hundred-dollar video game system, and it's just not the kind of values I want for my kids. But in the city, because I choose not to spoil them, I get a lot of nonsense: 'Oh, my friends have that.' Here there's no kids next door with a Sony or Nintendo."

I spent a cold night in the trailer and woke early, which was just as well because the children were waiting to come in and have their morning cereal. It had not been apparent the previous night that this was the breakfast wagon and family gathering room.

"I'd seen it coming for years," Melinda told me as we sat in the trailer talking about the credit crunch over breakfast. At least, her children and I were having breakfast. She was having coffee and her first cigarette.

Through the low, narrow window, the desert stretched away toward the mountains in the far, far distance. In the other room of the trailer a huge dog was hurling himself against a closed door, and I was having trouble concentrating for fear the animal would crash through the flimsy wood. Outside a noisy generator was running at full speed.

Because they still have no solar setup, Melinda and her brother crank up the generator each morning to charge their laptops, cook breakfast, and power the satellite dish. I didn't ask what it cost them in gas. "If I was a millionaire, I still wouldn't go on the grid," Melinda said. "I just have a personal problem with power companies. I think they're extortionists." I couldn't argue with that.

The Internet connection is via Wild Blue, a satellite Internet service sweeping rural America. At sixty dollars a month—compared with at least three times that for other, less reliable competitors—it is probably the family's main expense outside of food and gas.

"I was hanging on by a hair." Melinda, perched on a stool at the breakfast bar, returned to the subject of the economy. After the morning meal is over, this spot becomes her desk, where she works doing online research for a few bucks an hour while simultaneously smoking hand-rolled cigarettes and looking after her youngest daughter, who has Down syndrome. "The econ-omy they have been building is not sustainable," she said. "It's a bubble based on consumer spending, and spending is based on debt," she added, quoting from articles she had read online. "The mantra was 'spend yourself to prosperity,' and a lot of people bought that."

I refrained from accusing her of falling into the same trap.

"The FDIC is almost out of money. After the housing crash, the credit card debt is next," she said over the buzz of the gen-erator. "They have less than ten percent in reserve." Melinda's personal reserves didn't amount to much either, I sadly re-flected.

The early-morning sun was hotter now and cigarette smoke was curling in the sunbeam coming through the window. Still wearing multiple layers of fleece from the cold of the night be-fore, I needed to cool down. I jumped out of the claustrophobic trailer and proceeded past the broken children's toys, old pots and pans, non-working fridge, grill, tables and chairs, and porta-potty. I pulled clean clothes from my trunk, changed, and walked a long way into the desert, as there seemed to be no toilet facility other than the porta-potty on offer.

As I returned to the trailer across the flat desert, I was able to view the Secor Ranch in its wide-angle entirety. It was sparkling in the morning sunshine. The big mountains looked closer than they had appeared in silhouette the previous night. The flat top of one of them had recently been acquired by Anheuser-Busch as a corporate entertainment area for Budweiser.

There are four trailers scattered about. Way over on the right is David's. A few hundred yards straight in front is a trailer re-served for her sister, a co-shareholder in the land purchase; she was away at the time. The main trailer, closest to me, is where I slept, and the other is for the kids. Next to the main trailer are the generator and the satellite dish. Melinda came out and we continued chatting in the morning sun.

Together with her sister and another brother (also absent), the family had raised twenty thousand dollars to buy the fifty-six acres of featureless desert upon which we were standing. "It's four households," she answered when I asked why on earth they would want to own so much hopeless, arid, parched desert. "We want to grow food, keep livestock, have room to spread out." Sure, they could probably keep one or two cows here, but it didn't make economic sense to me. This is not some prime piece of Kentucky countryside. Just the cost of the fencing would keep them in beans and rice for years. Unless they plan to start a gated community in this wasteland, I can't help feeling that the fifty-six acres is just fifty-six acres of headache. Isn't 1.5 acres per family all the spreading out anyone could wish for? After all, they don't really need to own the land in order to walk across it. Nobody minds. Nobody even notices.

Melinda seemed not to hear my question about the large space, so I changed tack. Would she like to see a population expansion in the Big Bend area? "If it were people who are willing to leave the city behind," she replied, rolling an American Spirit. "Treat it with respect." She thought some more and it dawned on her that more homes might mean more kids, which would be a good thing. "There's not a lot of kids—graduating class at the local school this year was just eight," she added. Families with children tend to stay in the area just for the length of the hunting season—Thanksgiving to New Year—an act of collective selfishness on the part of fathers who drag their families to this godforsaken place to go shooting while the kids stare at the desert.

"There's too many of us to keep living the way we are living and still have anything left of our planet," Melinda added a little piously.

Her oldest boy had been sitting on a pile of tires, listening. He got tongue-tied when I asked him if it was better here than in Schenectady, but after a pause the young teenager said, "There's no violence here like in New York."

Melinda broke in quickly, as if afraid my questions about Schenectady might remind the boy of what he was missing.

"He didn't have the freedom to go out on his bike. There's a beautiful bike trail there, but a lot of kids were beaten and mugged, so I had to keep him under my thumb. My son misses television more than anything. He hasn't had any TV for more than a year, but to me that's one of the biggest benefits, sparing him from pop-culture garbage. They have learned an awful lot about not taking things for granted. They've learned about conservation, to simplify, that you don't need so many things."

Her worries about drugs, the violence around the corner, and the effect that they could have on her kids had been the tipping points. "Justin fell into the wrong crowd," she said, more to the boy sitting with us than to me. "He was hanging with kids who were heading to drugs, and he's a bit of a follower, so I wanted to get him away. It became clear he wasn't being educated at public school, just meeting friends who were leading him down the wrong path."

"What about education?" I asked. Celia, the middle daughter, had been homeschooled from the start. Melinda is decidedly unstructured. "I don't do a formal grade-level kind of education. I take what they are interested in and weave in math and science. For instance, my daughter has taken a recent interest in dinosaurs, so we find dinosaur bones in the desert. We read about arrowheads and fossils and so on, science, and even some math. It's more of a natural progression of learning. But they will have those basics of reading and writing and math." I was skeptical, more of homeschooling in general than of Melinda's particular version of it. I had tried a couple of simple arithmetic questions on Celia a few minutes earlier, and she was hopeless. Perhaps she had been nervous. "She says she can't read," Melinda told me. "But she can look at the words and see what they are, and I try to explain to her that if you look at the word and you can see what it is, then that is reading."

Melinda and I spoke one more time back at the American Legion, on a busy night. She told me again about the values she wanted to instill in her kids, and the ones she had left behind. "Other parents are worried about the same thing: their children's unhealthy demands for the latest craze," she said. "In the most affluent suburbs the emphasis is on material things. People are very shallow and materialist, and values are pretty much lost. Most families don't even sit down and have dinner together anymore. Kids are shipped off to day care, and there's barely family interaction, never mind community interaction."

Although many urban and suburban families would like to raise their children in the country, it seems out of reach for most of them. Maybe living off the grid would allow more of them to achieve that goal. Although they would have less money, they might become closer as a family.

As befits a former nurse, Melinda is a mine of health information. "Kids in grade school have high blood pressure, heart problems, obesity from eating processed packaged food, from all the sugar. I don't understand it, because it is so much less expensive, healthier, and it tastes better to cook real food. Kids today are just pushed so hard. They go to school and then soccer, they eat their meal on the way at a drive-through."

Melinda was just hitting her stride when we were interrupted by Howard, a friendly old-timer wearing a blue-and-white-striped shirt that could have been made from deck-chair material. We were out in the parking lot, and he had just left the American Legion. He was wearing blue jeans held up on his skinny frame with a brown belt, and he looked as fit as a whip. His rough, graying ginger beard and eyebrows were topped off by a gray fedora at an angle, with a feather tucked into the black band. He waved a hand, showing a few ringed fingers. In his other hand was a can of beer. He had been about to jump into his white pickup, which sports a KINKY FOR GOVERNOR, WHY THE HELL NOT bumper sticker. But now he marched over to describe his afternoon spent posing as a gold prospector to entertain some tourists he had met on the ridge.

"You *are* a prospector, Howard," Melinda joked.

"You," he said, pausing meaningfully, "are about the same size as the girl I saw in Amarillo, and her pictures ended up in a magazine." I guess this was an authentic, down-home backwoodsman pickup line. Melinda laughed politely and joshed Howard back as he made for his truck. It won't be long before this poised, sassy New Yorker finds an admirer her own age in the wilds of Texas. For now she has to make do with the flattery of old-timers.

"The stress level is lower here," she said as Howard roared off. "I was spinning my wheels all my life, and this has been a good lesson that if things are not right, then you just have to step out and do something, rather than worry about it as my mother did. I'm at peace here," she laughed. "We are a lot more relaxed here than we ever have been before. We were very quiet, very stressed, insular people in New York, but everyone has loosened up and come out of their shell, and it feels like home. Like stepping into another world, really.

"Mom would probably be pleased that I stepped out," Melinda said, wiping away a tear in the semidarkness. "My mother always wanted to do things, and put it off. She was a very unhappy woman all her life. She would have been proud I stepped out."

We strolled back inside, where everybody was having fun. A three-piece band consisting of a banjo, guitar, and ukulele was singing cowboy songs and diverse ditties. The one everybody in the room loved was "'Zacly When Did We Become White Trash?" In this case it was true: As usual in rural America, they were all white—but they weren't exactly trash.

GENIUS OR CHARLATAN?

A large chunk of the people who choose to live off the grid believe that the American system is under grave threat from multiple pressures, many of them from within, and that the economy and social fabric of the nation may not survive in its present form. Global warming and other eco-disasters rank high on the list of fears, and thus the preparation for post-apocalypse life becomes crucial for these people.

Mike Reynolds's entire professional life has focused on preparing for that ecological emergency—and preparing the rest of us. He lives in Taos, New Mexico, and he owns and runs a large tract of eco-houses, just outside town.

He has probably built more off-the-grid homes than anyone else in the Western world, although when I asked to visit him in his own home, Mike was surprisingly reluctant. He is the inventor, or popularizer, of the Earthship, a particular kind of self-sufficient house made from used tires that have been filled with earth. Mike says he thought of the idea as a way of recycling used tires, of which there are millions, though some say he first saw the idea being developed elsewhere.

I have spent time with him now on two continents, and I still cannot figure the guy out. Is he a visionary environmentalist or an eccentric opportunist? Are his eco-buildings the solution we are all looking for, or a cruel joke being played on a gullible public? He has lost his New Mexico architect's license; are other architects embarrassed by him, or are they jealous of him, as he claims? (His national license was revoked, then reinstated.)

As I set out on my research trip, two very different documentary films had hit the festival circuit, both made within a few miles of each other. *Off the Grid: Life on the Mesa* is about the dog-rough conditions in the gun-toting, drug- and crime-ridden community out on the ridge just north of Mike Reynolds's settlement, which, incidentally, is called Greater World. The other film, *Garbage Warrior*, is a paean of praise to none other than Michael Reynolds. Its makers were not the first to spot the filmic potential of the subject; the late actor Dennis Weaver, who had lived off the grid in Ridgway, bought a set of

Mike's blueprints in 1980, built an Earthship, and produced a documentary about it. Mike appears in the film just once, for about fifteen seconds, holding his plans. Weaver moved out of the Earthship shortly afterward, when he discovered he was allergic to the gas the tires gave off, which seeped through the limestone walls.

Now I was about to visit Earthship central. There are about five hundred Earthships in the area, and at least two thousand households living off the grid, according to Jennifer Hobson, a New Mexico State press officer. "Seven percent of the total population," she reported.

At the Albuquerque airport I had my first taste of the local eco-consciousness. I stopped at the state-funded tourist information desk to ask for eco-friendly places to stay, places that were in keeping with my mission. From behind rows of glossy pamphlets advertising skiing and climbing, a very proper elderly lady—the kind I would expect at an Anglican church bazaar—peered out at me uncomprehendingly.

"Environmental places to stay?" she repeated with a puzzled expression.

"Yeah, like an eco-hotel," I prompted.

"Ah," she brightened up. "We got an Econo Lodge."

Even with all those off-the-grid residents, it seemed that the area had not yet taken eco-tourism to heart. Disappointed, I walked over to the car-rental desk, signed my contract, and headed for the Taos Mountains.

It was a freezing January morning when I arrived at the Greater World subdivision, sitting seventy-six hundred feet above sea level. Then the sun blazed forth and began its daily assault on the piles of winter snow. I struggled out of the car and took in the view. I didn't like what I saw. The land is just scrub, rock with half an inch of dirt on top. The mountains are fairly unimpressive and featureless. The wind is harsh. The lack of air made me dizzy, and as I was shown into my seventy-five-dollar-a-night Earthship, a wave of cold left me trembling.

Once I began to acclimate, I had to admit to myself that Earthships are visually extraordinary—each one is different. Many are built partway into the earth so that their true size is apparent only after getting very close to them. Mike's designs have little Gaudí-esque finishes, such as turrets, and ceramic mosaics on smooth, curved exterior plaster.

And within twenty-four hours, the uncompromising emptiness of the terrain had grown on me. When I saw the nearest mountain go pink against the sunset, my judgment of the area mellowed, but I remained skeptical. I could not understand what would entice anyone to move here to live off the grid. I knew that artists such as Georgia O'Keeffe had been inspired by the light, but they had moved under romantic and luxurious circumstances. What could compel settlers, who undoubtedly have the choice to buy land of comparable value anywhere in America, to opt for this? It's great for a visit, but would I want to live here?

Harsh in the winter and harsh in the summer, the best thing I have heard in Taos's favor is that there are no insects—because there is so little life to support them—and no humidity. Clearly some adore it. The residents themselves were at pains to say they love it for what it is rather than what it isn't. They don't want anyone to think that they are living here just because the land is dirt cheap.

I prepared for my meeting with Mike Reynolds by looking more closely at his Earthships, although not the one he lived in; Kirsten, his PR agent, explained that his wife was too ill. I took a drive to see some other eco-buildings in the area.

Mike's work, I concluded, is a combination of modern technology—such as solar panels—and the architectural style of Antoni Gaudí, the brilliant Barcelona architect of the early twentieth century. Reynolds's designs have a distinctively bulbous appearance, as well as turrets and roofs, that echo Gaudí's work. Modern innovations include huge, angled, south-facing windows to capture maximum sun, and, just behind them, indoor flowerbeds fed with the gray water coming from kitchens and bathrooms.

I began to identify a trend that goes beyond Earthships. Elsewhere in the area I saw straw-bale houses, designed in the eighteenth century, powered by wind turbines from the twenty-first. Cob buildings—a hand-mixed combination of earth, straw, sand, and water—had satellite dishes. Yurts had solar panels leaning against their circular walls, and the green light of a wireless modem blinked away inside. These are all combinations of ancient design wisdom and the latest technology.

In reaction to the solemn architecture critics and those who dismiss the off-the-grid life as a return to the Stone Age, I decided to call this style pre-postmodernism, and I tried putting these ideas to Mike Reynolds as we waded through the mud on a tour of his newest buildings at Greater World. "Yeah, I like Gaudí," he grunted. He pretended not to hear my remark about pre-postmodernism.

Mike is admired and despised in equal measure by his clients, who find his brusque style off-putting. And there have been accusations over the years of far worse than rudeness—broken promises and bad workmanship are two of the lesser charges.

I found my twenty-four hours as his guest to be difficult work.

It had started well enough. My first night at Greater World was on Super Bowl Sunday 2009, and a party was held in the Phoenix House, one of the largest and most lavishly outfitted building in the subdivision. For a community that lives on the edge of society, this was a truly all-American evening, with vast amounts of food and liquor.

I was made to feel very welcome. As soon as I walked through the door, a beer was thrust into my hands. Next I was invited to sample New Mexico's most pervasive crop, a joint made of locally grown marijuana.

Mike's crew of twenty to thirty adoring young employees were all present, along with his wife, Diana. Although I had been told she was ill, she seemed perfectly well, quite up to a visit from me.

As the staff milled around eating and drinking, I looked for Mike, and found him sitting with Diana on a sofa in front of a giant flat-screen TV that had been installed as part of an attempt to cater to an upscale rental market. I said hello. Only a slight tilt of the eyebrow and the faintest of grunts acknowledged my greeting.

The game got under way and, as always, the ads were the very best the industry had to offer, especially the General Electric promo for the smart grid. I think it was the first time I had heard the phrase. The ad shows a spritelike scarecrow dancing and gamboling among the power lines as if they were daisies in a field. "They should have shown him getting scorched," Mike barked to his wife.

Mike turns out to be a bizarre and socially dysfunctional character. He looks like a drummer from a once-wild but now all-too-predictable rock band. His white hair is long and shaggy. His close-cropped beard covers a pendulous face too big for his body.

He runs and bikes and likes to hang with the young, so it's easy to see how he lures in countless interns, not to mention the naive filmmakers who portrayed him as a hero.

I thought I was the only one who had received the peremptory treatment, but he is like that with everyone. Mike takes an aggressively antiestablishment line on almost everything. The only time he switches out of monosyllabic mode is when he gives his sales spiel.

We met a day later in his design office, and he ranted away for hours, from the moment I sat down, telling me that the LEED standards (Leadership in Energy & Environmental Design) for eco-houses, drawn up by the U.S. Green Building Council, are "fucking bullshit," and how to save the planet from disaster—which, of course, involves Earthships.

There is just one way, says Mike, to ensure that America

switches to eco-housing in general and his beloved Earthships in particular. And that is to "declare martial law." Was he suggesting, I pondered later, that there is a national emergency due to a severe glut of used car tires, or is it the housing shortage that requires the declaration of martial law?

I asked him to expand on that answer, and, whatever else you may say about him, Mike is certainly not afraid to go out on a limb. "Well, we have a national emergency, if not a global emergency," he said, "so they can deploy martial law to allow people to apply the Testing Site Act, so that anyone who is doing something green gets their permit in one hour. And there are safeguards, conditions—like it has to be off grid, has to stay off grid."

According to Mike, one of his greatest political triumphs is that he somehow persuaded the New Mexico legislature to pass a law called the Sustainable Development Testing Site Act (2007), which he says he wrote and which enables a residential home to be built off the grid with little or no code as long as the purpose is "to reduce the consumption of and dependence on natural resources by residential development." It should be called the Earthship Act, as it is framed so as to enable Earthships to be built, and is so specific as to be of little use to anyone else. It requires an additional license for use of rainwater (New Mexico is a dry state), and the Act itself will expire after a period of ten years. So although the Act sets the framework for eco-homes to be built, in practice it essentially prevents this process for buildings other than Earthships.

Nevertheless, according to Mike, the Testing Site Act, in combination with martial law, could enable the building of thousands of Earthships. "Yeah, I mean they did it with the atomic bomb. It was built during a state of national emergency; we destroyed thousands of lives testing it. We developed it really quick, in time to save our ass. They said, 'This is how it's going to be. Fuck all the owls and everything. This is how it's going to be.'"

Settlers of all ages and income levels are moving onto large swaths of land on the nearby mesa, but not because of the Testing Site Act. People with very little money are building cabins on land of dubious ownership, and living on Social Security, sometimes for the rest of their lives. I spent a couple of hours with Bill Reed, an eighty-year-old pothead and self-professed former successful drug dealer who has ended up with nothing save his immense charm.

Lucid and amusing, Bill seems to be one of the most popular characters in the scattered community. He spends his days touring the yurts, cabins, and houses, joshing the punks and hippies with the lugubrious delivery of Walter Matthau. In wet weather he has trouble driving to his tiny cabin, which is held together by willpower as much as by nails. He has a solar panel and an outhouse, and stays in touch with the outside world via a phone line and the Internet.

Bill is one of the more outspoken local critics of Michael Reynolds. "His problem," said Bill, "is building at a reasonable amount per square foot. Those tires, they're labor intensive. He says friends and relatives can help ram the earth in, but that takes a lot of time."

The Earthship PR person made a big fuss about the work Mike did in the Andaman Islands after the tsunami. Bill and other locals, however, accused Mike of "milking that tsunami thing to the max."

While I was on the mesa, I also met John Kejr, a broker for the local realty company Dreamcatcher. I wanted to learn if there is a ready market for the small plots of land on the mesa inhabited by Bill and his neighbors, and John had probably sold more off-the-grid homes than any other broker in New Mexico.

He drove his 4x4 to the place everyone uses as their meeting spot, at the edge of the mesa, next to a water tower by the highway that takes you past the Rio Grande Gorge and on into Taos. I could just about see Greater World from there, with its high concentration of Dreamcatcher signs. Owners of Earthships, like everyone else, are struggling to shift their homes during the recession.

John told me straight out that he refuses to deal in the tiny plots of land that change hands on the mesa for between two hundred and fifteen thousand dollars. "These quarter-acre lots—on Two Peaks and Three Peaks—were given away at the World's Fair, or sold in the back of *TV Guide*, and they were bought by people who have never even seen them. They think Taos, they don't understand there are no roads going to these areas. The infrastructure is nonexistent. There are title issues that make it very difficult to sell."

I already knew the harsh New Mexico climate was not for me; still, I was playing with the idea that with land so cheap, I might decide I could live with the drawbacks. "What if I buy a piece of land for a few hundred and then build a ten-thousand-dollar home on it?" I persisted. Is that not a relatively smart gamble? I was interested in making this kind of a gamble myself (though probably not in Taos). And I was also inquiring on behalf of hundreds, perhaps thousands of mesa landowners who think they have a tradable home. They might be rather horrified to learn otherwise.

"It's not going to be to code," was John's reply. "They will have problems. They might be surrounded by other similar homes which are dilapidated. It's a little bit Wild West out there. There are oftentimes other people living there who, because they don't have ownership, are a little lax in other areas of the law as well— maybe fugitives hiding out there or something."

The stars of *Off the Grid: Life on the Mesa* are, from one point of view, the vanguard of the new eco-living revolution, showing the rest of us the low-carbon way forward. But one could also see them as America's Most Unwanted—scroungers, criminals, rejects, and dropouts, reacting to the crash by forming a new kind of Hooverville, made of more durable materials but still a symbol of their sense of rejection by mainstream society.

As part of my visit to Greater World, I shadowed Mike for a few hours. I watched him work with his builders to complete houses, listened to him deal with clients on the phone, and sat amazed as he discussed sales tactics with his office staff. At one point we passed a group of guys hard at work hammering earth into tires on the first wall of a sixty-foot-long building. "That's our new educational center," Mike said as we passed. "We got five hundred thousand dollars from the Governor's office for that." I was impressed.

A few minutes later, I listened in on a phone call as Mike took the credit card number of a former rock star in southern Ireland who had decided to try and build an Earthship resort. It was the culmination of a long negotiation. Mike finally persuaded his new client to make a down payment of a few thousand dollars for the time spent coaching the Irish in their attempts to get the project off the ground. "He's been told to be careful of us," Mike said. The problem, as Mike saw it, was that his former business partner in England, officially the sole European franchise of the Earthship Biotecture brand, had lost faith, and was putting out the bad word about him. This was later denied by the British entrepreneur, who said that he had needed to "tweak" the Earthship design for the European climate, and that this had led to "creative differences."

At any rate, this was hardly my first inkling that Mike's reputation is less than sterling. Mike says that the complaints are from early clients, when Earthships were still at an experimental stage, and that the loss of his license was a hidebound profession's reaction to his groundbreaking ideas. Now I was learning, and by his own admission, that even his own partners are turning against him.

Mike had been persistently evasive about whether I could visit his home. At one point he seemed to say that I could meet him at his house the next evening, despite his wife's alleged illness. At the end of the day, the plan changed; Mike had to attend a board meeting.

"You can't go on your own," he said when I asked. "The dogs'll tear you up." His once-adorable puppy is featured in the embarrassingly hagiographic *Garbage Warrior,* an "independent" film so smarmy that Mike routinely sends it out to potential clients along with his sales pitch. I wondered if it was the same dog.

I found out where the Reynolds house is located and was brought there by a local guide. There was no dog, just a large house, near the San Geronimo Lodge Hotel, in a ritzy part of Taos called Cañon. It's not a very nice house; it's an untended, unloved house, with a rather ugly, unkempt front yard full of junk furniture. And it's on the grid—all of the grids: power, water, sewage, even cable. I doubt that Mike will worry too much about being exposed. "All my life," he told me, "I am handed a plate, and one side is chocolate mousse and the other side is dog shit. It's the story of my life, so I don't get too excited when people say good things about me, and I don't worry too much about the bad things."

Mike is an unusual part-time off-gridder. He works off the grid and lives on the grid. He does also own an off-the-grid second home, what he says is his eventual retirement home, in the REACH community (short for Rural Earthship Alternative Community Habitat), many miles from Greater World, up a long dirt track that he told me is impassable most of the year. I heard rumors that he cannot visit there because the community is full of angry residents who feel he has broken his promises to provide a road and a well. I pulled the papers at the local court-house and found there were some lawsuits in the nineties as Mike tried to silence his critics in the run-up to the loss of his architect's license. I never found my way to REACH.

At the time, Taos County still had an outstanding case against Mike, dating back years. It stems from building violations. They seem to have lost interest; the county attorney never returned any of my calls to discuss it. The lawyers representing the clients Mike has sued over the years also did not come to the phone.

I was beginning to understand how the New Mexico legal

system works—even the lawyers are lawless, and rather uncommunicative.

I did manage to squeeze a few answers from New Mexico Governor Bill Richardson's office. "It appears that no money has been given to Mike Reynolds or to Earthship Biotecture," I was told by budget administrator Kim Gonzales. I had asked for confirmation that Mike had somehow been awarded five hundred thousand dollars for his education center. "I have searched our database and we don't show him as a vendor." As Mike's office later explained, the amount was only three hundred thousand, and it had been granted to Taos County, not directly to Earthship Biotecture—the county will own the building, though Greater World will operate it.

So is Mike Reynolds a genius or a charlatan? The answer is both. He has developed a vision of environmental living, and has succeeded in sharing it with two to three thousand paying customers around the world, who have either bought his plans for Earthships and built them on their own, or commissioned him to do so. He has created his own worldview, one that a surprising number of people wish to subscribe to, even if they don't agree with him entirely or even like him at all.

The problem with many architects, both great and not so great, is a tendency to display condescending indifference to their clients' budgets, and Mike appears to do this as well. Unlike most architects, he frequently deals with individuals on low budgets, but that simply increases the pain they feel at cost overruns and design problems. But Mike has a string of happy clients, as well as unhappy ones.

Antoni Gaudí, whose work so clearly influences him—although Mike seems unwilling to acknowledge the debt—regularly bankrupted his clients as he built his gemlike apartment buildings and cathedrals around Barcelona and elsewhere. But Mike Reynolds is no Gaudí. The Earthship concept has so many hidden costs and experimental niceties it's like taking on an extra family member.

In the end, Mike might be best summed up by his own words,

when he said that his life is a two-sided plate of chocolate mousse and dog shit.

"That's been my life," he told me in his world-weary way. After distilling the opinions gathered from clients and locals, it may be that it's the plate he gets because it's the plate he deserves.

THIS WAY MADNESS LIES

Jonathan Traister is one of Mike Reynolds's less-than-happy clients. He has been coping with personal disasters of one sort or another since 1993, when his uninsured home in Topanga Canyon, near Los Angeles, was destroyed by a forest fire.

He and his wife, Alison, moved to the Northridge area of L.A., and they began to rebuild their life. Their first child was only a few months old when their new home was destroyed by an earthquake. In a fit of superstitious fear, the couple literally fled the city. They were both twenty-seven at the time, according to a long report about their plight in the *Los Angeles Times*.

Then the press clips go quiet for a while, until 1997, when Jonathan and Alison resurface in a string of reports about artists selling their wares at art fairs around the country.

I happened upon Jonathan at a gas station in Taos, where he told me how to get to the Earthship village. He has movie-star looks and charisma: huge blue eyes, a haircut like Davy Jones's in the early Monkees days, bubbling charm, and a smile that has probably encouraged many an art purchaser to seal the deal.

Our chance encounter led to another meeting at his house, where I gained the impression he and Alison are a former golden couple for whom life has turned very sour. They had recently closed down their art gallery in Taos, and the contents of the store had hurriedly been moved to their house, where it sits in piles. As we spoke, the phone rang constantly, and each call seemed to be a demand for money.

Sitting at a large oak desk squeezed into a tiny study, Jonathan stroked a credit card machine by his side as if it was a pet cat, and fiddled nervously with a pair of credit cards, shuffling them like they were precious little friends who were about to take their leave.

After their escape from L.A., he told me, the pair discovered Earthships and their fear turned to optimism. Never again would they be disconnected from power and water, wondering how they would keep their children alive. They would have their own power and water, and they would be free of the system.

I had been buying Jonathan's story until this point, but he was about to reveal an unexpected streak to his philosophy. "I realized that how man has placed himself in relation to the earth is totally backward. We rely on systems that are so far away for our security, it's a kind of enslavement. The same people who print the dollars, the investment elite, the bankers—they are the real terrorists." I filed this away for the moment, but it was a harbinger of stranger things to come.

Reminiscing about his arrival in the area, Jonathan said that he and his family were one of the very earliest to settle in Mike Reynolds's Greater World. "I had this idea that we would all work together to build a better world, a real community here," he said as we sat in his study. In the intervening decade, he built one of the finest off-the-grid homes I visited. But it had not been easy, and now I wondered how he would hang on to it.

Before he arrived at Greater World, Jonathan had imagined "construction parties where we were all going to get together and hammer tires. But it wasn't anything like that." He paid Mike Reynolds sixty-five hundred dollars for a set of generic Earthship plans and waited a few months for a community to form. "Nobody had spoken to me, and when I had my first construction party only one guy turned up, smoking a joint and asking, 'Where's the beer?'"

That sounded exactly like the Mike Reynolds I know. I had joined one of these Earthship work parties myself, outside Valencia, Spain, in 2005. We volunteers arrived to find Mike and his team—or "sons," as he referred to them—playing Grateful Dead music and sucking on cans of beer they pulled from a five-foot stack of cases. The cans became part of the construction materials as fast as Mike and his sons could empty them. To be fair to Mike, the disappointment Jonathan felt when the community did not rally around him is not necessarily Mike's fault. It could be as much to do with a response to Jonathan's peculiar philosophy.

Now, more than a decade later, Jonathan lives inside this elegant, curvy brown adobe-walled garden. His Earthship, heavily modified from the original plans, feels like a comfortable, stylish home. His two boys were playing happily outside (tormenting one of their school friends) while his wife was rearranging the piles of artwork. They still have their connections, their skills, their good looks, and the stock from the gallery. In theory they could keep working and trading.

Sadly, the reality it is not quite so simple. After being debt-free for fifteen years, the previous year Jonathan had taken the surprising step of arranging a large loan against his home. "I thought I would never, ever put this home up," he told me. "The reason why I did was because I feel like America right now is at a time just like Nazi Germany before Hitler came to power, except that it's not on a specific country scale—it's on a global scale." A sinking feeling came over me as I listened to this rambling mixture of economic analysis and conspiracy theory. "The real problem we are facing right now is not because of some mortgage crisis or some credit issue; it's because of the system that controls us—the debt system." I knew what he meant, but if this is indeed the case, I didn't understand why he had taken out a loan against the house.

"I really do believe that the forces who created Nazi Germany are at it again, creating a global new world order—a global, economic, fascist dictatorship, doing that through the system of money and credit," he said, still toying with the plastic cards.

I still didn't understand where the new mortgage fit in.

"I felt there was an economically controlled crunch coming. So before the trapdoor opens up, I wanted to get the equity out of the home." This sounds logical, if not fully reasonable. Why not simply sell the house? "What's in my heart is to start a community which is off the grid, but with a lot more food production, a lot more complete self-sufficiency."

So, a year earlier, Jonathan had traveled down to the Baja peninsula, in Mexico, to view a two-thousand-acre ranch he had in mind as the place to start his own community. "A place with hot springs an hour east of Ensenada. I love hot springs," he told me, his boyish charm reasserting itself. "But I wasn't sure, and I thought, I will get on the land and I will know; the land will talk to me. So I got my kids out of school, and went on down there. I got on the land, and I didn't know. I was totally stressed out, so I turned to God and I said, 'Lord, I need some help here,' and he said, 'Son, you *do* need some help here; go to Georgia, to the seminary.' So I went."

Since his return from the seminary , Jonathan has become a holy man. "I turned my life to God, through Jesus Christ," he said, still sliding his fingers over the card machine. "And my wife says to me, 'Honey, don't you know there are two kingdoms out there?' And I would say, 'Gee, it seems that way.'"

Jonathan believes the Devil's spawn are ascendant. "Our world is run by thirteen elite families—like J.P. Morgan," he believes. "You know, making up diseases, impregnating them into the population, empty concentration camps. You have all these things—it's all too evil," he said, fixing his huge blue eyes on me. "A lot of people would call me a conspiracy-theory nut," he admitted, "but where did that term come from? It was designed to create a wall so that the guy in the street would not listen to me."

For someone who believes the godless world is wrong and has been brainwashed into not listening to him, an isolated, off-the-grid location is the ideal fortification in terms of protecting this belief system from being assailed.

I tried, many times, to speak to Jonathan again, but never managed to. Perhaps he was keeping his phone off to avoid his creditors. I heard from him by e-mail only once more, and he said he was working hard to get the house rented out, then heading to the island of Tonga, in the South Pacific, to start his new community with his family. You can hardly get any further off the grid.

Jonathan, it seems to me, has been driven mad by the darts fate has thrown at him. Unable to face a relatively minor financial setback, he appears to be sacrificing what really matters—his home, his sanity, and his family—on the altar of a demented god.

Not every attempt to take God off the grid is doomed to ridicule. Later I visited a few communities successfully combining remote living and religion, while remaining healthy and wealthy.

Still, my heart goes out to poor, confused Jonathan, both out of sympathy for his predicament and because I suspect he represents many tens of thousands, both on and off the grid, who are unable to come to terms with the gap between the real world and their own failed ambitions. He took drastic measures that many would say amount to running away.

7 Running from the Rat Race

> "I found that by working six weeks a year, I could meet all the expenses of living."
>
> Henry David Thoreau, *Walden*

Stories like Jonathan's or Melinda's might suggest that those who commit to going off the grid full-time and forever are running away from something, or have run out of road financially, or have ended up off the grid by default. But standing in contrast to this notion is Vonnie Mallon, a woman for whom going off the grid was a totally positive choice, arising out of financial success. Vonnie had had everything she could have hoped for in the on-grid world, but she was still missing something that she would never find there.

I met Vonnie by chance during a brief break from the adversarial setting of Mike Reynolds's Greater World, and hoped to drive a few miles to another set of hot springs. This time, however, it would be a public hot spring found at the end of an almost inaccessible track, known only to locals—and mountain-dwelling locals to boot. The idea was to spend the day up to my neck in a warm pool, naked except for a woolly hat, staring up at a blue sky from the bottom of the Rio Grande Gorge. Several locals had recommended it, saying it was neither too hard nor too hazardous to find.

I got lost almost as soon as I set out. Before I knew it, I was in a tiny town called Carson, little more than a post office and a small store set back from the one road. When I walked into the place, it looked like a cross between a grocery store and a café, with a couple of Internet terminals thrown in. The customers, all guys with baseball caps and checkered shirts, were sitting at the two or three tables gossiping and drinking beer, occasionally popping out for cigarettes. Behind the counter was a dark-haired, immaculate woman with "big city" written all over her sculpted, masculine features. Vonnie isn't standoffish and has no air of superiority—she was one of the most approachable people I met in my travels—but she does have the style and sense of distance I recognized as the result of maintaining a carapace around herself in a city full of strangers, a protective shell unnecessary in the rural Southwest, but that she has yet to quite throw off.

Vonnie lives in a small, isolated Earthship community, six miles out of Carson. The STAR (Social Transformation Alternative Republic) community, as it's known, was founded years earlier by none other than Mike Reynolds, in his most experimental days. It now has about twenty residents.

Vonnie travels along a near-impassable road to work at the store, Poco Loco, a few days a week, partly for the money, and partly because she needs to make the ride anyway. Her ancient Toyota truck eats gas at the rate of about a dollar a mile, so whenever she can, she rides in on a 100cc trail bike, which takes her fifteen minutes, compared with thirty in the Toyota. The truck is a ridiculously wasteful vehicle, but it was all she and her husband could afford after their brand-new hybrid SUV bit the dust. (How they came to lose the hybrid is a long story.)

For now, my interest was focused on the fact that Vonnie had been, until she came to New Mexico, vice president of marketing for Urban Outfitters, working out of their headquarters, or "corporate campus," in Philadelphia. To me Urban Outfitters seems like a hipper version of the Gap. The stores feel less corporate, and the "look," to the extent there is one, is more diverse. That's their devilishly clever allure, but they are just as corporate as any other big, faceless company.

Vonnie invited me to stay at her place, and we agreed I would return after my trip to the hot springs. One of the bar's patrons suggested I give myself a break and go to the touristy version at the Ojo Caliente Mineral Springs Resort, a few miles up the road. Yes, this was exactly what I needed after my grueling stay with Mike Reynolds, so I headed over to the little tourist town with its famous hot springs.

My first encounter was not promising. A couple of fierce biddies at the front desk scowled at me as though they would frown at any sign of fun, and the large, fussy, overstated marble lobby seemed the opposite of what I was hoping for from the place. Once I had put my bag in my room, donned my robe, and walked the quarter mile back to the pools, I was pretty pleased to relax on the grid for a brief spell.

There are several pools on the compound, each with a different naturally occurring mineral in the solution, such as iron, sodium, arsenic, and lithia. The temperatures peak at over 100 degrees.

I was visiting on two-for-one night, when the normally empty springs are inundated with locals. I spent a couple of hours lounging in the arsenic pool and was thoroughly relaxed, but by this time the place was buzzing. Part of the buzz was caused by the large number of teenagers who ignored the "whisper zone" rule. I also realized, when a couple slid into the water beside me, that this place was not as sedate as I had expected. I lay in the iron pool for a while, with only my head above the surface, the taste of the water on my mouth reminding me of blood. To my left, a woman slid her legs around her male friend and leaned toward me; directly opposite, a pair of women swam into my line of vision and began fondling each other, one with her back to the other, and both of them facing straight ahead.

I looked at them with curiosity, and received contemptuous stares in return. Whether they were a lesbian couple or a pair of prostitutes strutting their stuff was not something I wanted to discover.

I moved to yet another pool, but pretty soon the ten p.m. curfew alarm sounded. This, I realized, is the main reason for using the free springs, at least in New Mexico. They may be difficult to access, but the free springs are open past bedtime, all night if you wish. It seems monstrous to charge for the privilege of using what was once a free, publicly available pool and then close it down at ten p.m. This is a rule devised entirely for the benefit of the resort, not the guests.

I had a final soak in the arsenic pool the next morning and headed back to the Poco Loco store in Carson, where Vonnie was waiting to ferry me along her impassable road to meet the other members of her community. During the entire twenty-minute drive I clung to the handhold with one hand and pushed the other into the ceiling, to prevent my head from hitting the roof as we went over the bumps. At times there was no road, just a few tire tracks over the earth.

As we drove, Vonnie yelled a well-rehearsed biography at me over the roar of the engine. Hers had been a high-powered, demanding job, taking her all over the country, she said, and she had been good at it. Like most American executives, she had been expected to work very hard. "It's a great company, but they definitely find ways to take more than you can give."

She would arrive in the Urban Outfitters corporate office at seven-thirty each morning—earlier if there was a problem—as would the other members of her management cadre. Her direct supervisor had been a woman who grunted a lot and never thanked anyone for anything. "They make you feel like this is what you have to do to be on top and everything will be OK. They stretched you real thin," Vonnie said as we finally pulled up at the end of the bone-shaking ride. "You looked around the office and the males were all reading magazines! The girls were running all over the place. It's not that we couldn't manage our time, but there was too much to do. We never got to talk to each other."

I wasn't sure whether this last comment was a reference to her female colleagues or to her husband, Pat, or both. Vonnie was perfectly open in explaining that their marriage had been under strain as a result of her work commitments. It wasn't just the long hours but her weekly road trips to oversee in-store launches and promotions.

Vonnie had met Pat when she was nine and he was eight. They had been inseparable ever since. "But we didn't fall in love until I was thirteen," she added.

Pat is now thirty-four, with graying stubble, longish brown hair, and a nice smile. He has a lean body, hardened through a couple of years of building, decorating, gardening, and doing without. When we arrived Pat was standing in the garden in front of the house, next to a pair of tall, heavy wooden doors, open now and locked each night. They had been installed after a home invasion, the one that had led to the damaged SUV hybrid.

Pat is not the corporate type—he is a tortured artist and writer. Where Vonnie is effusive, almost a chatterbox—though with plenty of insight—Pat is laconic, shy, and distant. He lives inside his head. It is, he told me, a place he likes to be. He had been attracted to the monotonous sagebrush landscape of the Taos area because it taught him that rural beauty is a mere diversion, a way of "avoiding confronting yourself."

"This kind of non-scenery forces you to be with yourself," Pat said. "There's nowhere else to go." For Pat, civilization is the history of man's long march away from himself, and our attempt to divert ourselves from the moment of confrontation. His pen name is Von Pat, a nice tribute to the virtual melding of his identity with Vonnie's, a process that began with their childhood tryst.

"When we moved here, we wanted to live on our own one

hundred percent—and that's what we are working towards," he said, like a twenty-one-year-old experiencing the intensity of his first love affair. Of course, it still is his first love affair, since neither of them has ever been with anyone else.

We had been talking in the garden, which was still fairly scrappy, with just a few plants here and there in the poor soil. There are four or five Earthships within view, all of different shapes and design finishes, mostly quite small with just one or two rooms. Vonnie and Pat's is the largest, and Pat led me inside the long, single-story structure, another Mike Reynolds design.

The house had been a mess at first, so Pat spent two years on improvements, and now the place is perfect. *Dwell* magazine's editors would wet themselves at the sight of it: high concrete interior walls as smooth as a baby's cheek, painted in clean basic cream and beige. Some of the concrete was sculpted with soft corners to create alcoves and a breakfast bar. The wooden ceilings are all tongue-and-groove, dotted with skylights that pull open to disperse the sun's heat during the warmer months. A purpose-built recess houses the sleek, full-size silver fridge (pre-postmodernism again), and another recess contains shelves full of tea, herbs, and natural medicine. The breakfast bar on one side of the kitchen and the bulbous fireplace in the opposite corner complete the room.

The front door of the house opens onto a large sitting room, equally meticulously designed and finished, with the big sloping windows and indoor plants common to most Earthships. Turn right and you are heading for the kitchen. Turn left for the bathroom, complete with odorless composting toilet, and then the bedroom. Vonnie and Pat have friends from back east who want to come and live in STAR community, so Pat is planning another room or two for guests. (I myself stayed in a nearby mini-Earthship.)

The couple had made the move from Philadelphia two years earlier. Vonnie had planned to keep working until they had set themselves up financially, but it was not to be. She had fought hard to be able to live and work from her Earthship but still travel to the in-store promotions. Her boss had hated the idea, but she was a trusted senior staffer, and the company eventually agreed. It was the local Internet supplier, Taos Mountain Electronics, that ruined her plans, although, in a way, she is grateful to them now.

The couple was short of money after paying for the house and the move, and were still keeping an apartment in Philadelphia. They had already paid Taos Mountain twenty-five hundred dollars for a satellite phone and Internet, but when they arrived, it simply didn't work. "There was a lot of going back and forth to town and begging them," Pat said, "but the company said, 'I'm sorry, you bought it.'"

They took Taos Mountain Electronics to court—and won. But getting the money back was hardly compensation when you consider that it led to the early end of Vonnie's job. For a brief period of time, she had traveled an hour to Taos each day, trying to work in an Internet café there from seven-thirty a.m. to seven p.m. "I was having anxiety attacks and in tears constantly—I was fading." Her sacrifice was not enough to quell the corporate politics, and Vonnie was forced to resign. She had planned to keep the job for no more than another year, so they could build up a decent savings to then carry out their self-sufficiency plans, but it was a nice stream of income that simply dried up.

She has no regrets. "I thought I needed the money to do the other things then. You get out here and they just fade away. All those things you think that you need, you don't need them at all. We have a community and that's all we need."

Food is high on their list of priorities, and it's a special subject for Pat. "Right now food is a big deal. It's a big journey to get food together," he told me. As part of his "horrific" childhood, Pat was fed sugar a teaspoonful at a time. "It was slipped into my mouth—instead of meals." Just six months before we met, he had discovered that he was addicted to sugar. It happened when he fasted for the first time in his life, alone for seven days on a nearby mountaintop. After the first few days he was so crazed that he forgot to even drink his water supply. When he eventually came back down he was half dead. He pulled through and has not touched sugar since. But it was a battle. "I couldn't move for the first three weeks. I was bedridden, with thoughts of suicide. Being here saved me." Since then they had begun planting their garden and built a plastic walled greenhouse and were harvesting vegetables. They plan to have chickens and year-round vegetables, but there is a long way to go.

Pat was on antidepressants when I visited. He had slowly come off them since arriving in New Mexico, but he still needed them occasionally. "I always thought [my problems] were in my mind, but now I realize the role my body played," he said, sitting at the kitchen table in his tranquil home. Thoughts of his body and its inner workings are, in and of themselves, enough to give him a panic attack. "This thing is a piece of meat, and its name is Patrick," he would say to himself.

Vonnie had been on the road for six years by the time they moved to Taos. And Pat was "in a very dark state" influenced by his diet. Their relationship had all but broken down. "Our motives for coming here were love and freedom," she said. "Freedom, and through that, love—reconnecting with our relationship. We catapulted a spiritual awakening. I needed to be silent within myself, and get rid of all the distractions around— the constant society expectations, the work expectations. It was easy to lose myself, continuing in this forward manner, never really being in the present."

For Pat, there was another aspect to the move. "I wanted to get away from what was unnatural—the city and what goes on inside of it," he said. "I had this picture in my head of nature, which I knew nothing about, although I knew the city never made sense to me. It functions but the keyword is *function*. I didn't want to just function—I wanted to live. Coming here, my preconceptions were slapped in the face by the wind and the rain and the snow. Everything started to fall away, and I didn't want to go back to the city at all. Even if you are committed to living in the city, you should be fundamentally conscious of it." (This is what Thoreau would call "living deliberately.") "Where does your water go, where has your food come from? It seems like we don't want to know these things; they are too difficult to face."

Vonnie and Pat were now at the end of the second year of their new life. I asked what they thought they had learned. Pat answered, "If you can afford land, then anybody can build an off-the-grid shelter for hardly any money at all. I realize that now. The materials are on the ground."

There had been highs and lows. The low point was what the STAR community believed to be a xenophobically motivated home invasion (like many in the area) of one of their number, a middle-aged nurse named Patricia. A year earlier, a gang of Latinos had forced their way in and demanded to know where the drugs and money were. They kept Patricia hostage for four hours, telling her, "You hippies don't belong here." It ended with Pat and another resident pursuing them in Pat's new 4x4. They flipped the car, destroying it. So, for a while, Pat and Vonnie had no Internet and no car—the two key items in their survival plan.

In retrospect, Vonnie is able to see the incident in a positive light. "We came together as a community," she said. Nobody was hurt, but it took them all a long, long time to feel safe again. Now they are permanently ready for trouble—all of them are armed. Vonnie showed me the gun she keeps close to her at all times, a small silver pistol.

The community had meetings to prepare to defend themselves against future attacks. (None have come yet.) They held a second set of meetings to decide what to do about the nonexistent road. "Mike [Reynolds] turned up," Pat told me, "with his band of goons. He was drunk, he slobbered over the free sandwiches, demanded a hundred-dollar-a-year [subscription to STAR community] from each of us, made all the same promises he makes each year." Then he left, and has not been back to the community since.

THE MOUNTAIN HERMIT

Whereas Vonnie and Pat are trying to build a community, Andrea Johnson is working on a more solitary mission.

Andrea lives outside Ridgway in a two-hundred-square-foot cabin, ninety-six hundred feet up in the mountains. There are roads, but once the winter snow arrives it's only accessible on skis or snowmobile—it's a ski-in. She grew up in Charlotte, North Carolina, where her parents still live.

She wrote via Off-Grid.net, telling me about herself. She's an award-winning camerawoman, she said, and was the youngest member of the documentary team at the PBS station in Tucson, Arizona—and the only woman. Like Vonnie, Andrea says she was exploited; eighteen-hour days were expected of her. "It was very bittersweet; it was a dream job. But I am still recovering from it."

At last, in her late thirties, she has found her calling. She has taught herself how to use a chain saw and a bow saw; how to fell a tree; how to cut, stack, and chop firewood; how to rid a cabin of mice "herbally"; how to set up a 12-volt solar electric system; how to cook on a wood stove; and how to keep her springwater both snow- and frost-free.

Andrea is tall and fit, with mounds of corkscrew hair and a huge, gleaming white smile. "The day Barack Obama became the U.S. president," she said when we met, "I was in my cabin, knowing that in so many ways being an African-American woman, with the privilege to live this way, the way I've chosen, challenges and all, it brought tears of joy and fear to my eyes."

I never did make it up to Andrea's cabin when I was in Ridgway. The snow covering the road was too thick for me to drive, and there was no time for my only other option—a two-and-a-half-mile snowshoe hike on the same road, followed by a six-hundred-vertical-foot climb from there.

Instead we spent a pleasant evening together near Telluride, sharing a bottle of wine while she told me of her off-the-grid odyssey. She was wearing a figure-hugging sweater and a white knitted cardigan, acquired from the Ridgway animal shelter thrift store, where she works two days a week. She had searched almost the whole of America, forty-nine states in all, to find the perfect place to go off the grid. And she had chosen Ridgway.

Before extracting every last nuance of her reasoning during our conversation, I studied a photo of her compact, modern cabin, an A-frame with a dark green pitched metal roof and two guitars hanging on the wooden porch. The view from the front door shows dreamy, snow-covered peaks towering above the green tips of fir trees.

Andrea's father was a senior IBM engineer and mathematician until he retired. He was demanding of his daughter. "It was only as an adult that I found I was not an idiot at math," she said.

She went to film school at NYU. "I was driven once I discovered film—just out of there and into the world, thinking that everything was rosy with a camera. Then I got really burned out." The long hours she worked were exhilarating, she said, but "being young, I had no other life other than work. I didn't know how to take care of myself mentally, emotionally, financially. I was working for PBS making a quarter of what I should be making." She didn't mind, though. After she finished with PBS, Andrea became a scuba-diving instructor. Her most recent job, prior to coming to Ridgway, was as a long-distance truck driver. She had her own rig, and as anyone who has seen the inside of one of these truck cabins will tell you, it's a lot like being in a sailboat—or living off the grid.

"I've been self-employed in a lot of different things," she said, "but truck driving was the most lucrative. I lived in the truck and put all my stuff in my parents' garage. It just made sense. I made a list of all the things I enjoy, and I've always been a driver. You have everything you need in your truck, and it's all twelve-volt, same as off grid."

I pulled into a Flying J (one of the larger chains of truck stops) after this conversation, and marveled at the gadgets one can buy that plug straight into a car cigarette lighter. Even though few drivers use the lighters for smoking anymore, the sockets are still standard on every vehicle, and some of these rigs have two or three of them. The truck stops sell inverters with ten times the power of the one I carry around to charge my computer. They can run a half dozen 12-volt gadgets, all available in the truck stops: fax machines and scanners; mini-fridges and frying pans; coffee mugs and heated blankets, lights, and shavers; coffeemakers, ice cream makers, blenders, pizza ovens, slow cookers, and popcorn poppers; TVs and DVD players; the list goes on. My favorite accessory of them all is the plug that turns a cigarette lighter into three cigarette lighters. (Although the first time I used one it blew out all the car's fuses. Luckily I was still in the rental parking lot, so I was able to just change vehicles with no fuss. It wouldn't blow any fuses in a truck.)

"There's a lot of truckers who want to live off grid, and you see subdivisions for sale in trucking magazines," Andrea said by way of introduction to the story of the two-year road trip that eventually led her to Ridgway. She had begun by studying a large road atlas. "I decided I want to live in a place with a population of no more than twenty-five hundred—so immediately it was the smallest dots." There were a few other necessities, of course. "There are some beautiful places that I, as a single woman of my ethnic background, would not want to live in or put up with the energy. Particularly in colder climates in the United States, rural equals Caucasian. I wanted snow part of the year."

She also considered her potential locations in relation to others. "Two hundred miles from a large center is too far, depending on how you want to live, but ten miles is too close. In ten years they'll be at your back door. So I started drawing circles on the map. I grew up on the East Coast, and I didn't want to live there. [On] the East Coast I could always feel the hum, no matter how far out I got." She told me that the northern tip of Maine would have been an exception, but it breaks the two-hundred-mile rule.

"To begin with, I wanted to live as far as possible from civilization, where the weather was always warm, but once I lived in a small town, I realized I wanted to be part of that [kind of] community. And there is something about the Southwest that fits my energy—people tend to be friendly and open."

She was homing in now: a small town in the Southwest where she could be alone, and where there was snow part of the year. She added, "I always wanted a bathhouse—preferably built over a spring. Just before I found this place, I had narrowed it down to New Mexico or southern Colorado. I knew the other side of Colorado was too desertlike. In a lot of ways it makes sense to live in a more temperate climate if you want to live off the grid. Arizona is high on the list—it's good for animals. Florida's awesome." Things grow so easily, her family in Florida can eat homegrown food almost "without having to garden . . . but I didn't like the humidity. Land is still cheap [there] but not as cheap as the Midwest—Kansas or Missouri." She had almost bought land in Missouri. "There's a lot of off-gridders in Missouri because it's not too cold. A lot of people who are not Midwestern end up there."

We were on the second bottle of wine now, and Andrea returned to recounting the highlights of her American off-the-grid tour. She "accidentally" lived in Texas for eighteen months. "I hate Texas. It's not my state of mind. There are little ranchette subdivisions where you can buy cheap land. There's no mountains, and sometimes water's an issue. Having lived in the desert, I really appreciate being able, through my own knowledge and technology, to get water."

She had decided that California is too expensive. "It's got great spiritual and artist communities; it just wasn't my home. It has the best range: the beach version, the mountain version, and everything in between, the hippie-artist thing or the rancher." What had put her off was the real estate prices and the restrictions on building permits. "What works for one little patch doesn't really work for another little patch. In New Mexico you get the same deal in all the rural areas."

Oregon: "I had some spiritual connections there in rural areas. They are saying, 'Bring it on.' There are whole communities there, not communes."

Alaska: "I went there specifically looking at a property, and a business. It's just too far away. You might think your are tough but you are not that tough." She understands her limitations. It was in Alaska she realized that she would be happy in a small town, "as long as it's the middle of nowhere."

Montana: "Good place, liked the people, but I didn't happen to find the town that spoke to me."

Now at last she has found the town that speaks to her. She enjoys the ski-in and the challenge, and for the time being, at least, she is journeying alone. "I have hermit tendencies," she said, "but I am not an isolationist."

Her primary interests in life are her intellectual and psychological quest. "A lot of it is the spiritual, introspective, and meditative aspect of being alone. It is a very meditative and contemplative life, grounded and mindful, which are the guide-posts of my personal spiritual path, allowing a moment-to-moment face-to-face with my deepest self—being confronted with what I think and do, and why I think and do those things." Here is someone who can fairly be said to be living in "selfish isolation," but it feels right to her.

So is her traveling over? Does she think she has really found her journey's end? "Yes," she said, clasping and unclasping her large hands. "I was nomadic because I was looking for my home. Now I want to plant a tree and watch it grow. I have not been more than twenty-five miles from here for over two years. I never had a dog when I was growing up, and now I do. It meant I was choosing a life."

I was still wondering exactly why she had chosen this life. I knew it was what she said she wanted, yet she is clearly a communicative and confident woman who likes to be part of society. So why does she think this solitary life is the antidote to her bad experiences in the corporate world?

"I came out of the womb wanting this," she said flatly. "Call it karma. There is nothing in my childhood to explain it. It's just been my way, my dream—a knowing that it suits me."

Perhaps unconsciously we all choose our lives at an early age; our later actions are just ways of playing out the earlier choice. I was still puzzled as to how Andrea could have gone from Emmy award–winning camerawoman to truck driver, so I asked her if I could ring her parents and get their take on it.

I caught her dad one Saturday morning and asked what he thinks of his daughter's lifestyle. While making it clear that he has no wish to go back to his own off-grid childhood, he recalled he had spent the first six or seven years of his life in a house with no running water or electricity. As to what Andrea had been like as a kid, he told me a revealing story.

One time he took her with him to his office at IBM on a Saturday morning, to pick up some papers he had forgotten. "She was about ten at the time, and we went up to my floor and we were walking down the long corridor with office doors on either side. Just a normal office floor. She said to me, 'Oh, Dad! How could you work in a place like this? I could never work in a place like this.'"

I knew what he meant. Andrea is a free spirit for whom corporate life is a prison. Her father simply confirmed she has always been that way.

Post-consumer Society

"Spoken or printed, broadcast over the ether or on wood-pulp, all advertising copy has but one purpose—to prevent the will from ever achieving silence. Desirelessness is the condition of deliverance and illumination."

Aldous Huxley

If American culture since 1980 has focused on conspicuous consumption, the 2010s may one day be characterized as the time large numbers of Americans began to think about consuming less—both for the good of the planet and for our own spiritual well-being (not to mention the impact of a distinct lack of money). Of course, there has always been a frugal backlash against the excesses of consumerism. But the new austerity is entering the mainstream in a way that may be irreversible.

My encounter with the couple as they were being married at Walden Pond was as lucky as it was charming. The reason for their pilgrimage gave me an insight into the divide between Americans who see consumption as the reward for all the struggle and hard work and those who are, frankly, slightly embarrassed by it.

The pair—let's call them John and Jane to spare their parents' blushes—had expected to marry in front of their respective families. But after they announced their engagement, it became clear to the happy couple that they wanted a minimalist wedding, with little in the way of the traditionally lavish send-off, while both sets of parents wanted, nay, demanded, a chance to push the boat out. The twenty-seven-year-old bride's father, until a recent layoff, had been the banquet superintendent at one of Nashville's fanciest hotels. This sort of celebration is in his blood. And John's parents are wealthy, semiretired professionals who contribute to their Episcopalian church and to the Republican Party. They worked hard all their lives, are the opposite of flamboyant, and spend carefully. For them, John explained, a wedding has to take place in a church and be followed by a reception with a large number of guests, who, the hosts believe, also expect things to be done in a certain way. A very expensive way.

John, age thirty-seven, saw it differently. He felt that the church had brought him up to value "quietness, smallness, and simplicity." It is an ethical and spiritual belief. "Simplicity is active," he said. "It is something found in moments or in actions or in specific choices. It is not a lifestyle." Like Thoreau, John tries to live deliberately, meaning with awareness of the consequences of one's actions. The deliberate consumer refrains from impulse purchases and resists cheap goods that will need to be replaced in a few years, favoring instead reliable items with a lifetime guarantee (such as the Leatherman pocket tool).

These are the values John and Jane wanted to celebrate when they married, and they could not, they believed, vow to live this way together for the rest of their lives while participating in a traditional American church wedding followed by a traditional American wedding reception.

The insights I gleaned from John and Jane (who do not live off the grid, I should point out, although they would like to one day) were echoed repeatedly on my trip across the country.

THE GIFT ECONOMY

There are many great things about the United States. To me the greatest of all is that everything is happening here, and all at once. All the social trends, all the time. While millions pursue the capitalist dream seeking extreme wealth, millions more are trying to live a less materialist life—what Sarah Smith calls "the gift economy."

Sarah lives in Portland, Oregon, and her details have been changed to protect her identity for reasons that will become clear. She is living on land that does not have residential zoning and conducts most of her life through barter. She uses money as little as possible, swaps her time with others via a local time bank, and grows a bit of pot, which she barters and gives away as often as she sells it. Sarah is not, however, the first to use the term *gift economy.*

At the Burning Man festival each year in Nevada, thousands gather in the desert to throw off the shackles of consumerism. First-timers to the event are always amazed by the generosity of the Burners, as those who attend the festival call themselves. Burning Man cofounder Larry Harvey explained it this way during a public lecture at New York's Cooper Union in 2002: "We discourage bartering because even bartering is a commodity transaction. Instead, we've originated both an ethos and an economic system that is devoted to the giving of gifts. This is a radical departure from the marketplace that we're accustomed to. . . . The marketplace invades every crack and corner of our lives today. A gift economy is founded on principles that are diametrically different from those that dominate our consumer culture."

Sarah lives only partly in the gift economy—at least for now. She earns about two hundred dollars a week working in a restaurant and is paid in cash. She has no car and cycles or takes public transportation around Portland. She tries to live at least part of her life in keeping with the principle that, in her own words, "we exchange and give to each other without necessarily expecting anything in return, while simultaneously receiving and having our needs met." She doubts society will be transformed in this way in her lifetime.

The time bank consists of a few dozen individuals whose time is valued equally, and every hour of work carried out via the time bank is seen as a donation to the group rather than as a unit to be traded. The key function of the time bank is its social events, when members can meet each other. The entire concept will work only if there is a strong, trusting bond between the members.

This kind of time bank, which is widespread all over America, can be considered part of the gift economy. Each hour its members give to time-bank activities is an hour they are entrusting others with (i.e., they trust that the hour will be returned to them in the form of another service). Because the hours owed are unenforced and unenforceable under the group's constitution, the IRS cannot tax them.

The IRS has ruled that "time bank hours" are not taxable, and they cannot be seen as barter so long as they are not legally binding (i.e., as long as they are backed only by a moral obligation) and are always measured as an hour, regardless of what service is offered. (Barter is technically taxable, although there is no way of enforcing occasional exchanges between individuals.)

This definition is disheartening for those who see an hour as a unit to be bartered. But for those who see it as a gift that they hope will be returned, the IRS can't do anything, nor would they want to.

Sarah is thirty-one, with a design degree from Portland. She likes to dress well in thrift-store clothes and has never hustled in a high-earning job.

There are tens of thousands of thirtysomething men and women living in cities with the same perspective as Sarah's: caring, community minded, idealistic, intelligent, hardworking . . . and squeezed out by the financial system. Some of them simply leave and move to low-cost small towns or rural communities, making the cities poorer by their absence. Others cave in and work high-paying jobs they don't believe in, and still others stick to their guns in rented accommodations, which usually means that they'll get squeezed out in the end.

Sarah has found another way.

In 2009, she sold her car for three thousand dollars, withdrew her savings from the bank, and, for sixty-five hundred dollars, bought an acre of woodland on a steep slope at the end of a quiet road on the edge of Portland.

With no more savings, Sarah decided there was no point in having a bank account or a credit card. So she closed both and opened a loadable Visa account, "just for things where they insist on a card, like online purchases." She didn't care about her credit score, and she still got owner financing for the part of the land cost that she hadn't paid in cash.

Sarah thinks that her community, and America in general, will face significant challenges in the next five to ten years. Her new home allows her to prepare for that day, and to continue to live in the gift economy. "I am not a survivalist," she explained, "but this is what everyone is talking about right now." This was mid-2009, and many individuals and groups were making plans for the bad times ahead, whether it meant stockpiling food, guns, or water, or paying down mortgage debt. She believes that in the near future "individual communities will begin to be affected by some major issues—whether that's cities in Texas that dry up because of drought or the whole financial system crashing down, or a combination of other things." There is no bunker mentality here. Her primary motivation is not fear; it's a kind of generosity. "From day one I thought of [my small piece of land] as having the resources set aside for friends and family should we ever need to use them."

Sarah doubts there will be recovery, and those of us who can remember the late seventies after the shock of spiking oil prices will remember the reappraisal of values that situation caused: the priority of human relationships over money, and the community over the individual.

Despite her assertions to the contrary, Sarah is, in a way, a survivalist, part of a group who are plotting communities rather than mountain bunkers, and who MSNBC called "the new survivalists." "New survivalists are living normal lives while trying to protect family and friends from threats that now seem very real," the reporter, Jonathan Dube, said in a July 2009 report. "They want to do more than simply survive. They want to make sure they have something to live for." That neatly sums up what Sarah is aiming at. She wants to do more than just survive, she wants to be part of a community that gives each member something to live for.

LOCAL CURRENCIES AND CAR SEX

A decade earlier, based in Austin, Texas, Lyndon Felps had developed self-styled bank notes, called Dillo Hours, that could be traded between individuals. The notion of gift exchange was absent, but a community grew around the Dillo and the currency briefly garnered some national media attention, and then sank back into obscurity. Part of the reason may have been Lyndon's refusal to adopt the Web as a way of keeping all the members in touch with one another. That was in the early days of the Internet, when it had fewer users than today. Lyndon was uncompromising in wanting the Dillo Hour to be a personal network based on trust, and at that time he didn't trust the Web.

To my mind, the biggest challenge in terms of entering the gift economy, or the post-consumer society—or whatever it might be called—is figuring out a way for goods or time to be exchanged, so I was intrigued to consult an expert and hear how he thinks it might succeed.

Lyndon Felps lives at Earthaven in North Carolina, one of America's oldest and most successful off-the-grid communes. The difference between a commune and a community comes down to the members' level of involvement in one another's lives. A commune usually operates by a process of consensus and has rules about many aspects of members' lives, from the hours they spend involved in work for the commune to the number of days per year they can rent out their homes.

An off-grid community, at least as I define it, is largely governed by the laws of the land. It's more like a subdivision that does not happen to be connected to municipal utilities. Residents are free to do what they want within their property line, and any communal tasks are entirely voluntary and spontaneous.

In North Carolina I discovered another treasure trove of scenery. Yet again I asked myself why anyone would buy fifty acres in West Texas or New Mexico if they could find two acres in North Carolina, which is far more temperate, more livable, but of course more expensive.

There is a five-mile-per-hour speed limit, and as I drove in I immediately felt like I had entered a unique combination of building and vegetation. It's totally unlike a suburban housing development because the buildings are too architecturally diverse: a trio of hand-hewn bungalows here, a terrace of modernist, zero-carbon apartments there. Each of the homes has solar panels on the roof, and most have solar hot water.

In the center of the 320-acre compound are a small store and post office, where I stopped to ask the way. There is also a community kitchen that becomes the center of all social activity every day at lunchtime. The whole building is hydro-powered from the local stream.

Earthaven is near the town of Asheville. Like Portland and Austin, it's a liberal enclave in a largely conservative area. I drove into the rolling countryside of the Black Mountains and made straight for the commune. At the end of an anonymous road a few miles from the freeway is an official-looking green and white street sign bearing the name ANOTHER WAY. A few feet farther there's a hand-cut, hobbit-sized wooden sign with EARTHAVEN written on it in gaudy paint.

I passed a few mini-mansions standing on their own, each with its own vegetable garden—in some cases a huge vegetable garden. It is all so distinctive and widely spaced that it has the ambiance of a recreational space, an upmarket resort or health spa, rather than a residential development.

I was headed to the Medicine Wheel, a big three-story house that has yet to be completely finished. As I arrived, Lyndon was puttering about in the vegetable patch, a fenced-off area of several hundred square feet. A wispy, almost insubstantial vegetarian of about fifty, with kind eyes, Lyndon had traces of a beard, wavy graying hair, and glasses up on his forehead; he wore jeans, a red work shirt, and gardening work boots. He put down the tools and we walked into the house for tea and a chat.

It feels like a student house, partly because of the rough-and-ready decor, the odd pieces of crockery and furniture, and the big kitchen where residents often eat communally, though rarely at the same time. As Lyndon proudly showed me around, he pointed out the plywood paneling on the ceilings and walls that he had claimed "from the waste stream" of a lumber company that had decided it was cheaper to give away the wood than burn it.

Medicine Wheel is home to half a dozen Earthaven members, including Lyndon. He had been living part-time at Earthaven for many years, but is now making the move to full-time, leaving Texas behind much as he left the oil industry behind after a promising start in exploration and then refining in the seventies.

By 1981 he had become an organic gardener, he told me, and in 1982, the year Jimmy Carter installed solar panels on the White House roof, Lyndon built his first panel and started learning about permaculture, the holistic approach to gardening that is slowly taking hold among the American green movement and goes hand in hand with localism.

"I am not as in the street as I used to be," he said over a cup of herbal tea, his eyes crinkling as he recalled his days as an activist. "The best place to be is in between, where we challenge the system and give alternatives at the same time."

All through the 1980s and 1990s, his main concern was green trade: How would neighbors trade and barter with each other as local economies became more important? What was the solution to the anomaly in which trucks traveled thousands of miles to bring us goods we could perfectly well grow ourselves? In the mythical future, would the truck journeys slowly be squeezed out of the system?

In 1992 he started the Dillo Trading Club in Austin, named after Texas's official state animal, the armadillo. "It was a way of keeping wealth local. We had a lot of developers coming in at the time," Lyndon said. Austinites took to the funky currency, and the timing was good because the mild recession of the early 1990s had increased receptivity to local initiatives. There were also parallels with earlier bouts of austerity. According to Lyndon, at one time, in the 1930s, "there were twenty-five currencies in Texas alone. People still had their labor. They still said, 'I want to go out to work today.' But there were no dollars. So they created their own."

By 1996 the Dillo Hour was firmly established in Austin, with about five thousand dollars' worth of hours in circulation at any one time, honored by a mix of self-employed trades and small businesses, such as alternative health. "We had a booklet called the *Dillo Times*. It listed names and phone numbers, and it became like an *Alternative Austin* listings mag," Lyndon recalled.

Eighties-style greed soon reasserted itself, and although the Dillo group had peaked at about 140 members, the Dillo died officially in the late nineties, but he cannot remember exactly when. As mentioned earlier, Lyndon had held out against using the Web as a networking tool to increase the ease with which members could trade, preferring to keep it all face-to-face and personal. I can understand why, but history has probably proved that his skepticism of computer-based interaction was wrong.

In retrospect the Dillo was both too small and too big. It was too small because it never achieved the critical mass of members that ensured they would all stay confident in the system: Just like with real-world currency, they needed to believe that their Dillos would be tradable in the future, and for a wide variety of goods and services. With membership barely into three figures and, as always, some misusing the system (taking out without putting in), confidence began to wane. On the other hand, the Dillo was too big in the sense that its members were widely scattered around Austin, so they found it inconvenient to meet each other casually in order to maintain the intimacy and trust that were necessary to a successful local scheme. And there was an extra-distance overhead cost each time a service was exchanged. Until barter trading is hyper-local, the cost of doing an hour's work includes traveling to the place where the work is done.

Lyndon held up a childlike pink slip of paper with black lettering that read ONE LEAP. It's the currency in operation at Earthaven and a sample of his latest project. It is working well, being used regularly for internal transactions between members, such as work on-site. "There's more incentive to spend it here, because who wants to drive ten miles to go to the store?" Lyndon pointed out.

There is always a danger that the IRS will take an unhealthy interest if the Leap ever becomes too successful.

According to Lyndon, there are three rules to follow to satisfy the Internal Revenue Service. One, the currency doesn't look like a U.S. dollar. Two, none of the bills are worth less than one U.S. dollar. And three, there is an exchange rate with the dollar. At the moment it's fixed at ten dollars to a Leap, and Earthaven residents are paid one leap per hour for the time they spend on community projects.

By now it was time for dinner, the weekly potluck at the community kitchen. I retrieved a three-Leap bottle of pinot noir from my SUV and we headed over.

I met a dazzling array of characters that night, a sampling of the ninety or so Earthaven residents. There was Bruce, a brilliant young former Caltech mathematician with a clipped, urgent delivery, who had abandoned academia for organic gardening; a lady whose name I have forgotten, who had been part of the feminist avant-garde based around *Spare Rib* magazine in London in the 1970s; and Gasparo, a mystical chiropractor who shares with Lyndon an interest in the gift economy and alternative currencies. Gasparo has helped launch several currencies in his long life, and travels with a self-designed gift note in his wallet—a document he can present to anyone announcing he is offering them a gift. When he finished his meal he sat at the table and licked his plate clean. No doubt it saved both energy and water, but I'd never seen anyone do that before.

I spent part of the evening talking to Mana, a tall, sexually charged Dutch woman who had recently joined Earthaven with her husband, Johnny, a tree surgeon from Arkansas. They had spent years traveling around America in a small pickup truck searching for their ideal community, and Mana had even written a master's thesis on the subject. It emerged that she could also have written a thesis on how to make love in a low-roofed truck (a Mazda B2200), which became a key skill as they covered three hundred thousand miles touring America. "We were having fires every night," she said, "swimming in every river we could find on the map, eating great food, drinking bottles of wine, and sleeping in the back of our little pickup. And I mean little; lying down, both of our hips barely fit in between the wheel wells. And little was no problem for us; we made love anyhow. Neither one of us could sit up, but we got creative!"

Through talking to Mana and the others, I realized that this particular eco-village has successfully placed itself outside and beyond the consumer society. Apart from using its own currency, the community is engaged in "cultural relanguaging," meaning its members are working to iron out untrue assumptions from everyday speech—false beliefs such as the primacy of man, or the vital importance of material possessions.

MAX'S POT

Back in his day, Lyndon was part of the thriving alternative culture in Austin, Texas. The city is both the liberal and cultural beacon of the state of Texas. It may not be the only place one can buy a latté—the real money is in Houston and Dallas—but Austin has the cool credibility. And while Texas has a reputation as the most redneck of the states, it also has Austin to demonstrate that even in Texas everything is happening all the time.

The presence of Pliny Fisk is part of the reason for Austin's preeminence as a thinking person's green city. His Center for Maximum Potential Building Systems is known locally as Max's Pot, a fifty-acre compound loosely affiliated with Texas A&M University. There is a wide variety of zero-carbon buildings on the grounds, including some wholly off-the-grid cabins for interns, and grid-tied offices and a home for Pliny Fisk, its owner, founder, and guru.

Max's Pot is one of four groups that formed in America in the seventies to institutionalize the idea of the off-grid home. The others were the New Alchemy Institute, in Cape Cod, the Fair Loans Institute, in Berkeley, and the Integral Urban Home, also in Berkeley.

I arrived early for the weekly open house and cocktail party, joined by Marcus Ottmers and Ted Norris, two of Austin's leading permaculturists. Pliny lives there with his wife, Gail Vittori, chairman of the Green Building Council, the body responsible for handing out the official green ratings to LEED buildings all over America. And although that makes her the more "successful" of the two, it is Pliny who is the guru.

A small, wiry, bespectacled professor of architecture, with a fearsome intellect, Pliny specializes in low-cost buildings and eco-design. What remains of his hair grows down to his shoulders, and he was wearing a combat jacket as he led students around the center.

As I arrived, Pliny was advising a group of Mexican students on their entry for the Solar Decathlon, a competition for the best solar-powered off-the-grid home. The U.S. Department of Energy organized the first of what has become a biannual competition in Washington, D.C., in 2002. There are various criteria for inclusion, one being that the building must support a typical Western family. To that extent the whole concept is doomed to failure—the typical Western family would have to seriously adjust its behavior and truly want to reduce its carbon output if the solar-powered home is going to become a viable proposition.

Pliny has competed twice, and we were sitting inside one of his entries. "This house we are sitting in cost $176,000," Pliny said of the eight-hundred-square-foot white tentlike structure, a rigid outer shell held in tension by a system of scaffolding struts. It contains a living room/office, a dining area, a full bathroom, and a bedroom, and it placed second in the 2002 Decathlon. The German winner (also eight hundred square feet) cost $2.5 million. "That's about three thousand dollars per square foot," Pliny pointed out. "The AIA [American Institute of Architects] committee for the environment gave us first place."

He wanted to stress an underrated but, in his opinion, vital feature of good eco-design: This building has been disassembled and reassembled several times. From his perspective, living off grid is merely a subset of his overarching metatheory of eco-design—what he calls the "life cycle" approach. It is only by analyzing a building, or anything else, over its entire life span that one can truly say whether it is or is not ecological.

Pliny's advice to would-be off-gridders such as Marcus: You need to inject ideas into the system like a virus, and do your best to ensure they take over the host organism. He was dismissive of Mike Reynolds's Earthships: "He doesn't have good criteria for designing his buildings. They totally overheat." The right criteria for a building, Pliny told me, depend on where it is located. "In an area of water shortage, it's different from somewhere that's wet all year round. And then are you talking house scale? Community scale?" He does, however, approve of trailers, because they "bring in the key services, the kitchen and so forth, and then you build around them for your roof, water gathering, storage, and everything else."

The wind was howling and the building shook at this point. The struts vibrated like the strings on a double bass. I bade farewell to Pliny Fisk, certain that our paths would cross again.

THE SULTAN OF SCROUNGE

In Portland and Earthaven, among other places, I had met people who had little interest in accumulating personal possessions. As strange as it sounds, it is, on the opposite end of the spectrum, possible to be a post-consumer materialist.

Steve Spence, the survivalist who canceled our meeting after he accidentally shot his son in the hand, had, by way of apology, introduced me to a friend of his living in upstate New York. Jim Juczak, a high-school teacher, is known locally as the Sultan of Scrounge. He goes to extraordinary lengths to garner free building materials from local businesses and the local dump.

So it was that I found myself on a seven-fifteen train from New York's Penn Station one fall morning, luxuriating in the big, wide seats and eating the deli breakfast I had put together on the way to the station. Across from me a pair of fun-loving twentysomethings were returning to the suburbs, having partied all night by the look of them. Their phones kept ringing, and I don't know who was more annoyed, they or I. Because they had their eyes closed, I could not even ask them to turn their phones off.

The sun came up as the train slowly journeyed north along the Hudson River as far as Albany, then west up the barge canal. It was the first day of November, and the trees were every shade of red, orange, and green.

By the time I made it to Jim's eighteen-sided home, in rural Jefferson County, it was growing dark. The sultan himself came out to greet me and show me around what he calls Woodhenge—

the fifty-two-acre former gravel quarry he bought for a shade over forty thousand dollars, twelve years ago.

Problem sites, such as mined-out quarries, are a good target if you are trying to get off the grid on the cheap. "Crack houses are another good target," Jim said, if you are looking for an urban setting. They are treated as toxic until they're cleaned up, and have usually had their wiring and plumbing ripped out, reducing their value sharply.

"Half of this was moonscape when we bought," Jim said as we walked over to the guesthouse, a former motel that he had snapped up for twenty-five hundred dollars. He had then transported it on a semi to its current location and had it re-erected for another twenty-five hundred, including the cost of the police escort. Pliny Fisk would be impressed. "Design open buildings that can be reused in part or in whole so that the structure can be easily maintained" is one of his core dictums.

Then I met Phil, a taciturn Vietnam vet with a denim jacket and tinted aviator glasses who lives in a steam-cleaned ten-thousand-gallon kerosene tank facing Jim's house and half buried in a mound of earth. Phil and Jim had converted it into a snug, if windowless, bedroom/sitting room. It has a little extension done up to make it look like a conventional house from the outside, with yellow walls and white wood window frames. "I'm back from two wars to Fort Drum," Phil told me. "I'm not interested in an immaculately finished twenty-five-hundred-square-foot place with a little yard built for status. It's not my vision. I want somewhere agriculture is easily incorporated."

Another building near the main house, known as the Common House, contains more guest quarters, reserved for those building their own houses elsewhere on the acreage. It doubles as a workshop.

Lee Brown is the latest to join Woodhenge, with her husband and three children. The trailer she bought "has a sponge floor and a leaky roof." She is hoping Jim will soon let her start building. "I have a very nontraditional way of looking at things," she told me. "My goal is to find a community that shares the same vision. Our main goal is to sustain ourselves. People do not have a backup except calling Pizza Hut on a Friday night," she added. "The probability of mass famine is getting closer every day."

Lee and her husband, both age forty, are looking forward to abandoning their working lives. "Retirement means being able to live comfortable without having to punch a clock. It costs fifteen hundred dollars a month to pay your bills if you own your house. If you grow your own food and your home is paid for, you can be self-supportive on almost the same lifestyle for $150 a month."

Jim and I continued on the tour. I marveled at the root cellar, made according to a design by architect Malcolm Wells, with sand-filled tires—almost an Earthship. Wells is the architect who first came up with the concept of the earth-filled tires as building blocks, later popularized by Mike Reynolds.

I could tell Jim is a teacher (as is his wife) because he talked at me nearly unstoppably, as if addressing a classroom full of children. And he was wearing a long-sleeved T-shirt with the slogan "If the speed of light is 186,000 miles per second, what is the speed of dark?" To call him barrel-chested would be an injustice to barrels. Let's just say he is almost as wide as he is tall, with bright, intelligent eyes, red hair parted on the side, and a bushy red beard.

Jim finished the tour with a look at the henhouse out back. His thirteen-year-old daughter is responsible for the dozen or so chickens. "I trade a couple dozen eggs a week for some stale bread from the local baked-goods place, enough to feed the chickens, and then they lay more eggs." Although Jim is doing all he can to develop a bartering and trading ethic in his community, there is still no network of other locals willing to circumvent the cash and credit system.

Back at the Juczak main house, built from all sorts of scavenged parts, he proudly showed me the seventeen double-glazed windows that line the huge circular building on both the ground and second floors. They were all mis-filled orders, bought at an eighty percent discount.

The house's central column is seven feet wide and made of twenty-three discarded steel-reinforced concrete manholes. The twenty-three-foot-tall hollow tower supports the roof rafters and second-story floor joists. The tower is also a radiator, albeit a rather unsuccessful one. Jim had built a two-ton wood-burning stove at the bottom of the cylinder and then filled the central column with sixteen feet of sand, making a thirty-five-ton heat store. But it isn't as efficient as he had hoped—in order for it to store enough warmth to pump out real heat, Jim has to burn a fire "continuously for five days and nights."

The manholes are also secondhand, costing $550 including delivery and stacking. The rafters are from a defunct bowling alley. "I saw them demolishing it and walked up there with my hard hat and a clipboard—bought ten one-hundred-foot trusses. Ten thousand dollars, for fifty to sixty thousand dollars of wood." Thanks to these bargains, Jim has ended up with a larger home than he had intended, and this goes against one of his key beliefs, that new American homes are unnecessarily large. The average size of a new home has almost doubled in the past twenty-five years, he told me. Meanwhile the cost of heating has also doubled. And the cost of construction materials has risen sharply, although not for the Juczaks.

Jim's outside walls are made of concrete embedded with old wine bottles, ends facing inside. These let in multicolored light without the thermal loss of windows or the expense of high-quality double glazing. Instead of mortar, the house is held together with "papercrete," a concrete made from his own recipe using recycled paper sludge from a local paper mill, which is only too pleased to allow Jim or anyone else to take it away for free—forty cubic yards a day is thrown away. Jim makes the sludge into mortar by mixing it with masonry cement, about twenty percent by volume.

It's not all that simple, however, to take free paper sludge. Jim had to prepare a "hold-harmless" agreement with the paper mill, and he needed an agreement with the New York State Department of Environmental Conservation to "interrupt the waste stream between a manufacturer and the tri-county landfill." I called him a few months after my visit and he was helping *Good Morning America* produce a segment explaining how to make papercrete.

The ground floor of the nearly circular building consists of a huge kitchen and living area taking up exactly half the floor space. On the fridge is another piece of the bumper-sticker wisdom Jim so loves: "Due to cutbacks, the light at the end of the tunnel has been turned off." The first floor contains two more rooms: Jim's office, which takes up a quarter of the area, and a utility room and storage area.

Each flushing toilet has something I had never seen before—a sink and a tap built into the top of the low-level flush unit. After each flush, the tap above the sink opens to let the correct amount of water flow, via the sink, back into the holding container of the flush unit. So as long as you're quick, the water you use to wash your hands is instantly recycled to flush the toilet. Jim's water is a scarce resource, coming from a spring and also from captured rainwater. It makes complete sense to build the sink into the toilet tank.

"I am not ecological," said Jim, "just logical." I think he had just found his next T-shirt slogan.

Up a flight of stairs, made by Jim's senior-high manufacturing class from two military bridge-building I beams, are the couple's bedroom, two bathrooms, their daughter's bedroom, and a spare room. It's a spacious home for someone who has turned his back on the consumer society, but in a way that is what makes it special. It shows that one does not need to cower in a Thoreau-style ten-by-twelve-foot cabin just because one has abandoned materialism.

Jim admitted that if he was doing it again, "it would be smaller. Easier to heat, easier to maintain." His wife had wanted it bigger and lighter than he had. "At the time we were considering adopting more kids, and my mother-in-law had a few spills, so space was an issue."

He appears to have things in perspective. "Yes, we are both natural cheapskates," he openly confessed, speaking of himself and his wife, Krista. He does not buy bargains for the sake of it. He hoards building materials, food, and food jars, the kind with a screw top much favored for canning fruit and meat in the summer months. Jim simply finds it fun to live on as little as possible. It's like an intellectual challenge. He also has a genuine anger at the system—the tax system, the corporate system, and big government and big business in general. And he is passionate about peak oil and America's new role as a debtor nation.

Jim originally went off-grid ready as a result of a twelve-week power outage in his Watertown home, caused by the ice storm of 1994; he had no water, heat, or power. Afterward, he and Krista bought a secondhand wood burner and added a hand pump to the well. They stocked up on dry foods in storage. "We learned to can a lot more, and began to experiment with things like making mead to preserve nutrition and have a nice drink available. It was always a very secure feeling to go into our larder and pull out a small jar of something we had made ourselves." In 1998 there was a two-week outage, and this time they stayed in the second house.

Back then he was still a registered Republican, and ran for town justice. These days, just about the only group he belongs to is the local Freemasons. Jim voted for Ron Paul in 2008, because he felt that nobody else was being honest about what would be needed in the long term. He foresees a slow "spiraling down" toward a calamitous collapse. "The longer we forestall it, the deeper the recession and the bigger the energy crisis will be." There may need to be a natural disaster or an epidemic to bring it on, but he is fairly sure a crisis will emerge. "The American work ethic seems to have shifted to the American take-it-easy ethic, and not worry about the future."

Jim has a year's worth of food stashed for the desperate times ahead, and expects to give much of it away to whoever turns up.

His supplies are held mainly in the form of rice, barley, and oats, which he feels are low-risk in terms of being seized by looters. "Seventy-five percent of the American people would not know what to do with those foods," he said.

In "hyper-suburban" areas around New York City, Jim expects the residents to be completely incapable of fending for themselves. Even fleeing the city will be too much for them, said the Brooklyn-born fifty-year-old. He had headed for exurbia in search of less stringent building regulations and to escape from neighbors who had freaked out about the effects his activities in Watertown might have on their property values.

His biggest immediate fear is not global warming, peak oil, or economic collapse, but that the state might interfere with his way of life and tell him that he is not allowed to make electricity, convert his car to fuel he can grow on his property, manage his land the way he wants, or build the buildings he wants. The new international building code, which recently became law across the United States, attempts to standardize plumbing and wiring. Jim also cited attempts to impose a certain kind of lumber on DIY house builders.

Jim is in the process of retroactively gaining his building permits. He appeared before the county planning subcommittee and gave a presentation, which was helped greatly when he learned that there is a simple form anyone can fill out to say that they have a philosophical problem with obeying the normal rules. "Every state has to have a religious and/or philosophical exemption to the building rules. You simply state, 'I don't believe in indoor plumbing,' and they can't make you put it in."

It sounds as though Jim gave a bravura performance to the local commissioners. "They were all looking at me as if it was a drug-using commune. I said, 'Come on, guys, look at me. I have been a teacher for twenty-five years. I belong to the Masons.'" He tried to persuade the board to see the social benefits of schemes like Woodhenge in terms of closer families. "Look at all the parents who are getting a bit older," he told them, moving on to one of my favorite issues. "They want their children to look after them but they aren't allowed to build a house next door so their kids can keep an eye on them."

As time goes by, Jim told me, he feels increasingly aligned with the Amish, and admires their ability to sit down with the people around them for their entertainment. He believes we could all benefit from the Amish sense of family and community.

At breakfast the next day, Jim was wearing a new T-shirt. This time the slogan read, "Clothes maketh the man." The word *clothes* had been crossed out and *power tools* had been inserted. It read, "Power tools maketh the man."

We sat at the table and I looked around, admiring two hundred bottles of preserves, sauces, canned meat, pickled vegetables, a few dozen baskets of root vegetables, and other goodies hanging from ceiling hooks, not to mention the artwork on the walls, most of it by Jim's daughter.

He gave me homemade apple preserves, made from apples gleaned from neighbors' gardens, spread on home-baked bread. Over coffee, which wasn't homegrown or even fair trade, Jim started giving me the technical specs of his power system. He said he traded the twelve 50-watt solar panels in return for a sixty-five-dollar rifle. He walked me around the house, giving the provenance of every item of equipment, and would probably have done the same for the entire fifty-two acres if I had let him.

The main house cost about forty dollars a square foot, compared with a national average of around $150 per square foot. The motel cost about five dollars a square foot, and the former kerosene tank was more like fifty cents.

"Don't try to recycle cast-iron baths," he advised as he showed me the en suite bathroom, "unless you want to incur the equivalent cost in hernia surgery."

On my final morning there, Jim wore a T-shirt bearing a picture of a drill with the slogan "I do my bit."

It's fair to say that Jim depends more than most on the detritus of modern society. If there were no consumers, he would no longer have access to their castoffs. Is this, as Daniel Staub believes, a crucial inconsistency? I don't think so. There will still be avid consumers for years to come; Jim is just showing us all a possible alternative. In the event of continuing economic decline, many more will need to behave like Jim. The big retailers and producers of brand-name goods have a vested interest in making his kind of behavior seem eccentric at best and penny-pinching or counterproductive at worst.

Jim, despite his many flaws and inconsistencies, is the harbinger of a new consciousness. His is the way forward, whatever the future holds. Either the economy takes a turn for the better, in which case we all need to be reminded that it is ecologically absurd to go on consuming at our present rate, or it fails to recover (or even slips further back), in which case many more of us will be forced to scavenge for a living.

Jim recently took a sabbatical from his job teaching workshop skills to the eleventh grade in order to explore a career writing and lecturing on the subject of cheap and eco-conscious living. I can't help feeling he would be better off opening a personal-shopping service for post-consumer consumers. It would be an invaluable service, and his fee would pay for itself purely in terms of new discounts this resourceful man seems to attract just by getting up in the morning.

Power and Freedom

> "None are more enslaved than those who be-
> lieve they are free."
>
> Johann Wolfgang von Goethe

The post-consumers have a mix of
spiritual, ethical, and political motivations. This next group is
more about economics (although all these categories are ap-
proximate, and most off-gridders fall into more than one). The
desire to have complete dominion over one's own life, and freedom from the state and other powerful busybodies, is only
natural.

I hit Texas as President Obama was giving his first State of the
Union Address, promising enormous sums for health care and
education. Meanwhile, millions of boomers were wondering
what they would do if their savings were wiped out. Driving
toward Fort Davis from the Midland airport, I listened to the
car radio as one pundit estimated that if pensioners were paid
all their current entitlements, by 2041 the pensions' trust fund
of two trillion dollars would be wiped out. For the first time, I
stirred uneasily at the thought of a pension-less future.

I was on my way to visit Wretha, a woman from Dallas, now living in a "mountain resort" with her husband, Bob. Before meeting her, I had enjoyed her honest blog, on which she writes about her attempts to go off the grid in Texas, how she and her husband, known as Mountain Man Bob, save money and make do, and their plans to grow tobacco. From what I already understood of their life, relying on a pension was not something they had factored in.

It was late evening at the Midland airport when I started the four-hour drive southwest. The rental was the smallest compact I had ever seen, and although I usually managed to sweet-talk the clerk into upgrading for free, I hadn't worked my magic this time, so I would be sleeping in the driver's seat in a few hours. After plugging in the inverter to charge the phone, I set off toward Fort Davis.

There was thick fog and a little snow as I drove down endless straight roads with tumbleweed and sagebrush billowing in front of me on the high winds. This was not one or two isolated plants; at times the road was seemingly alive with tumbleweed dancing madly in the headlights like bizarre puppets. It was like watching a western on a bad TV set.

In a few days I was set to meet a guy who lived in his car, and I decided to give myself a brief preview of the experience. At two-thirty a.m., I saw a sign for the Cactus Motel in Balmorhea. It has a large car park with plenty of bushes, so I slid the car into a dark shadow, wound back the driver's seat as far as I could, pulled on my sleeping bag, wrapped a goose-down parka around my head, and slept like a king. When I awoke early the next morning under a clear, cold sky, I spent a half hour using the motel's free Wi-Fi, relieved myself in the bushes, decided not to push my luck with the free breakfast, and got on my way.

An hour later I found Wretha waiting for me in her black VW Beetle at the entrance to the mountain resort. I followed at a distance along mile after mile of dusty, bumpy road. We zigged and zagged across the subdivided ranch, and finally came to a halt in a small, sheltered canyon with three or four houses within shouting distance of each other.

Like Daryl Hannah on Brown Ranch, Wretha and Bob are the only homeowners in their mountainous subdivision who have not connected the power the final few hundred yards from the road to their house.

There the resemblance ends. Wretha's home is a higgledy-piggledy, handmade wooden box raised on the side of a steep hill, a few hundred yards past the house of their nearest neighbor, who sits much closer to the road. The neighbor allows Bob and Wretha to "look after" his grid-connected place when he is gone, which is more often than not, and this gives them a strange part-time on-the-grid status. They use his fridge, his TV, and his spare room, for storing their dry and canned rations, hoarded in the event of total social collapse.

Wretha made tea in the neighbor's kitchen, then she and I sat on camp chairs while Mountain Man Bob, wearing no shoes, sat cross-legged on the ground, chain-smoking Philip Morris filter tips. The cigarettes had been imported via the Internet from Moldova for a mere seven dollars a carton, versus forty dollars from the local store. I accepted his offer and tried one. At an altitude of six thousand feet, I instantly regretted it.

Once the dizziness passed I could appreciate the romance of the spot. It's a rocky, tree-lined gulch, and the lush vegetation suggests there is enough water around. Peace and the isolation are the main attractions, plus the lack of humidity, which makes it one of the few places in the United States where one does not need air-conditioning in the summer. Bob realized this when he first visited the area, in the eighties.

When their time came to flee the city, Bob remembered his trip and brought Wretha to have a look. Cities may be the well-spring of human civilization, cauldrons of creativity and commerce, but Wretha and Mountain Man Bob are refugees from the cold, hard side of urban life, examples of the many who will inevitably and always be unhappy in the concrete jungle.

Out here, in almost total poverty, Bob and Wretha are truly

happy. Their happiness is due in large part to being in control of their lives for the first time. "I have had it with the Man," Bob would say later. "I take care of myself as much as I can—doctoring, energy, building, gardening."

They began to tell the story of their miserable existence in Dallas. They had met, as many do these days, via the Internet. It was less common in 1999, when they were both in their midthirties. Wretha worked as a stock girl for Best Buy, and Bob fixed the kitchen equipment for a number of branches of Red Lobster in the Dallas–Forth Worth area. They each lived alone, worked long hours, drank moderately, and, apart from sleeping, visiting their families, and seeing each other, had no disposable time.

Their common bond was a feeling of oppression, of the system grinding them down. Bob was self-employed. He undercharged and over-delivered, and as a result was hugely in demand in the Dallas–Fort Worth restaurant community. "He was like MacGyver," said the manager of the Dallas Capital Grille when I phoned later. Bob could have raised his rates and hired an assistant, but he didn't believe in leading his life in a businesslike way. It would have been disloyal to his esteemed clients if he had let anyone else attend to their heating and equipment requirements, was how he saw it. Of course, society as a whole does not necessarily share this viewpoint, so there was a mismatch between Bob's own beliefs about how to play fair and the way others behaved toward him, a mismatch that usually operated to his disadvantage.

A year before my visit, the couple bought their six-acre lot for $11,500, using Wretha's share options from Best Buy. Since then they have lived in a more intimate world of one-to-one human relationships. Bob is in his element. His joy in helping others and his manual skills make him a valued member of the immediate community. Now he gets back exactly what he puts in—even a little more.

As we sat there, Bob in the dusty red dirt, they talked of their plans: Grow some tobacco, add a well, expand the vegetable garden, and finish the root cellar. They would have already drilled the well, but their neighbor gives them all the water they need. They plan to end their dependence soon enough, Bob said as he showed me up a steep path, past an old pickup and a travel trailer.

The main house, if you can call it that, began life as a sixteen-by-sixteen-foot room, approached via an outside wooden staircase. It had been built within a fortnight of their arrival. With their basic shelter taken care of, and the neighbor being so generous, there was little urgency to complete the work. As a result, the place is a permanent construction site, and one suspects that it will be for years to come. A thirty-by-thirty-foot area in front of the house is a mess of old appliances, salvaged lumber, and other junk—quite natural when there are just two of you, a deserted mountainside, and a big construction project to finish.

In the year since the initial building effort, Bob and Wretha have added a small guest room and a west-facing viewing terrace looking out over the mountain range. Under the raised platform, Bob is making progress on the root cellar and the cool room that will provide their shade during the hottest part of the summer.

Wretha took me for a quick visit to the country store so I could pick up some snacks and a bottle of wine for dinner. There was nothing I would consider eating, except some fresh croissants. When we returned to their unfinished cabin, she began to prepare dinner while I opened the wine.

The culture gap yawning between us all day opened wide. I asked for wineglasses and was given three plastic cups. I stared at the cups for several seconds, as if through willpower alone I could transform them into glass. They stayed obdurately plastic.

Wretha began opening cans and packets, and Bob showed me the emergency supplies, several months' worth of "stuff that doesn't require refrigeration"—chili beans, canned food, ramen noodles, rice, diced canned potatoes, and "a bunch of those oatmeal bars."

I asked about the stuff that does require refrigeration.

"Oh, the beer?" Bob asked. "That's in the fridge down at Glen's place."

We sat down for drinks, served in the plastic, and Bob began to explain why he really left Dallas. At the heart of it all is anger. Bob is an angry man, angry about what this society is becoming, and angry when the system won't let him, a law-abiding, tax-paying citizen, do what he wants with his own home. He had lived in Dallas in a double-wide trailer he'd bought in the 1980s for twenty thousand dollars, and when Wretha moved in he had wanted to add a tiny extension to give them more room, and a little picket fence around the trailer so they could have a sense of their own space in the trailer park. Of course, he was not allowed either—the extension was disallowed by the local zoning, and the picket fence was nixed by the trailer park people. Both these brushes with authority left him with a depressing lack of control over his own life. Out here, he felt fine. "I like being able to build what you want without having to get permission from Nanny," he said of his new home. "Here you don't have to ask anybody for permission. Nobody has to come out to inspect it and tell you it's OK."

Until the recent credit crunch, the Bobs of this world were looked down on as failures, while the rest of us busy folks were thinking, There, but for the grace of God, go I, as we rushed to meet our next deadline, whether it was picking the kids up from school, getting the car out of the lot before the time expired, or keeping the boss happy at work. Now we have *all* been dumped on by the system and our money handed to the bankers so they can continue paying themselves huge bonuses. We are all angry now—although not necessarily about the same things.

Bob and Wretha also expressed their frustration at the way their Dallas neighborhood had been overtaken by a new ethnic group. "Where we used to live it was like little Mexico. It wasn't even bilingual anymore; it was all Mexican," Wretha told me.

"And people are so afraid of offending or being seen as politically incorrect."

Bob joined in. "They get the vote, then begin to make the rules, and pretty soon they rule themselves in and you out. We find ourselves being the outsiders and the outsiders are now the new insiders."

Around the time Red Lobster had decided they could not risk their Dallas outlets being maintained by a one-man operation who was undercharging them, Bob began noticing "all these illegals riding round in new cars and living in new houses. And I thought, How does that figure?"

"And there's people just waiting at the border to help them," Wretha chimed in. "A Mexican woman will drop a baby—they call them 'anchor babies'—and if it's born here, it's an American citizen, and some white liberal will make sure she gets legal representation. . . ." she trailed off to serve dinner: chicken stew, on paper plates.

Paper plates? Plastic cups? I couldn't believe it. It seemed to me that they weren't understanding key elements of the term *ecological*. I lamely concluded that they were doing it to save water by not having to wash up. I was aching to tell them about my trip to the American Legion in Big Bend, and to ask them 'zacly when did they become white trash, but the words wouldn't form in my mouth. Mechanically, I raised the food to my lips, and to my amazement, it was delicious.

I complimented Wretha on it and asked for the recipe. I almost choked when she recited the following:

2 cans chicken soup (with veggies)
2 cans chicken meat
2 cans chicken stock
dumplings made with Bisquick and chicken stock

Twenty cigarettes a day and a high-salt diet of canned food—before long, Mountain Man Bob is going to need all the self-doctoring skills he can lay his hands on.

"It's going in the direction of the Nanny State," Bob said when I asked why he attaches such importance to self-doctoring. "I can't stand depending on somebody else, and I can't stand somebody telling me that if I can't jump through this hoop and that hoop then I'm not going to get what it is I need. I got a broken arm, I need my arm fixed, I'll be darned if you want my social security number, you want my name. You're not going to help me if I don't? You're going to let me die if I don't tell you what my name is? OK, I'll go fix my own broken arm.

"You won't give me water?" Bob moved on to a new hobbyhorse. "I was a month late paying my bill 'cause I got laid off. You're going to turn my water off because I can't pay my bill? I'll get my own damn water."

The final straw had come when his neighbors were beating their dog so badly that Bob called the police. The cops came, all right—and arrested Bob. After a night in the cell it transpired that Bob was being held "at the request of child support," for failing to keep up on his payments to his ex-wife and their son. His ex wrote a letter confirming that his stopping payment had been by mutual agreement, but it made no difference. Bob had failed to inform the authorities in the proper manner; therefore he was guilty, and a law-abiding Christian American had become a criminal.

"When a few things like that happen I ain't got no more use for the Man," Bob said. And now here he was. "I'm happy as I could be without dying and going to heaven and finding out it's as good as I thought it was," Bob said, Wretha nodding her head in agreement.

THE LAST AMERICAN MAN

Bob and Wretha are pleased to have thrown the Man off their back. Eustace Conway has set up a little kingdom where he teaches others to do the same thing.

Over the potluck dinner at the Earthaven commune, someone had casually mentioned Turtle Island Preserve. "Of course,"
she had said, "you know Turtle Island, the other side of North
Carolina?" No, I didn't. "And the Last American Man? You must
know about the Last American Man."

"Tell me more," I had said, and she'd told me of the book of
that name, by Elizabeth Gilbert, published a few years earlier,
about a man of such intense and exquisite masculinity that
women flock to him, a man who makes other men look like
girly-girls, a man who lives off the grid.

I read Eustace Conway's story. It's of a man who has some
blinding insights on how we humans could and should live on
this earth. Before he even started studying anthropology in college, he had moved into a tepee and learned to hunt, trap, and
fend for himself in every way. It was then that he decided to
dedicate himself to living this way for the rest of his life.
More important, he decided to lead by example, to make his
life an open book and his home a study center. This is what
transformed the gawky student into someone his female colleagues found exciting and attractive, and whom his male com-
patriots found threatening and potentially humiliating. In the
decades since he began living this way (he is nearly fifty now),
tens of thousands have passed through the front gates at Turtle
Island Preserve.

To meet Eustace I first had to go through Desiree, a curva-
ceous, dark-haired Coloradan with pouty lips and smoldering
eyes. She had spent a few years "traveling and camping" before
arriving to live at Turtle Island Preserve. "That was when I
learned the delights of a cold shower," she told me. I was very
curious about their arrangement. Was she Eustace's personal
assistant and gatekeeper, or his girlfriend as well? And if she
had a sexual relationship with the Last American Man, was she
his only girlfriend or just his main girlfriend, merely one of
many? These were questions to be left until I got to know her
better.

We were sitting facing each other in the café of the Earth Fare grocery store in Boone, the big town closest to Turtle Island Preserve. It is easily the best grocery store I've found in all my time in the United States, a smaller version of Whole Foods, run by kinder people. The food is exemplary, and the prices are reasonable, especially on the bargain shelf, which is restocked hourly. The prices in the café are the same as in the store, and it has free Wi-Fi and excellent bathrooms. No wonder the entire off-the-grid population around Boone uses the place as a clubroom.

I had been e-mailing away on my laptop until Desiree turned up and slid onto the bench opposite me. I explained my mission, and she said that Eustace was very busy at the moment; I could ask her any questions I might have.

My first was whether he really does believe that we are witnessing the death of masculinity in modern America. She quoted from one of his favorite books, *The Sibling Society*, which she admitted is "a bit dry." Eustace agrees with its basic analysis that "instead of an ambition to grow up and mature and reach the status of an elder, we are much more directed, these days, into being youthful and immature and unaccountable, careless and selfish." He also agreed with Dr. Seuss, that "America is a society of obsolete children."

To me this seemed to be more about a decline in wisdom rather than masculinity, but I began to see what Desiree was getting at. "Eustace sees full-blown masculinity rarely coming to fruition," she went on. "It's becoming harder to find role models, elders, hunters, really masculine men."

So are men becoming wimps?

"It's not that they are all wimps," she said, now relishing her role as the voice of Eustace. "It's that they stay boys." She ended with a defiant stare, almost a challenge to me to prove that I am not one of these lady-boy kidults infesting America.

I tried to look solemn and wise, and took my own voice down an octave or two. "Do the multitudes who come to Turtle Island to learn building, bushcraft, and land-husbandry skills include any real men?" I asked with a growl.

The answer was that it is all too rare, especially among the self-selecting group that visits the preserve. Presumably it's an awareness of their shortcomings that leads them to seek help from Eustace. Apparently "as soon as the boys get a splinter, everything stops while they get a Band-Aid. Nine times out of ten," Desiree said, "Eustace will choose the strongest females in the group to work closely with him."

I bet he does, I thought to myself.

This seemed to be the appropriate moment to raise the issue of Eustace's continuing attractiveness to the opposite sex. Desiree reported that there is "still a steady interest from women, who phone to ask, 'Does he have a girlfriend? Is he married?' I just pass the messages on to him," she said casually, in a way that left me unable to tell whether she couldn't give a damn or whether she filters the messages first, perhaps subtly changing the phone numbers or discarding the ones that seem too enticing.

"And is he still attractive to women?" I asked, throwing caution to the wind.

"The body is just the image that reflects the attitude," Desiree replied elliptically. "He doesn't like sugar or get excessive on snacks."

As I pondered that one, I was delighted to hear Desiree invite me for breakfast the following morning. I thought that any further questions about his sexuality had better wait until I had at least met the Last American Man himself.

I had one call to make before then, to a student at the university in Boone. Eustace's story has, intentionally or otherwise, inspired an entire micro-generation of students to follow his example. I was off to meet one of them.

Eddie Lemke is not what I had expected. He picked me up in the parking lot at Earth Fare and we headed up to the campus in his small two-door sedan, the backseat piled almost to the roof with clothes and books. "Uh, it's, uh, the best place to keep them dry," he explained, in tones so laid-back he was almost talking out of his nostrils. We drove up to the top of the campus and parked behind a mound of earth that is part of a building project. Then we walked through a wooded area for five minutes, and there on Appalachian State University property was Eddie's tepee. It was about fifteen feet tall. He had placed it there in winter without realizing that the hydrangea bushes all around it would provide him with excellent cover most of the year. As a result (his fellow students confirmed this later), he had gone undetected for eighteen months.

Eddie seemed like a pretty normal student to me, except for the strangely laid-back way of talking and an annoying little goatee. He did not seem like the typical kind of guy who goes back to the land. His main interests in life, as far as I could tell, are kegs of beer.

It turned out that his initial motivation for the campus tepee was mainly financial. His parents had cut off his allowance due to overspending. He had made a deal with them that if he could survive on no money for a semester, they would restore his monthly payments. That was when he came up with the tepee idea. He built the tepee largely alone, at almost no cost, he said, with no reference books, and it had worked out fine. He had even made a fireplace out of an old oil drum that was installed so it peeked out of the tepee, allowing him to shovel in wood from the outside; it kept him warm as toast on the inside. He had some help from his parents once they saw he was serious. His mother had even sewn the canvas tepee pieces together for him.

This was all impressive, but Eddie is no eco-revolutionary. He told me at length about his current source of income, a Web site that allows students to compare the prices of a keg of beer at the many outlets in and around Boone. He hopes to take the idea national.

He had agreed to show me the tepee only because his final semester was almost over, so security was no longer all-important, and I had the impression that he was going to be pleased to see the end of it. There is little overlap between Eddie Lemke and my image of the Last American Man—except for one thing. The tepee,

Eddie told me, may have been cold and damp and lonely at times, but it was a "babe magnet." He pulled out his cell phone and showed me photos of the previous night's party. Correction: It was a two-babe magnet.

The drive from Boone to Turtle Island Preserve later that afternoon was ravishing. This is a place where anyone could be happy living off the grid: rural, relatively remote, and yet only a thirty-minute drive from a university town, which means libraries, bands, and bars. Turtle Island Preserve is set in some really great countryside, lush and green, with rolling hills and fields like the ones seen in ads for shampoo and butter. A ranch on the preserve is approached via a stunning mountain road that meanders through an enclosed valley dotted with fields where horses graze and past well-maintained homes with neatly kept lawns. It's a lot like England, both in the kinds of trees—willow, oak, and ash—and also in the way the fields are laid out.

By the time I turned onto the bumpy track that leads to Eustace's estate, it was dusk and it had begun to rain. It continued to pour for the rest of the visit. This will sort out the men from the boys, I thought as I parked the SUV and walked across a bridge over a fast-running stream.

With my car-dwelling lesson drawing nearer, I decided to take a page out of Jassen Bowman's manual (which appears later in this chapter) and stay overnight in a parking lot. It proved far more atmospheric than most campsites I've been to. I would be ready to meet Eustace bright and early, but first I took a walk into the preserve before bed.

Eustace started with one hundred acres when he first set up Turtle Island Preserve. Over the years, through simple purchases and deals with neighbors to swap one parcel for another, he managed to lift his holding to roughly a thousand acres of prime North Carolina real estate. He makes a handsome income offering residential courses in old masculine skills, such as spoon carving, blacksmithing, horseback riding, cooking with wood, and using a "log builder's tool kit."

As I walked down the main path onto the land, I was under huge trees; tulip poplar, oak, locust, maple, basswood, and hemlock abound. On the left are bushes. On the right, the path opens out to reveal huge lawns sweeping away to a small valley with various pine, spruce, and fir trees on the opposite slope. I passed several high wooden buildings, hand-built by Eustace and his many interns. There is a woodcutting barn with a bio-diesel wood saw, and a stable that looks ancient. I learned later that the stable had been made of recycled wood within the past few years.

As the rain intensified I headed back to the SUV, where I spent a couple of enlightening hours with a glass of wine and a copy of *The Last American Man*. I learned that while Eustace had been living in a tepee as a university student, elsewhere in North Carolina he had held natural-living courses for his fellow students. He had told them that "reduce, reuse, recycle" is a good concept. "But first," he would say, "apply two other often-overlooked principles: reconsider and refuse—do you really need this consumer product?"

It was still raining at seven-thirty the next morning as I retraced my steps onto the preserve. In one of the stables, a man and a woman struggled with a number of wet and steaming horses. Those interns again. Reproduction antique wagons are lined up under the cover of another stable. A third shed looks like a henhouse, and even has an authentic Foghorn Leghorn–style rooster running between wobbly handmade stools, crooked shelving, and other artifacts that are clearly the products of lessons in masculine self-reliance.

I continued straight on to the biggest building of all—an eighty-foot covered open-sided kitchen and dining area, with several long rows of tables and a huge fireplace at one end, and a big, crowded kitchen at the other, all in a dark wood finish that added a layer of gloom to the dank atmosphere.

As previously instructed, I waited by the fireplace for my hosts to arrive. It was bucketing down now, warm and steaming wet, when a 4x4 came into view through the trees, traveling from the far side of the land. Desiree and Eustace disembarked.

Grateful for the invitation, I had come prepared with the mangos and pineapple Desiree said he likes. As he ambled in, Eustace looked like a very different person from the alpha-male stud I had expected from the book's title and the snippets I had read the night before.

He has an almost timid demeanor, still gawky after all these years. He's tall but stands with his shoulders slightly rounded, the way some tall people get when they stoop a lot to listen to shorter companions. His body language was controlled, self-contained. He didn't stride or strut; he walked softly, and probably silently, though the rain on the wooden roof was too loud for me to be certain. He had a cheap blue nylon jacket to protect against the rain, worn over an orange fleece against the cold, and a white cowboy hat jammed down on top of his blond hair, worn in Native American–style plaits. He has a ragged graying mustache and beard, shaved just above the chin, and a saintly smile. I say saintly because he beams goodwill out to the world through that smile. It is a smile of kindness, not humor or self-certainty. I immediately sensed that Eustace is a good man of almost entirely altruistic motivation, and nothing he said later caused me to change that view.

He had bought the first 102 acres of Turtle Ranch some three decades earlier for eighty thousand dollars, specifically as a place to practice his twin urges: to live close to nature and to introduce others to nature. He leads extended hikes and sweat lodge sessions for adults, and courses in husbandry and bush-craft for adults and school-age kids.

At first Eustace's motivation was based entirely on the majesty of the natural world, the need for us to reconnect with what he called "the magnificent truths and inspiration and peaceful feeling of the correct way." This has now changed.

He often receives letters from twenty-one-year-olds telling him they have moved into tepees. Having seen how even Eddie had adapted to tepee life, I asked why it isn't more common. "It's about American norms," said Eustace. "Your parents saying, 'What are you doing?' People want you to conform, to be like them." Eustace's answer made sense; Eddie had lived in the tepee as a solution to a problem after his allowance was cut. And his lateral thinking had given him a powerful bargaining chip with his parents, who had quickly resumed his allowance. Recently, Eustace told me, he had stopped talking about the skills themselves and why they are important, and was instead focused on reminding the world about the loss of both skills and freedom we have suffered as individuals in a society that infantilizes us in order to control us. "I have been realizing the bigger picture," he said. "Every corrupt government has, step by step, achieved the plan of taking away the freedom of Americans. The propaganda we get is that we have the greatest freedom, but after studying I found that we have just an illusion of freedom."

By this time Desiree had been joined by Brett Butler, a part-time bushcraft teacher at Turtle Island Preserve. He quickly had a fire roaring in the hearth. "I had a cook staying here who grew up in communist Poland," Eustace was saying. "And after living in America for a decade, he was sure that the communistic lifestyle has much greater freedom than Americans'."

To put it simply, he believes that the American social system is in terrible shape. For this Eustace blames corporate leadership, which has us where they want us. As he sees it, Americans have become a herd of sheep marching compliantly to their own destruction. "The economic and social structure of North America today is succeeding beautifully in producing non-thinking, incapable people—the perfect candidate to be the mindless consumer who doesn't even see who they are or what they are doing."

Desiree chopped and served the pineapple. Eustace sighed

with satisfaction at my little offering and kept talking. "I like the freedom and peace of being off in the natural world, with friends and nature. I am probably one of the freest people in North America—or have the ability to be."

But on one level he is not free. He explained, "I am like a martyr giving my time and energy up to share with other people. It's a politically incorrect thing to admit, but I don't totally enjoy it."

So why does he do it?

"I could make a choice any day to just walk off into the forest and never be seen again. I don't really like being around people, but somebody has to step up to the plate, because nobody else is."

His philosophy has changed over the past decade. He has dropped his goal of persuading ordinary Americans to live without electricity of any kind. Naively, he had believed the book about him by Elizabeth Gilbert, and his occasional appearances on *Good Morning America* and shows like it, would help move large swaths of the population to adopt his lifestyle.

And there was another, deeper error in his thinking, he told me.

"I had the allure of self-sufficiency," he said in his halting style. "It's an American trait—it's not community sufficiency; it's all about individual freedom. I like being by myself and I'm very capable, but along the road a wise man pointed out it's not really about self-sufficiency; it's about community sufficiency, and I thought, Yeah, that makes perfect sense. Humans are social creatures. I have been following the wrong path."

That's when Eustace started using electricity (though not from the grid); until then he had relied on wood and muscle as his only two sources of energy. "I started telling people it's not about self-sufficiency—we need something which is a better model, which is more broad. One of the problems is that we don't know how to interact with each other anymore. Our social situation has fallen apart—even our vocabulary has fallen apart. For the last fifty years we have been shown how to be a success, be a leader, be a decision maker. It's all about me, me, me—now, now—me, now. It's horrible. We are not being taught to be good community members."

I found that very interesting. For Eustace, it explains why many Americans feel that they are trapped, yet also feel like they have nowhere to escape to. In a society of individualists, Americans need communities to take them in. But there are none—or, at least, not enough.

Does that mean all these young men living in tepees, like Eustace Conway did, have got it wrong?

"When young people come to me and say, 'I want to follow this model,'" he said, waving his hand to indicate that he was talking about his current landed lifestyle, "I say, 'No you don't. You could grow a large amount of food on a small piece of land.'" He thinks a very workable solution is about eight people on two acres of land.

"I am almost doing a disservice to give a model of this grandiose thing. I didn't sleep for years—hardly just a few hours a night—and worked like a maniac. It does not represent a healthy model. If I was a young person who had the wisdom, I would [adopt] radical models of land ownership, such as not owning any land, moving around. . . . There's a root crop called Jerusalem artichoke. It does very well. Let's say a group of young people had a mobile lifestyle covering, say, a ten-mile area, moving so they don't get caught. What you do is plant maybe ten or twenty plots of that. It takes care of itself, so when they do come back, they get food there. That's what I would be researching if I was a young person: greater mobility and greater freedom, true hunting and gathering."

Another alternative Eustace suggested is "moving around half the year in state forests, hunting, maybe, then you come back to your own piece of land that gives you a legal base." That way you have the benefits of both staying in one place and mobility.

I asked him if, now that he has discovered the power of community, he will invite some like-minded folks to come and share his one thousand acres.

"I have thought of inviting some people to live here," he replied. "But that's not my motivation. I am a little bit more selfishly interested in more space for myself. I think that space and the beautiful wild is one of my greatest motivations. I am also selfishly motivated in that I don't want to become a babysitter. I am in that role to some extent because of the people I brought in here."

I remembered again that the *New York Times* had characterized Thoreau's experiences at Walden as "cold and selfish isolation."

He went on. "The mass of people in North America are extraordinarily incapable on many levels. I am almost afraid to tell people how horrifically incapable they are. They don't know how to grow a garden or plant a seed—they don't even know what a seed looks like. So our social system is not in a good position. The higher level of corporate leadership is succeeding in getting us where they want us."

Eustace then moved on to talk about the issue for which he is best known—the collapse of masculinity. "The women, especially the younger women, are more and more capable. The men are horribly incapable. You would die if you could see through my eyes how incapable the young men in North America are today, whether it's social, or personal strength and courage, or whether it's physical ability, like how to run or walk or climb a tree, or anything in science or physics or thermodynamics. They are the most unbelievable example of incapable human beings that ever walked the planet. They come and offer help—in fact they can be no help at all. I think, Oh no, please. You can help a lot by staying away. I know that's horrible, but that's a fact."

Eustace despairs of the modern American social and economic system. "A catastrophe is the only thing that's going to move the masses. It's unfortunate because they could make the change today—they have the information." I find this admission interesting, because it means Eustace, like many professional environmentalists and social theorists faced with little support for their campaigns, is waiting for social collapse. He has been waiting a long time.

At this point Eustace revealed an unexpectedly radical side to him. "The government doesn't want people to do this," he said, sounding like Mountain Man Bob. "It doesn't want people to have the freedom. We are set up to be slaves who look after ourselves. The government doesn't want people to know how to grow their own food. If you know how then you have freedom; you are not dependent on the system. The corporations that control the government tend to lose money if the masses are not tied into their system."

Eustace is, like many of us, a bundle of contradictions. He has his freedom, has worked and struggled for it. Yet he feels trapped. His life is on many levels a vindication of his beliefs, yet he feels like a failure. And the larger his empire grows, the more out of love he becomes with corporate America.

ON THE ROAD AGAIN

In November 2010 Jassen Bowman will run on the Libertarian ticket for a seat in the U.S. Congress as a representative of the State of Colorado. He told me his political plans as he drove me around Boulder, pointing out the locations where the car dwellers—like Jassen—sleep. This was during the height of the recession, though the shops and restaurants were full due to the high proportion of well-paid government employees at research establishments specializing in the environment, such as the National Center for Atmospheric Research.

When we first met over the Internet, Jassen had lost his home to foreclosure, following a divorce. He had wanted to let me know about his lifestyle, and why he was doing it.

"It goes by many names, such as car camping, car living, van dwelling, boondocking, full-timing, and dwelling portably," he wrote. To Jassen, it's all about freedom. "Sure, I could move in with a couple guys in a college town," he wrote, but instead he had decided on what appears to be a much less appealing choice. "I'm going to sleep in my car. That's about all I do at home is sleep, anyway. Otherwise, I'm out living life, which I believe is what humans should do."

Over the past eleven years, Jassen has spent a total of about three living in either a car or a van, usually for a few months at a time. "My longest stretch included two months in a compact car, followed by eight months in a van, right after my divorce in 2005," he wrote.

Now I was due finally to meet him in person. He was to pick me up at the Boulder Outlook Hotel, where I had spent a rare night on the grid. We would then tour the Boulder area in his car, the car he sleeps in, learning about his car-dwelling philosophy.

Jassen is five feet eight inches and in his early thirties. The light brown hair sticking up from his chubby, childlike face is almost a military cut, a holdover from six years in the Navy. Tinted, round wire-rimmed glasses give his pasty skin an intellectual air.

The first thing he showed me was the car itself, an inconspicuous silver four-door Saturn sedan with tinted windows. It is smaller than I had expected.

"I don't live in a car," he told me. "I live out of a car."

The reasons he had selected this particular GM model were: 1) reliability: Jassen had done 230,000 miles in the car over the previous seven years with hardly a hiccup, although the clutch was starting to go; and 2) fuel consumption: about forty miles to the gallon, compared with—at most—twelve for an RV. Jassen had owned more than a dozen vehicles since starting to live out of a car at the age of nineteen. For him, at least, the Saturn is the optimal solution. "If you live in a car, you should be using your car, traveling, enjoying the opportunity to go to interesting places, and that means gas consumption."

Leaving, for the moment, the question of exactly why Jassen

has chosen this lifestyle, I was interested in the practicalities of car dwelling, the dos and don'ts and the essential gear.

"Homelessness is illegal in most cities in America," he told me as we cruised through Boulder. "I believe everyone should have the right to sleep in a cardboard box if they want to, whether they need to or not." I had to remind myself that this queer fellow is running for public office. Boulder is unique, Jassen explained, in its tolerant attitude toward car dwellers: There is a city ordinance that says anyone can sleep in their car one night in every seven.

That particular early-spring week, with the thermometer hovering around the 30-degree mark, it transpired that Jassen had not actually been living in his car; he was living in his office. In fact it is not even *his* office, but a tax advisory business, owned by a couple of Brits, where he recently had become employed. His daily mission, as he sees it, is preventing the state from getting its illegitimate hands on individual clients' money in the form of taxes. It makes him proud of his work, he says.

As it was Saturday night, and despite the cold, Jassen had decided not to go back to the office; instead he wanted to head out of town (easily done in Boulder), park on a mountain road, and wake up to the smells and sounds of nature.

So Jassen is not homeless, exactly, and he certainly does not *need* to sleep in his car. "You see these?" he asks rhetorically, reaching into the backseat and pulling out a pair of pink ice skates from among the debris. "They cost me five hundred dollars. I love to figure-skate, but it's an expensive hobby that I couldn't afford if I paid rent." To my amazement, Jassen has been an avid figure-skating fan since the age of nine. His life's ambition is to become a figure-skating judge, traveling from one competition to the next. Until that day arrives, he takes part in amateur events in Boulder on a weekly basis.

"It's a beautiful, elegant, graceful event," he told me. "You have got to be a pure athlete—also graceful and artistic." I didn't doubt him, although glancing over at his pudgy, bullish form as he sat behind the wheel of his car, I could see he is clearly none of the above. But for all I know, when he's ice skating, in the theater of his mind the ugly duckling becomes a swan.

We stopped briefly to inspect one of his favorite overnight spots, a dead-end street on the edge of Boulder, with two motels next to each other and a craggy mountain towering above. The street is parallel to a larger road and twenty feet higher. We parked a few yards from a set of steps that leads down to the lower street, where there is a twenty-four-hour public toilet. The motels mean that local residents are used to unfamiliar cars pulling up at all times of the night, and they may have other benefits, such as a laundry room or a snack machine. Or, just as important, a free wireless connection for the laptop.

Jassen told me that, in his experience, the best place to park in an urban situation is likely to be on a residential street next to a commercial area. "The residents will be used to seeing strange cars parked overnight," he advised me. (This would come in handy a few weeks later.) It's hard to generalize, as this depends on many factors, the kind of town being one. Salt Lake City is apparently one of the worst towns in America to spend a night in a car. Its God-fearing, curtain-twitching citizens almost always reported him within a few minutes of his settling in for the night.

In places where he doesn't know the lay of the land, Jassen said, his strategy is to find his spot during the day, and then arrive there at twilight, park, and sleep. He suggested moving around inside the car as little as possible, and not to get out to stretch your legs. He also said to leave the area immediately upon waking the next morning. Other tips I gleaned included not parking under a streetlight and not parking near a construction site, as they have their own security that will be on the lookout for strange cars with drivers in them parked nearby.

Jassen also has his favorite parking lot, a huge one run by 24 Hour Fitness, the gym he depends on for his once- or twice-daily shower. It's full during the day, of course, but was fairly deserted when we pulled up at ten p.m. We parked on the perimeter, the only section that is screened from the road by some high hedges. Next to us was an old white Volvo Estate with a bicycle strapped on top, the backseat folded down, and a jumble of cardboard boxes inside. "One strategy is to have a lot of clutter so you are not very visible while you sleep," he explained.

Because he was driving me around, Jassen had reinstalled the passenger seat. When he is on his own, he removes the seat and replaces it with a specially cut piece of plywood, on which he can stretch out and sleep. If he's stuck sleeping in the driver's seat, he winds it back to its fullest extent. In his car, as in most, the front seat does not go flat, so he tries to park on a slight hill facing upward, at an angle of about ten to fifteen degrees, to compensate for the tilt of the seat and to "prevent the blood pooling in my stomach."

Now it was dark, so Jassen took me to the place where he keeps the plywood car bed and various other possessions. His storage unit, on the edge of town, offers twenty-four-hour access. As we drove in along a row of cinder-block units, each large enough for a small 4x4, Jassen pointed to the two or three that have residential occupancy, unbeknownst to the storage company. He flung up the sliding door of his own garage and flicked on the light. "This is how I live," he said apologetically. "It's by no means glamorous." I don't know if he was expecting me to contradict him. I said nothing.

Two bicycles hung from the wall. A camping bed, ready for use, with a pillow and blanket, sat invitingly on the floor. (It was late by now.) There was a 250cc motorbike, a shelf of books, and a rack of clothes. There were storage boxes with papers, camping equipment, and more clothes. Jassen has organized his belongings so that there is room to drive the Saturn into the space. This way he can remain inconspicuous when he spends the night here.

He keeps his possessions grouped together in large plastic boxes so that he can simply put a particular box into the car depending on his plan. A long trip out of town requires the clothes box and the cooking/camping box. A business meeting requires the smart-clothes box. And so on.

On the surface, Jassen's reason for car dwelling conforms to a twisted sort of logic. I wondered about the real reasons he had lived this lonely, dislocated life for so long.

Although Jassen had responded to all my inquiries spontaneously and openly, he didn't entirely like my next line of questions. I asked if as a child or teenager he'd ever felt he didn't really have a home.

He answered yes immediately. He also revealed that his mother is currently on her fifth marriage. "She was very nomadic. There was a time when we did live in our station wagon, for a few months when I was six, seven, eight. When I was a kid, home was not really home." Hardly the ideal preparation for life. Without a home, I believe, there is no center, and therefore no sense of self.

As if reading my thoughts (which were fairly clear from the question), he suddenly said, "I don't care what some shrink wants to say one way or the other. I am a motormouth. I love partying, but I am also perfectly comfortable by myself. I was kind of a latchkey kid when I grew up, and have no qualms moving from place to place and living frugally, no matter how much money I have."

Earlier, Jassen had told me about his own short-lived marriage. He'd had trouble adjusting to living indoors again after the wedding, and when they fought, whereas the stereotypical man sleeps on the sofa, he slept in the car.

"She wanted children and I didn't, plus she was a devout Mormon and I wasn't. There was a tremendous amount of pressure to have a kid. I learned a lot from that relationship, including that I don't want to be with somebody that's a homebody."

Jassen Bowman's car-dwelling life feels exciting to me, albeit slightly artificial. Sure, he is playing with the idea of being homeless, but he is also genuinely removing a huge habit we all have in our lives. Deciding afresh where you will sleep each night certainly adds a little edge to your day. I wonder why more of us don't live like this, especially younger singles.

Jassen, no matter what his motives, is one of society's explorers, the advance guard, an early adopter. Call him what you will; I do not think he is simply an aberrant one-off. Jassen and fellow van dwellers are, forgive the pun, road testing another, perfectly legitimate lifestyle choice on behalf of the rest of us, and in doing so adding to the richness and resilience of America's social mix.

10   Closer to God

"I went to the woods because I wish to live deliberately."

                        Henry David Thoreau, *Walden*

The off-the-grid culture is largely hidden and obscure, often deliberately so. Those who choose to live off the grid tend to be private. They often want to leave the mainstream world far behind. They may have been drawn to the lifestyle for positive reasons, or been driven away from the grid-connected world by cruel twists of fate, like Jonathan Traister. Most of the Christians I met, however, have embraced the off-grid life for the soundest of reasons, and although I am an atheist myself, I have total respect for them.

Some have an entire philosophy to back up their decision. Others might have acted on a mix of faith and impulse, like Rebecca and Caleb Simon, the caretakers of Bill Bieber's second home, the giant Colorado ranch. When they were offered the position, they were living in Creede, where Caleb was a skilled electrician in high demand. There is always something electrical that needs to be done when you're running your own power plant, whether it's checking the batteries, changing a fuse, or, as happened on one occasion, dealing with a direct lightning hit on the main inverter, the box converting the power from Bill's hydro plant into usable 110 AC.

Caleb was kind and hospitable when I turned up unexpectedly on a cold winter's day. Wearing a dark beige microfleece with a matching peaked cap, he showed me around the pristine estate and its brand-new traditional-style wooden barns and log cabins. Although the place isn't their own, the Simons have all the accoutrements of Western society in their lives: a huge pickup truck, a big garage and workshop, and a big house. They're off the grid but very much inside the system.

"It's a good place to raise kids. We have two boys, five and eight," Caleb was saying as his wife wandered up to join us outside their sizable log cabin, which looks across the valley to the enormous house the Bieber family occupies when in residence. Rebecca is a fresh-faced blonde in her early thirties, and was wearing a cap similar to Caleb's, along with a fluffy fleece. She had moved from Tennessee to Creede ten years prior, working as a white-water rafting guide. The conversation immediately took an unexpected turn.

"Don't you think it comes back to God, though?" she said, more to her husband than to me. "To have not such a busy lifestyle and to have our children as close to us as possible, no day care." The school week in Creede is just four days, so the Simons enjoy three-day weekends with their children. The boys work on the ranch through the school holidays and so are exceptionally close to them. "It's important to teach our children how to work, as far as serving the Lord," said Rebecca, ignoring my question about green Christians, who see themselves as stewards of the land. "The work ethic, I think that's serving the Lord. They get the education of being out working. They hang out, help feed the horses. The eight-year-old is pretty good with an ax, so he splits all the logs."

"And what if the little fellow should split his leg instead of a log?" I asked.

"I'm a nurse," she replied. So that's all right, then? I thought. "My heart is in taking care of people, she added."

An electrician and a nurse. Bill Bieber had chosen wisely.

Despite, or perhaps because of, her religion, Rebecca seems unwilling to allow herself any enjoyment of the beauty around her, or any lifting of the sprits from being with nature. "It's a lot more spiritual up here, and healthier, I guess," she admitted. "We want to raise our children ourselves. We are busy here in the summer, and having the children here by our side, that's part of our belief."

STAIRWAY TO HEAVEN

There is a group that shares Rebecca's belief in the godliness of hard work at a young age. Possibly the best-known off-gridders in the United States today, besides Daryl Hannah, are the Anabaptist Christians, also known as the Amish or Mennonites. Every morning TV show, at one time or another, has featured these quaintly dressed anachronistic Americans going about their business in a horse and buggy, or making cheese the old-fashioned way. America has more than 350,000 Mennonites, and the number is growing quickly, because Mennonites have large families—after all, they need all the workers they can get.

Mennonites divide into many sects because they are forever having schisms over the correct interpretation of the Bible. The off-the-grid sect, known in Mennonite circles as Old Order Mennonites, who eschew electricity, are the ones you see in nineteenth-century costumes. Their code is simple: Dress plainly, without adornment; renounce vanity.

But if Leon Martin walked into New York City's Soho House looking like he did when I saw him in his dad's yard in Kentucky, he would be besieged by women and probably by modeling-agency talent scouts.

I had driven past a knot of Mennonites fixing a truck in their front yard. I stopped to engage one of them in conversation, as I wanted some basic information. I was under the impression that their religion banned them from driving cars, which rely on electricity to power their engines, and had to ask for clarification.

Leon was standing closest to the gate. He has cropped brown hair, blue eyes, a small, very straight nose, and a big, self-deprecating smile. He was wearing a pair of sturdy blue work jeans—not Levis, and not dark blue, but a middle blue that says (in New York, at least), "a little bit cheap, almost slutty." He also wore, like the other men and boys around him, a checkered shirt and suspenders, which are narrow compared with the "greed is good" banker's suspenders—about a third of the width.

All this was topped off with a well-made—and probably expensive—light-colored straw hat. Each man present, I later learned, owns exactly two hats—the straw one and a crush-proof black homburg made out of some seemingly indestructible material.

These were all Old Order Mennonites. So none of them would dream of walking into Soho House or any other nightspot. The only thing they would consider more unpleasant would be watching TV, which they compare to an open sewer running through American homes.

Leon, however, does ride in cars, and he does live on the grid. His family is part of a faction that has divided the usually tight-knit Mennonite community in this area in middle Kentucky, outside the town of Liberty.

The Martin family had came from the Philadelphia area at the same time as the Weaver family, whom I was due to meet shortly, and all had belonged to one church. But then a breakaway group, led by the Martin family, had decided that they would not be any further from God merely by taking advantage of modern amenities. Having electricity did not imply they would listen to rock music, or watch bad programs on TV, or even watch TV at all, they argued.

Leon agrees that the off-the-grid families are in the majority. "It's kind of a young-versus-old thing," he said in a languid, lisping, almost Andy Warhol kind of a voice. "They are the breakaway faction. Where we all came from, in Pennsylvania, we were all on the grid. I know a lot of young people who are part of the off-the-grid church, and they want to join our church, but their parents won't let them."

I was in the area to meet one of those parents, Ammon Weaver, the fifty-six-year-old head of the Weaver clan, which, although I had no idea at the time, is the biggest, wealthiest, and most devout Mennonite family in the neighborhood. I thanked Leon, who went back to work, but now with many stares from the others, all curious to know what we had been discussing. I continued toward Ammon's place. All I had known when he agreed to meet me was that he runs a horse-drawn "sweep" to power his home and a neighboring machine-tool workshop. I was aware that he is a Mennonite. I didn't know exactly what a sweep is.

I had driven through on a rainy May morning, and as I neared the eighteen hundred acres Ammon has accumulated over the years, the sun blazed on immaculate lawns, smooth as putting greens thanks to the gentle nibbling of the horses. Nature seems at its most profuse here. There is every variety of tree, from hardwood oaks to soft cedars. There were dark blue jays, bright red northern cardinals, and yellow grosbeaks darting through the trees.

As I turned in to the front gates I saw an empty courtyard in front of me, a large factory building on the left, and a house set back across a lawn on the right. Everything is tidy and in its place. I parked between a long hitching post and a small wooden cabin about the size of an outhouse.

I was to see several of those cabins in the next forty-eight hours as I toured the Mennonite community. It turned out to be a phone booth, situated close to the office and far from the house. The door was open, and inside was a woman of about thirty, wearing a long dress down to her ankles and a white bonnet on her head, talking and taking notes. This was Ammon's eldest daughter, and she placed the call on hold long enough to send a younger sister off to fetch their father, who was having lunch in the house.

Ammon is a kindly-looking man with a mop of gray hair and a face like a squashed potato, his mouth at a slightly crooked angle because he has less than a full set of teeth. I cannot take a photo of him because Mennonites "do not pose for photos."

This was my first lesson in the Mennonite belief system. Later I put the various things I was told together: They do not pose for pictures because the Mennonites reject any form of adornment or artifice. They sing in church, but there are no musical instruments, because music can be used to play the Devil's tunes as easily as the godly ones. (They must sincerely believe the old saying that the Devil has all the best tunes. And all the best TV shows, movies, and radio programs, not to mention Web pages.) Radios, along with the Internet and TV, are banned from this Mennonite community because of the temptation to which they might lead. Automobiles, as Ammon calls them, are prohibited for the same reason. They have phones because "it is not fair on others to be unable to contact us." Old Order Mennonites rarely phone each other, however. They visit by horse and buggy, or by bicycle if only one person is traveling.

We sat in the anteroom of the machine shop, the office's reception area. If I squinted my eyes so as not to see some new books on the shelf to my right, it could have been the nineteenth century, with two bookkeeping daughters behind a high mahogany desk and Ammon at a round, veneered table with fine old bookcases behind him. Ammon had been up early that morning for a meeting with two businessmen from Detroit, who had arrived by private jet to ask for a quote on a gadget to allow them to prototype a new kind of mass-market washing machine.

I was amazed. I had not expected this level of sophistication. Ammon said later that one of his machine customers is a manufacturer of titanium prosthetics, requiring the highest standards and razor-sharp accuracy.

He explained why he had come to Kentucky. "I chose to live a simpler life," he said matter-of-factly. He'd had a business in Pennsylvania in the eighties and early nineties, making steel parts for the manufacturing industry, as he does now. The business did not survive the downturn. He could have declared bankruptcy. Instead he slowly repaid all his debts over the following years, starting with the small creditors.

He blames his business problems on three things: borrowing— or over-borrowing (I could not work out which); not living a simple lifestyle and instead being seduced by overhead costs, such as cars and electricity; and being dependent on a hopeless unionized (non-Mennonite) workforce.

The problems began in the 1980s when Ammon expanded and moved the business out of his immediate community in Pennsylvania so that he could draw on the Pittsburgh workforce. "I had led a sheltered existence. I did not realize that there are people who think they are doing you a favor by turning up for work." Ammon complained that they spent their weekly paychecks in a few days, and would fight over borrowing money until the next check. After he shut down his plant and laid off his workers, several committed suicide. He said he saw this as a sign of their weakness.

So his answer is never to borrow again, never to employ outside the Mennonite community, and to stay off the grid. He is therefore dependent on none but himself and his community.

I can see why he does it, and it has worked for him. He now has annual revenues of over three million dollars, has voluntarily paid back the debts that forced him out of business, and has started borrowing again from the bank, just small, short-term loans when his working capital is tied up preparing large orders.

The Mennonites are probably among the richest members of this rural community. Kentucky has sixteen of the poorest counties in the United States, outnumbered only by the much larger Texas, with seventeen. It is no surprise, then, that the Monticello bank in Liberty has a gazebo specifically for horse-and-buggy parking.

A sweep, I learned later, is contained in a circular area about the size of a fairground carousel, but with real horses. The animals clip around smartly, attached to a central spindle, and the movement generates power. "It's real green energy," Ammon told me. "The horses eat grass, and they turn it into energy."

The Weavers are nothing if not cautious. And although the whole reason for my visit was to see the sweep, I didn't get to do so until the second day, when I was about to leave. Ammon himself had taken me on a horse-and-buggy tour of the area, and when we got back to his property he issued a few commands in Pennsylvania Dutch, at which point one of his six sons scurried off to hitch up the horses.

First he showed me the one-horse version—a very different design from the sweep. The horse stands on a treadmill, an upward-sloping machine made of wooden boards with metal reinforcements between the boards. There are rails on each side, so the horse cannot fall off, and the whole affair is covered, so rain or sun won't affect the animal. Once the horse was moving at speed, Ammon brought me through his house to the room where the motive power of the horse is transformed into mechanical power, via a spindle running from the treadmill and into the building. I watched as Ammon switched off the power, which meant shouting "whoa" and drawing on a pulley that set a brake on the treadmill. When he wants to switch the power back on, he shouts "giddyap" and yanks on the other pulley to release the brake.

He showed me how he can run a washing machine, a corn thresher, and an "ice bank," as the family calls their primitive refrigerator, a Coleman cooler filled with water that is charged (by the horse) three times a week for four hours, until there is enough ice in the bottom, and then recharged when all the ice has melted. It stores milk and meat to feed the family.

The horses do not generate electricity. Instead the energy is linked directly to the actual driveshaft of whatever machine it's powering. Forswearing electricity, the Weavers buy ordinary electronic devices, remove the electric motors, and run them on the mechanical power from the horses.

I describe the Weavers' horsepower arrangements in such detail not because they are relevant to a discussion of off-the-grid lifestyle as it relates to godliness, but because they show how we could all live in comfort without electricity.

Ammon Weaver's machine-tool company is run entirely on mechanical power, supplemented by compressed air. When I called him a few months later, he had just taken his largest order ever, and was about to see his annual revenue jump to four million dollars.

I heard a similar story, if on a smaller scale, at the lumber business run by Ammon's son, whom I visited next. Arriving at Timothy Weaver's, I drove past a phone box on the edge of the property and into a huge yard. In one corner is a hundred-foot wooden tower. This is Timothy's solar kiln—built to dry his wood very slowly, making it high-quality lumber that is less likely to warp or snap. He had bought a set of plans for twenty dollars (not via the Internet), adapted them, and built a sharply angled ninety-by-sixty-foot roof, which he painted black. On top of the roof he attached some clear plastic sheeting. The roof has air ducts in it, so air is trapped between the black roof and the sheeting and heated by the sun. It then passes through and around the building into one of four kilns of different temperatures, where the wood is dried slowly and naturally.

Timothy has some big customers for this wood, especially the hickory, which commands a higher price because it is dried more slowly than wood from normal commercial operations. And the time spent drying the wood costs Timothy next to nothing. It simply sits in the kiln, being heated by the sun and the movement of the air—no energy required.

Out in the yard, Timothy works the sawmill largely on his own, using simple mechanical equipment to lift the logs into position. When necessary, he calls on his two sons, ages nine and seven, to help. He also has two daughters. While I was there, he was sawing fifty-foot tree trunks into high-quality planks to make more treadmills. In addition to the fifty treadmills Ammon had sold already, the family typically takes orders for another ten or so at each horse show they attend.

We spent a while looking around his solar kiln, and then, because I had seen a sign for it on the way, I asked if he could take me to visit Zimmerman, the local cheesemaker. It turns out Elvin Zimmerman is a member of the same church, and he had recently ordered his own sweep to power the milking machines and the refrigeration unit in which he stores his cheese.

As with the Weavers, one of the older Zimmerman daughters dispatched one of the younger daughters to fetch Elvin and bring him to the cheesemaking building, where I had been asked to wait. A short and hugely fat man appeared, dressed in the same regulation garb they all wore: blue denim work bib and trousers, light-colored shirt and suspenders, straw hat, and work boots.

Timothy introduced me and they had a short conversation about the death that morning of a fellow member of their church; he had been crushed by a consignment of railway ties as they were being delivered.

Elvin motioned me to a chair. Seated opposite me, he looked like Humpty Dumpty in suspenders. I asked him why he had come to Kentucky to live off the grid. He paused for a long time. "I chose to live a more conservative life, a simpler life," he said.

I asked what he meant by "more conservative."

"I don't know how to put it into words real good," said the man who had, in just five years, built two businesses: cheesemaking with twenty-eight cows, and a timber business on the side, which is successfully competing with Timothy's. Pressed for time, he turned to rap out some commands, in Dutch, to his daughter across the room. "I'm trying to live a more common lifestyle," he finally replied.

"OK," I persisted, asking for the second time, "but what does 'common' mean? Does it have to do with being modest?"

Yes, it does, he said, yet he still was unable to explain exactly what he meant. So we turned to his product—the cheese. I bought a packet of the cheddar, which he had been taught to make by hand in Wisconsin. It was uncommonly, hauntingly good—very mild at first taste, with an unusually granular texture due to the unpasteurized milk used in the process. Then a tangy sharpness crept across my tongue and stayed there for a long time. Half an hour later I was still enjoying the lingering aftertaste. "It's because of the way we feed the cows," he confided in me. "[They're] just grass-fed." And there it was on the label of the cheese: "Zimmerman's raw milk cheese from grass fed cows." One can't get much simpler or more "common" than that.

He's making cheese from the milk of all twenty-eight heifers, he told me, and demand is so high that many of his regular customers have been disappointed. His herd is up from twenty-four last year and twenty the year before that. And he's even training his competitors: He gives courses in cheesemaking, at $150 a pop, to other farmers in the area who own dairy herds.

I asked if he would then sell their cheese to his contacts.

No, he replied; he would sell cheese only from his own milk, and his production is limited by his resources: the size of his farm and the size of his family—a wife and nine children, all working to turn the cheese out, or in bookkeeping or dispatch. Packaging is handled by his wife and two oldest girls, he said; cheesemaking by himself and his two oldest boys. Elvin also handles sales himself, traveling by horse as far as Lexington and Louisville.

I returned to his reasons for living this way. "We're Old Order Mennonites," he said, as if this is somehow a full explanation. "We're logging with horses on the mountaintop and you pull up the horses and there's no engines roaring and you enjoy it for a bit," he told me. That was the extent of his insight. "I'm not that good in English," he said. "I took schooling for eight years." This is the normal level of schooling for most, if not all, Mennonite men, including Ammon. But they tend to be well read—a product of the long evenings without music or TV. Ammon has donated a specially-built library of ten thousand books to the local community.

The combination of high quality and low price that the Mennonite clan brings to all their business dealings is very challenging to the competition, and sometimes causes bad feelings. Next Timothy took me to visit a Mennonite garden center, where I bought a half dozen packets of rare heritage seeds at knockdown prices. "Because we live life with no TV and no Internet and no electricity, we have lower costs, so we can charge less," he told me later. "But there are three or four other garden centers in the area and we have to be careful." He means they don't want to cause offense or drive the competition out of business.

"We try not to antagonize the marketplace," Ammon would tell me later.

I understood what he meant. In New York Jim Juczak had told me how he buys in bulk from the Mennonite foods store—rolled oats, brown rice, navy beans, barley, lentils, split peas, salt, kidney beans, in fifty- to eighty-pound bags. "The prices vary a bit from sixty cents a pound to a dollar eighty a pound," he'd said. "It's the same food you buy at the grocery store for ten times that price or more." Of course, nobody minds if the Mennonites undercut Safeway. For small shopkeepers, however, Mennonite competition is something to fear.

Timothy also took me to see their humble church, a former farm shed with metal siding. Inside, the walls are just as plain.

There are three hundred metal folding chairs squashed into the thirty-foot-wide room to accommodate the thirty-five families who belong to the church, along with two huge wood-burning stoves for the winter, and a desk from where the bishop officiates.

We returned to the timber yard just as Timothy's wife was coming home in the pony and carriage; she had been visiting friends. She had their five children with her, two boys and three girls. The boys wore the regulation hats and the girls and their mother had on black bonnets. Watching them there in the yard, though it is bristling with technology, from the solar kiln to the air-powered wood saw, I was almost taken back in time to the nineteenth century, when every farmer's wife would arrive home in just this way.

I asked again why they live without the essential aspects of modern life.

It became clear there is an issue of censorship involved. The Mennonites do not want to stand in judgment over individual works of music or film. "We don't want to be choosing which DVDs can and cannot be played," said Timothy.

They set great store in learning—Ammon had shown me his huge library. Yet surely the same argument that applies to TV or radio ought to apply to books. They are choosing, after all, which to have and which to avoid. It does not make sense.

They seem happy, and are by any standard successful, yet these Old Order Mennonites practice a form of isolationism that, once again echoing the *New York Times* verdict on Thoreau's Walden experiment, is "cold and selfish," albeit on a group level. They trade with the outside world, but they would never go on vacation with a non-Mennonite, nor run for Congress, nor, if Ammon was serious when he said it, employ a non-Mennonite. Although there is no doubting their sincerity, ultimately, it's hard to agree with their approach.

HOWLING IN THE WOODS

My other experiences with religion off the grid were mainly in Northern California, where I visited a Zen temple and a Yogic community and joined in a number of small personal spiritual quests. I was touring the San Juan Valley, still looking for any land for less than ten thousand dollars an acre (and finding some), when I met a guy who calls himself Hojji Firemaker. A former shaman of the woods, he has cut his hair and cleaned up his act, and now lives near North San Juan in a converted bus parked in a friend's yard. The bus is delightful and spacious, the perfect studio apartment; even with his wife and child it doesn't feel crowded. Most of the year they eat their meals under a patio umbrella outside. They have a long section of foldable brown fencing around the bus to give themselves some privacy.

Hojji is a temporary long-term tenant, paying to park here while he searches for some real estate to call his own; he and his wife are a bit tired of moving around. He is depressed. He has had to come down off his shamanic cloud to deal with the harsh reality of the California property market. Despite the recession, the price of land has skyrocketed in the area, due largely to a combination of pot-growing profits and demand from big-city weekenders. Even worse, his young wife had recently discovered that she has breast cancer and was going through treatment while I was there.

Hojji showed me Gary Snyder's place. The Pulitzer Prize–winning poet has a big off-the-grid low-rise house, set well back from the road. Returning to the area alone later, I came across Snyder's breathtaking Zendo temple farther down the lane. I have never been to Japan, but the temple and the grounds around it are how I imagine the country to be. The temple is square and made of light-colored wood, with a reddish corrugated metal roof. It's single story, but has a windowed pyramid poking up in the center that gives the mediation room inside it a vaulted ceiling.

The temple was unlocked, and I sat cross-legged in the meditation room on one of a dozen blue velvet cushions arranged in an oval, imagining what it must be like to be in the room with a group that has spent the past forty years meditating together. An extraordinary calmness and sense of beauty descended over me, and I was rooted to the spot. Out on the grounds around the temple, it's the same, a sense of time standing still, of not wanting to leave.

Outside the door of the mediation room, a giant copper bell hangs on the porch. It has intricate Eastern designs carved into it. Just as I was leaving, I picked up the soft-headed mallet hanging next to it and gave the bell one tap. It responded with a low, pure note that shimmered in the air for well over a minute. It had just about faded away by the time I had walked across the immaculate lawn and back up the driveway. For the entire afternoon I spent there, I did not see another soul.

Snyder had chosen the area because he had worked as a logger and now wanted to protect the trees. He bought the land back in the 1960s, with Allen Ginsberg, whom he had met in 1955 at the first reading of Ginsberg's *Howl*, a poem that would come to symbolize a generation. The third partner in the property purchase is Swami Kriyananda, spiritual leader of the Ananda Meditation Retreat, half a mile farther up the hill.

Ananda is an eight-hundred-acre colony of Yogic devotees living and working in a collection of thirty-seven huts, cabins, and domes, nestled in a forest three miles beyond the power and water lines.

It had been easy dividing up the land, said Nakula Cryer, Ananda's director. Forty-seven years earlier, Snyder, Ginsberg, and Kriyananda, now age eighty-two, had each walked on the land and "felt a special blessing in different parts."

Nakula said that the Ananda Retreat might well house the largest private utility network in Northern California, judging by the number of buildings served by the power sources up on the mountain. Greenfield Ranch, in Ukiah, serves many more homes and buildings, but each is served by its own supply, whereas at Ananda the power is centralized. There are several banks of solar panels, a wind turbine, and a propane generator (nothing green about the last item, but it is still off the grid).

Nakula seemed disturbed by my presence, and although he answered my questions and invited me to stay, I could tell he was searching for a motive other than my interest in off-the-grid living. He reached up to hand me a brochure without removing his eyes from mine, then sat back in his chair in his tiny office, housed in a construction trailer, part of a circle of assorted buildings next to the main dining room and kitchen.

"I hope you aren't going to distort what I say," Nakula demanded, his fleshy face contorted into a frown under his brown fedora. In the two days I stayed there, working, dining, or pacing the grounds, I never saw him without a hat.

He needn't have worried. The Ananda movement is quite startling enough without any distortion from me. Ananda is the apotheosis of the 1960s hippie spiritual-meditation movement. These days the saffron robes have been replaced with Birkenstocks, but the underlying ethos is much the same.

Kriyananda himself is a follower of Guru Yogananda, who wrote the classic *Autobiography of a Yogi*. Kriyananda has followed his master in predicting that "an economic catastrophe, together with a natural disaster, will require the world to move off the grid very soon now." This is according to Ania, a disciple I met later.

The Ananda Village, several miles down the hill on Tyler Foote Road, the main route into Nevada City, is planning to end its dependence on city water and the national power grid. That requires an up-front investment, but the residents are having trouble finding the money because the movement is still paying off the legal fees on a lawsuit brought by a different bunch of eccentric Yoga gurus, who challenged Kriyananda's right to teach in the name of Yogananda. The case revolved around complex copyright issues, on some but not all of which Ananda prevailed.

To raise the money and, they believe, to help save the planet, the worldwide Ananda movement has been working on a new kind of solar thermal power device that, according to its inventor, Ananda resident Ken Rauen, "breaks the second law of thermodynamics." The second law, he said, "has never been proven. It is just a rule of thumb, a guideline." For the moment, however, his research has "run out of steam."

In the meantime, Ananda is intending to launch an intermittent wage earner, the Green Energy Saver, a small box that plugs into your power supply and somehow reduces your electricity bill. "It examines the phase between voltage and current at the input of the breaker panel and corrects for inductive reactive power," Ken explained. Somehow I feel that Ananda is on stronger ground in its traditional area of expertise—meditation.

"It's not the land that's special," Nakula said. "Ananda is a state of mind first and foremost, and here is where you can tune in to that state of mind. We believe this world that you see is a manifestation of God and we are living in harmony with God. We don't hold [the environment] as something to campaign about, in itself."

I spent some time with young Ananda initiate Ania Gorna, who told me how she had traveled across America with no money to join the movement. She explained, "I wanted to know how my life could be used in the best way for the higher good. God gave me a life and I should return my gratitude—I wanted to serve. I thought the best thing I could do was help the environment." She clearly has her own interpretation of the Ananda philosophy. She approaches it as someone who has seen firsthand the strange effect religion can have. "My mother converted to [Christian] fundamentalism and was always going between different religions. Now she has married a Jewish guy, so she is a messianic Jew. She tries to be supportive of what I am doing, but she doesn't understand it."

Ania had come to Ananda from the East Coast at a time of depression in her life, and after reading *Autobiography of a Yogi*. I wondered to myself whether it is such moments of weakness that are the best recruiting agents for places like Ananda.

"The family really tried to keep me from going, crying and saying I was going to betray them," she told me. "Mom was sick at the time and I moved in to help her, but I was not happy at home. Nobody understood me," she tried to explain. "I thought, Why can't I be with people who believe in what I believe? Twenty minutes after I turned up here, I was signing papers to join the classes [in philosophy, community building, and Eastern mysticism]. I got some student loans, started working cleaning houses for people, doing construction. Now I have thirty-five thousand dollars of debt."

Ania had just graduated from Ananda when we met and found a high-paying job as a secretary for a nearby race-car designer. She seemed balanced and happy. She said she had been unhappy before, so Ananda has apparently had a good effect on her. Still, I was disturbed by this image of a penniless young woman walking into the retreat two or three years earlier, with no money, and leaving thirty-five thousand dollars in debt.

And then there's the curious suspicion of Ananda's director.

I asked around and found out that the lawsuit brought by the competing Yogis is not the only one that Ananda has fought and lost over the years. A decade earlier, when Swami Kriyananda was seventy-two, a female staffer brought a suit against him alleging "sexual harassment, deceit, and intentional exploitation of women, whom he had defrauded into joining the church." I learned that Kriyananda and the Ananda community were unable to claim on their insurance company, and the community filed for bankruptcy as it set about paying the $1.85 million judgment.

The movement's loyal followers continue slowly to pay off the debts, and today the retreat, along with Ananda Village, is as active as ever, albeit with a tarnished reputation. Swami Kriyananda, though no longer leader of the organization, still teaches and preaches at Ananda. His followers feel that he was unfairly pilloried in the 1990s media coverage.

The communities in this beautiful and spiritual part of Northern California are natural breeding grounds for sexual activities and experiments of all sorts. And so are the private homes. It might be selfish, or at least self-regarding, to ignore the world's problems and focus on exploring the boundaries of one's own sexuality, but for those who are under no financial pressure— maybe because they bought property when land was cheap— the dreamy, timeless stoned beauty of Northern California seems to foster the taking of sexual risks. One could almost say that sex was California's religion, at least until AIDS came along, and quite possibly since then as well, judging by my next encounter.

THE NEO-PAGANS

From Ananda I drove to the Grass Valley home of Jane Kesselman and Peter Galbraith, classic 1970s back-to-the-landers. "We are pretty eclectic in our spirituality," Jane told me. And the Grass Valley area reflects their values back to them.

She is a "neo-pagan by choice, and Jewish by birth and upbringing." The pair celebrate "the changing of the seasons and the moons, and always the winter solstice and Passover." Their real interest is in enjoying the company of others and living modestly.

Jane and I were talking in her yard, standing next to a twelve-foot-long line of large solar panels mounted at an angle on a frame. Someone was tinkering with the wiring on one of the panels, but as Jane did not introduce us I assumed he was the maintenance engineer. In fact this was her husband, who stopped for a moment to tell me his reasons for settling in Grass Valley. "I feel more comfortable with the social climate here," Peter said. "This particular area has been a place where folks from the Bay Area come to homeschool their kids, and engage in peace-type political activity."

Jane confirmed the importance of homeschooling in their decision making: "We moved to this area because of the high level of support for homeschooling—we didn't want to give up our children 'to the State' for the bulk of their childhood!"

Peter and Jane call themselves social anarchists. They believe a "cooperative, directly democratic form of self-organization will work for the good of all." They opted to go off grid because they are anti–nuclear power. "Energy independence was an important step for us," said Jane. "No, we wouldn't go for PG&E [the local utility company] even if they came down our road and hooked us up for free."

Their spread is twenty-five hundred feet above sea level and loaded with fruit trees. It has a hexagonal yurt, and an old trailer stored under an additional roof to keep the sun and snow away. (Eco-architecture expert Pliny Fisk praised that approach when we met.) There are several other outbuildings, from an outhouse and shower to a little music room for their fifteen-year-old daughter, Sage Po, who plays the harp beautifully and was preparing for an appearance on NPR. They had paid for the land outright thirty years earlier, with inheritance money. "We get away with just paying land taxes," Jane said. And since they have no "real" house, taxes are very low.

"We are very frugal," she added. She works in Grass Valley at Sierra Solar Systems a couple of days a week. The job pays all their modest expenses: food, fuel, thrift-store clothes, and "a few new things for our teenager." In most parts of America their income would be considered poverty level. Jane told me, "We are very rich in the ways that count."

Until a couple of years earlier, as they worked through their interest in communal living, they had a household of eight adults and seven children in four separate family units. The four families, three heterosexual couples with children and one lesbian couple, each lived in separate temporary structures on the land.

Jane and Peter had spent most of their married life in an open relationship. But one person's open relationship is another's adultery.

The happy-go-lucky, semi-communal arrangement fell apart when a man from one couple had a crush on the woman from another couple. The husband of the "crushee" walked out, and the husband who had originally caused the conflict was ousted. The fallout left just the lesbian couple and the two women with their kids at the residence, plus Jane and her family. Eventually the various families scattered to the four winds, leaving Peter, Jane, and Sage Po to enjoy a newfound tranquility.

"In being close to each of these adults," Jane said, "I knew they were unhappy in their relationships. They needed to break up. The commune living was just, like, a catalyst. I'm just glad we were here for the kids. They are all still friends."

Sage Po misses her pseudo-siblings, she told me after treating me to a virtuoso little harp performance. She said that there is one thing about communes that she hopes she will never have to experience again: the meetings.

As someone who's never been religious, I find it difficult to evaluate the various kinds of worship I encountered off the grid. Some will resonate with readers, and even without the order provided by organized or even semiorganized religion, there is a hugely spiritual side to the off-grid community. Whether it is Vonnie leaving her materialistic past behind, or Bill Bieber feeling the spirituality of the mountains in his ranch retreat, or Lynn Paget becoming more at one with the weather patterns—because it's the sun and wind that power her batteries—everyone who lives off the grid seems to experience the sanctity of life to a greater extent than the average person.

11

Under the Radar

"I have no desire to make windows into men's souls."

Queen Elizabeth I

The phrase "off the grid" means different things to different people. Sometimes I use it to signify stepping outside the system into a parallel place where different economics and value systems apply.

It can also refer to a break from electronic communications—not being online or available on your cell phone. And there is another, more interesting meaning to do with dropping off the radar of the surveillance society, something like Jason Bourne in *The Bourne Identity*. In this sense, being off the grid means not having an identity, not figuring in the computer records, not being listed—not officially existing.

All sorts of individuals fall under this definition. I came across four subcategories within it: criminals, civil libertarians, those building without permits, and the homeless.

SACRAMENTO STORIES

Sleeping in a car and commuting to work like Jassen does is one thing; sleeping in a tent in a disused lot in Sacramento, California, with no job and only a bottle of beer to look forward to at the end of each day, is quite another.

In early 2009 I read several media reports on the so-called tent city in Sacramento. It seemed *The Oprah Winfrey Show* had found just what I was looking for—a nascent community that had sprung up like the Hoovervilles of old. This was the new off-the-grid solution to age-old problems of unemployment and foreclosure.

A few weeks later I was on a flight to California's capital city, reviewing the newspaper reports. They tended to feature middle-class folks who had apparently been hit hard by the recession of 2007–2009. The fast-growing Tent City had almost become a permanent fixture, thanks to the media coverage. There had been other tent cities on the same spot in previous years, but they had been broken up by the city authorities. This time, the story had spread around the world, so they couldn't simply be moved on in the middle of the night—but it also meant the residents would be tired of talking to journalists.

It took me a while to find my way there from the airport. On the car radio, Edward Liddy, head of AIG, was in Washington, D.C., being raked over the coals due to the $165 million of taxpayers' money the company had just handed out in staff bonuses.

The first tents I spotted amounted to more of a Tent Village than a Tent City. There were a half dozen shelters in the far corner of a neatly fenced grassy lot the size of a large yard, and it could have passed for a campground if it weren't for the location: The lot is right next to the main parking area for Sacramento's police vehicles.

I walked over to the little group. It was a clear, sunny day, and although the yard is near a freeway, it was quiet and mellow, with birds chirping. A homeless man in the shade of a giant fig tree next to a cluster of tents watched me approaching. I introduced myself to a guy who seemed to be their leader. This was David Randolph Conn, a case of wasted human potential that is so common among the homeless. David is a former Navy SEAL with eight medals and citations earned during hunts for Soviet subs. As he told me these details, a voice came from inside a tent, confirming David's military claims. He ignored the interruption.

He said that the field we were in is owned by a local woman who allowed four ex-military men to share it, as a way of preventing it from being squatted on by less savory types. David wore orange sunglasses pushed back on his forehead. He has brown-gray hair that stretches halfway down his back, and a gray beard. He was sitting when we met, shaded by the big tree, with a high brick wall behind him. When he eventually stood up, I saw that he is at least six feet four, and thin as a rail. He was sucking on a can of beer and smoking a hand-rolled cigarette. Every so often he let out a terrible hacking cough. He told me that he makes his beer money collecting cans, about seventeen dollars a bag.

The four of them had been living here for more than three years. Yes, he knew all about Tent City, and yes, he could take me there. After a brief stop at the local gas station to buy more beer, we drove the two miles to Tent City.

We turned onto Dreher, a quiet side street, and then passed a casino with two police motorbikes parked in the lot. I passed the spot a dozen times in the next twenty-four hours, and there was always a police vehicle of some variety parked there. We stopped opposite some small, tidy one-story homes in what is mainly a black neighborhood. Then we walked to the end of the street, where the road turns to a footpath, crosses a bridge, and climbs a slight slope into the park that houses Tent City. As we reached the ridge of the hill, a long train was rumbling from right to left across my line of sight. To the far right is a huge industrial plant of some sort. In the foreground are the tents, divided into three main encampments.

It was early evening and the path was teeming with residents, mostly people under the age of thirty, both arriving and leaving. David seemed to know everyone. Clearly some of the Tent City residents have things to do in town, things that lead them to return here at around six p.m. Equally clearly, there are many whose livelihoods are entirely contained within the confines of this community. Young men on bicycles whizzed this way and that, literally taking off into the air as they went over the bumps. After an hour or so of walking around with David, I realized that I was seeing the same riders again and again, and that they are probably drug mules.

The picture that eventually emerged is the opposite of what the media coverage had led me—and the rest of the world—to believe. There are in fact three separate encampments in Tent City. The largest one is led by a bigmouthed, small-time drug dealer, David told me. It was his mules who were going about their unlawful employment, and his section was not one that David wanted to linger in for long, although we did walk through slowly, past junkie prostitutes and forlorn men giving us the stink eye.

We then passed into an encampment of what might be called professional homeless. Not only are they long-term homeless; they are activists whose aim is to raise consciousness about the homeless problem. This was where David was most at ease. He introduced me to Boyd Zimmerman, one of the organizers, who confirmed that there are few, if any, middle-class foreclosure victims on the site. Many of the residents have social or substance-abuse problems. They all know each other and relocated here for political reasons.

Boyd also happened to mention a tip for any would-be car dwellers out there: Don't live in a leased car. He had tried it, and when he defaulted on a single payment by just a few days, the car was immobilized via the GPS unit, and its location sent to a repo outfit.

Finally there is a small enclave of recent arrivals, about forty tents jammed close together, mostly desperate-looking men, but there was one attractive woman. Sensing a possible story in the making, I walked up to the woman, who was sitting on the ground outside her tent, and said hi. "I'm his," she replied, pointing at a furious-looking guy who was washing at a hose a few feet away. Whoops. With David at my side, I wasn't in any danger, and a brief chat with her "boyfriend" revealed that he is from a separate category, one that might be called part-time long-term homeless. I met others like him, people who move to rented accommodations when they have work, and conserve their money by using shelters and other free options when they don't.

To cut a long story short, the residents I spoke to were not people who had recently lost their stable homes and stable jobs. Reading the media reports carefully again later, I realized that there are no dates in the biographies of the interviewees. Yes, some of them had lost their jobs, and as a result their homes had been foreclosed on, but when was never mentioned.

It transpired that the entire Tent City phenomenon had been directed by two policemen from the Sacramento police force Homeless Liaison Unit; they are known to the long-term homeless in the area as Batman and Robin. They had been on that beat for twenty-five years and had become tired of being the bad guys who had to give the homeless a hard time. They were ashamed of the way their city was failing to deal with the problem of its homeless (a problem created by a very civilized tolerance of the homeless, which had only encouraged more to arrive).

Batman and Robin had begun directing everyone without a home to that spot next to the railway tracks, now known as Tent City. It had been a park that was primarily known as a haven for junkies and alcoholics. Then the *Oprah Winfrey* crew turned up, and the rest is media history.

As the trains rumbled by, horns blaring, I sat down for another chat with David.

"I was in for six years," he said, showing me the veteran's card that is his only form of official identification. "I don't know who my real family is, I honestly don't. No numbers, no addresses.

Something happened to me—too many strobe lights or something. I ran away from my dad when I was fourteen, went to live with Mom in Marietta, Georgia, and watched the manhunt [to find him] on TV."

He stopped to greet a passing woman of vague acquaintance. She called him Hippy—his street name. He told her he had just been diagnosed with emphysema.

He went on. "All I know is my real mother and father passed away. The people who adopted me were supposed to tell me where I was from. Somewhere along the line I was taken to meet my great-grandmother on a Cherokee reservation. My birth certificate says I'm fifty next birthday; other sources say I'm fifty-seven." He looks sixty.

The tale rambled on to include a chain of restaurants, Duff's "Famous" Smorgasbord, stretching from Ohio to Florida and owned by his adoptive grandfather, and a missing $250,000 life-insurance policy that had been due to mature two years earlier. Who knows what parts of the story are true? By the end of the evening, all I knew for sure was that David lives in the field where I had met him, that he uses the nearby gas station or the nearby McDonald's for his hygienic and nutritional needs, and that he would have spent his last two dollars on a beer had I allowed him. And that was that.

"You can't look back," he said. "You got to look forward. But I wish I could find my family."

TAKE BACK THE LAND

A very different kind of homeless campaign is being waged in Miami, Florida. A group known as Take Back the Land has also attracted many headlines since my visit, and for all the right reasons. "Why do you want to go there?" demanded a local cop when I asked the way to Max Rameau's place. "Six guys shot dead on that block. Last week."

I knocked at the battered storefront. Mothers were out walking with babies, a squad car prowled past at a sedate speed. The entire population is black, including the driver of the squad car. Max only laughed when I told him of my encounter with the cop.

Max is small and chubby, with a slight beard. He was wearing a black T-shirt bearing the logo of some long-forgotten political campaign. He makes money as a computer consultant, and has one of those very fast, very analytical minds that never need to pause to find the right word. His organization, as its slogan goes, reunites "homeless people with people-less homes."

As I walked in, Max was on the phone, dealing with a recently evicted family. When the call was over, we moved to the back of the store and sat down. So far, he said, they had moved one family into an off-grid home, because the power to that building had been cut off. But the cost of a fully functioning renewable-energy setup is beyond their budgetary means.

Max started by telling me of Umoja Village, an inspirational off-the-grid story with an unhappy ending. In 2006, he and the rest of the volunteers at Take Back the Land managed to build their own tent city on an entire city block, in the Liberty City area of Miami. They seized land that the city had left empty for eight years, and it became a rallying point. Limousine liberals turned up with clothes, soup, and money. City politicians were furious, but they knew bad press would ensue if they evicted the squatters.

Max and his team installed rainwater catchment and a well, solar panels, a generator, and solar showers (black buckets full of water that warms up in the sun). There was also a composting toilet. Six months later, the group announced that it had funding to build a series of hexayurts, autonomous structures that would, in effect, be permanent, high-quality housing. The next night a mysterious fire razed the entire shantytown.

Had it been, I asked, as they say in Ireland, "put on fire"?

"Yes," Max said. "We felt that it was done intentionally. There was a candle in someone's room and the official story was that it was an accident. The guy who was living there"—he pointed to a picture on the wall—"we couldn't account for him initially. One week after the fire, I was at the fence [the city] had built around the perimeter. I was standing there, and people were driving by and waving, and there, driving by in a practically brand-new Toyota Camry, was the guy in whose room the fire had started. So it's pretty clear that he went, within seven days, from living literally in a box to driving a Camry—a four-door sedan. It's one of the nicer cars," Max said ironically. "Probably runs twenty-five thousand dollars."

Max is too smart to get into proving guilt at this stage. In response to my questions, he explained that "a reporter met him, and said that he all but confessed. But he was acting so erratically the reporter concluded it would be unethical to report on his confession while he was, you know, out of his mind."

Max had created an off-the-grid shantytown at Umoja. "It was a well-thought-out design, and we were able to live off the land in a real way. We started planting the next day after we moved in, and regularly ate the greens. We harvested a little batch of greens every few weeks." The two groups, he said, that have most successfully followed the lead set by Take Back the Land are in Austin, Texas, and Charlotte, North Carolina.

Take Back the Land operates for families rather than individuals, distancing itself from the kind of lonely alcoholics I had encountered in Sacramento. And it will house families only in places that are "an improvement on what they had before. We therefore require [the houses] to have electricity," said Max. In the case of the off-the-grid house, "someone took the copper wiring out. So we purchased solar panels on that home."

It is usually cheaper and simpler for Max to pay the utility company. "The electricity company is concerned about your deposit and whether you are going to pay every month, rather than a copy of your lease or mortgage," he said.

The average cost of moving a family is $250, excluding security deposits on water. The solar setup, he said, added three thousand dollars to the total cost, and this is why there has been only one so far. If a friendly solar-panel maker wants to become involved, Max is easy to find.

"We want to do more off the grid," Max told me. "We want to be less dependent on those that have power over us and the people we are helping. The way we do that is by having as much independence from electrical and water [utilities] as we can."

Max said that he had been looking into doing "something similar" at Umoja, and had been in the process of launching an urban gardening program, "to teach people to grow stuff in their backyard, food they can consume. But also cash plants such as palm trees, which they can sell to landscapers. Sources of food and sources of revenue."

The most attractive thing about Max is his politely uncompromising stance against authority. Without any ranting or sloganeering, he explained that Take Back the Land does not negotiate with city authorities. It refuses any dialogue. "The social-justice movement is very wide," he said, "with different wings, and we are not interested in meeting or negotiating with the government or those who are in positions of power. We are not interested in tapping that. We want to create alternate centers of power. In that sense, we are off the grid of political power, because when they come to us and ask us what we want to talk about, we just say, 'Leave us alone.'"

The trouble with that approach, if Max's suspicions about the fire at Umoja are correct, is that the authorities are perfectly capable of playing hardball. "When the housing crisis really reached the worst here, and a media series came out about how government officials were stealing housing money, people got so angry, because the housing crisis was the worst in the United States here in Miami, and the money that was specifically to be used for housing, they were stealing it and giving it to their cronies. We had a meeting of several local organizations that were working on housing issues, and all they could think of was, What demand do we now make on the government? My position was, Why are we making demands of the people who are causing the problem in the first place? We need to figure out not what the government can do, but what are the things that our community can do by and for itself. Political power is something you can become addicted to in the same way that people in this country are addicted to other kinds of power— electrical power, certain kinds of access to water. We have to get used to doing without politically, as well as doing without physically."

I was so impressed by Max that I asked him when he would be running for office. He won't be, he replied, and told the story of his time working for an organization on behalf of ex-felons. "They would, all the time, say, 'When are you running for office?' And I used to say, 'If I ever run for office, shoot me.' One time, without missing a beat, the guy I was talking to says, 'In the foot or in the head?' So I don't say that anymore. But I still feel the same way."

RAINBOW PEOPLE—NO2ID

My conversation with Max was paralleled by an encounter I had in New Mexico, with the representative of another group that refuses to accept the authorities' idea of the way it should conduct itself.

The Rainbow Family are a group of utopians who have held an annual gathering in a different national forest each year since 1972. Those who attend adopt "rainbow names." There is no stage, no amplified music. Participants bring instruments and play to each other.

Since the mid-eighties, the U.S. Forest Service has tried to ban the gatherings, or insisted that a group-use permit be signed. The Forest Service says that this permit is normal for large groups camping on public land, and is meant to maintain public safety and protect the environment. Rainbow organizers say that the U.S. Constitution gives them the right to assemble peacefully on public land, and that requiring them to apply for a permit violates their basic right by turning it into a privilege. Many court cases have been fought on the issue.

The law-enforcement authorities detest the Rainbow-ites for many reasons, chiefly because they refuse to give their real names, and in some cases they have no official form of identification. In this age of the war on terror, that lack is likely to become a criminal offense.

I was driving along the ridge of the Taos Mesa with Vonnie when we passed a striking figure. This was Tony Laycock, a man who looks like Mick Jagger and talks like Keith Richards. He was sitting in his friend Steve's van, rolling a joint. We had met a few days earlier when I visited Bill Reed, the octogenarian pothead. Vonnie screeched to a halt and I jumped out to say hi to Tony, who is not a missing member of the Rolling Stones, but is a cool guy nonetheless, a British hippie who somehow got himself a permanent resident's status.

Tony and Steve were trying to decide whether or not to head to the nearby forest to cut firewood. It was not hard to persuade them that they should leave it for another day because it was about to rain. We went back to Steve's place, a converted mobile library a few hundred yards down the road.

Tony is about five feet six with long, straight, jet-black hair and strong weather-beaten features. He was wearing a jumpsuit of some kind, made of faux suede, adding to his rock-star style. The tan color of the jumpsuit is only a shade lighter than the mud that stretched around us in every direction as the snow melted. From a distance he looked like a Native American warrior. Close up, he has Mick's cheekbones, and Keith's accent and insouciant attitude.

Tony is a leading light in the Rainbow movement, and he has no ID to speak of beyond a Social Security number he has committed to memory: no passport, no driver's license, no credit card. "I would have to jump through so many hoops to get it," he reasoned.

He was, he said, pleased that word had gone out that the next Rainbow gathering was to be held in the Gila National Forest, in the south of New Mexico. In actuality, it would be held in the nearby Santa Fe National Forest; the organization merely needed to confuse the authorities, and every tiny deception helped.

The previous year, he said, he had been arrested at the gathering. He had also accused the police of having started a forest fire in order to drive the gathering out of Bridger-Teton National Forest, in Wyoming, an allegation that is still being investigated by the Inspector General. (The 2009 gathering eventually transpired and no arrests were made. Of the twenty thousand or so who attended, organizers estimate that ten to twenty percent had no ID.)

Living without an ID, Tony said, "is a bit problematic now." He and 230 others were arrested in July 2008 for camping without a license. "I was looking at being sent to Guantánamo," he said, flicking the long hair out of his eyes. "The Forest Service objected to my release for the reason that I had no ID, so I might be a terrorist. It took three hours for a real federal agent to contact his friend at Immigration and find out who I was, because they've got me on file."

The FBI man didn't leave Tony with anything to later prove who he is. "So I still ain't got no fuckin' ID," he said with a gap-toothed grin and a puff on a Marlboro. "Maybe eventually they'll give me an ID, say, 'Here, take that, and then we won't have to spend so much money establishing who you are.' I mean, they've taken clandestine photos of me about nine times."

Does he worry his fingerprints are on file?

"Why should I worry? My fingers haven't been anywhere they shouldn't have been. It's their little game, power-corrupting thing." Then he lapsed into a poem he'd written. I heard the phrase "anally and orally mind-fucked by those who want to own me."

People like Tony are a nuisance to the LEAs, as he calls the law-enforcement agencies. In fact, they are a nuisance to just about everybody. And yet Americans need to recognize Tony's right to exist as he does, or else the terrorists have won.

POT-GROWING NEIGHBORS

Lawless places such as the mesa in New Mexico, or Big Bend, Texas, or even wealthy Humboldt County, California, are not good places for terrorists. They are too sparsely populated either to hide out in or to be tempting targets. Such places do, however, attract pot growers, especially Northern California, which has a deeply embedded marijuana industry producing vast amounts of cash, some of which is recycled back into the community.

In Ukiah, almost everyone I met is growing grass. Even those who aren't are often connected to the growing industry in some financial way. Some growers only want to harvest a few plants and either keep it for personal use or make some pocket money. Others are doing it on an industrial scale. Mike Riddell, the social historian of Greenfield Ranch, is a builder by trade. As a result, he's been invited into many homes and knows many secrets.

Apart from wealth envy, the cannabis economy also sparks boundary disputes as growers vie for the most fertile pieces of soil. I heard of one case at Greenfield in which a man took some cannabis plants down with a machete because he thought a neighbor had planted them on his land.

Big money is involved. Land prices go as high as thirty thousand dollars an acre, unheard of for non-building land. I was regularly offered small plots of a third or a half acre with building permission for $150,000.

Driving into the appropriately named Grass Valley, one corner of California's Emerald Triangle, I switched the car radio to the local community station and listened to ads for head shops and a place called Grass Valley Hydrogarden, "serving the community since 2000" and selling plant nutrients, rockwool, "hydroton," grow lights, reservoirs, trays, timers, controllers, pest controls, submersible pumps, air pumps, trellis netting, and so forth. I was on my way to visit another of the station's regular advertisers, The Earth Store, one of the main suppliers of solar panels to pot growers for the past twenty years. When Earth Store founder Jonny Hill started the company in North San Juan back in the 1970s, he was selling off-the-grid equipment in the back of Mother Trucker's Store, the sort of place one could walk into and find the Grateful Dead buying their groceries. All kinds of people were moving into the area and building houses back then, when land was still cheap. And Jonny knew which ones were the dope growers. "Cash, Johnny Cash, he was our biggest customer," Jonny said. And that was the name he would write down in the accounts.

The present situation, in which drugs are illegal to sell yet legal to possess, could have been purposely designed to put money into the pockets of guys with Uzis—big-time dealers from Mexico and the Russian mafia, which have both recently become involved with the pot industry.

This is a concern for some who are thinking of living off the grid, because what could be more convenient than making ten thousand a year from growing a few plants—until, that is, they attract attention from the Uzi guys. In Northern California, I met several pot growers—and neighbors of growers—living up in the mountains. They were all very cagey and would talk only on the condition of anonymity, not because they were afraid of the cops—much of what they are doing is completely legal in California these days (though not the tax evasion)—but because of the other criminals, who might come to steal their crops. There had been numerous incidents in previous years, always around harvest time.

"Back in the day, we would scatter the plants around, on

the edges of fields, right deep in the woods," one of them told me. We were in the Ridge Stop Cafe, in North San Juan, a restaurant with a surprisingly gourmet menu for such a rural area, and I was recovering from a tiny toke on a joint someone had offered me in a backyard. They start the plants in small greenhouses, he told me, keep them warm with a little solar-powered heater, extend their day with artificial light, and then move the female plants outside once they're ready.

At harvest time, as spotter planes fly overhead, they move the trimmed leaves back into the greenhouse and turn on specially designed fans, about twenty-four inches in diameter, that run directly off a single solar panel, to dry the crop prior to transportation.

Recently, the whole industry around Nevada City has become more efficient and well organized. The growers do everything they can to cooperate with the local sheriff, knowing they will need him in the event of trouble. And the sheriff bends over backward to avoid bothering decent, law-abiding growers so he can leave himself more time to catch the growers who have chosen to operate outside the law.

The change was caused by the passage of a California law permitting grass to be grown for specified individuals who have a certificate from their doctor stating that they consume the drug for medical benefits. "All you need to do is go into surgery and say you are having trouble sleeping," I was told. You are allowed to nominate someone else as your official grower, but each grower is limited in the amount he or she can grow per certificate holder.

The way the law is applied varies sharply from county to county. Despite a loosening of anti-marijuana enforcement announced by Attorney General Eric Holder, the Nevada County sheriff's office offers a clear warning: Although it's legal to grow pot, with a license, of course, under state law, the federal government does not regard marijuana as legal under any circumstances, and routinely conducts investigations in the area. This was September 2009, and the official who talked me through the rules politely requested that if I was going to start cultivating cannabis, I laminate my license and "leave it in the garden somewhere, so that if we visit when you're not there, we can see it."

To be as helpful as possible, the legitimate growers in Nevada County rear their crops in as concentrated an area as possible, and in order to assist the sheriff's spotter helicopters, they mount their laminated certificates on poles, facing upward so the cops in the helicopters can literally read them from the air.

THE VALLEY GIRL

One of Greenfield's residents explained the setup to me. Twenty-one-year-old Lita Jarboe inherited her spread, near the clubhouse where Sequoia's wake was held. She grows a few plants and tried to explain the current regulations to me in more detail than the cop had had time for. "The law is all gray," she said. "They lowered the limit [on the number of plants an individual can cultivate], so nobody is sure they are legitimate. Time was you could grow up to ninety-nine plants. As of two years ago, it's up to twenty-five plants per parcel, and of those only six flowering per person [or certificate], and twelve in a vegetative state."

Because Lita lives with her boyfriend, Joe, who also has a certificate, they can have up to twelve flowering plants at any one time and another twelve that are getting ready to flower. This does seem in keeping with the spirit of the original law, but it's not good for the local economy and is very hard to monitor. Anyone with a certificate is allowed to sell "surplus" pot to registered cannabis clubs, which retail it for about twenty dollars a gram but pay about ten dollars a gram. This works out to $260 an ounce and about four thousand for a pound. Since it's possible to get as much as five pounds per plant per year, the theoretical income from twenty-four plants would be about half a million dollars. In practice the plants yield much less, which is why many growers simply remain outside the law and continue to grow hundreds of plants, just like they always did. I met one grower who said he holds about ten certificates for others. (They have to come and tend their own plants to stay within state law.) His mother-in-law runs a cannabis club in a different part of the state. It's a nice, cozy arrangement.

Lita feels that it's very unfair to restrict the number of plants that can be grown lawfully so drastically. "There's always the mold problem," Lita explained. "It can spread from the oak trees and wipe out half your crop. Then there are the bugs. There's so many things that can happen so you don't have anything in the end."

She said that, if she's lucky, with the size of her harvest and being clever about the time of year when she offers the surplus pot (i.e., not in October, when everyone else is offering it to the clubs), she might make fifteen thousand dollars a year, a much better day rate than she earns in the coffee shop, though hardly enough for a forty-thousand-dollar SUV (not that she owns a car of any sort).

"The way it works is you have to get a temporary certificate. You go to the doctor, you tell them, 'I got a pain,' whatever, which costs at least $130, and it's for a maximum of two months. Then you have to produce evidence, from your medical record, of a long-term condition."

She has a certificate because of long-term problems with her knees. Joe has a history of migraines in his medical record. "That is like the golden ticket," she explained.

Even if someone is operating within the law, a neighbor can complain. She told me, "The cops will turn up and probably seize your plants or tell you to destroy them."

Here in Mendocino County, Lita said, "young people think everything's great; they come in from across the country, find somewhere to live, and they smoke openly on the streets. And then they get busted. Or they talk openly about growing and get other people into trouble. The locals think, Oh my god, we don't talk like that here."

If anything, the law is stricter than it's been for years. "You don't realize how serious the cops are until you get into trouble, and then," she said, "you think, Oh, I shouldn't have done that."

So much money is involved—up to two hundred thousand dollars from a single crop in a small field—that the growers become very nervous around harvest time. And there are so many of them, each more nervous than the next, that everyone needs to be mindful. Elsewhere in the Emerald Triangle, I was given a warning: "You had better not be wandering around on back lanes enjoying the view at that time of year."

One person who "makes trips down to the city to get rid of it" told me that business with the wholesalers is hit or miss. "Sometimes the guy is there and sometimes not. Or they don't want to see you and you either have a wasted trip, or you drop it off and come back to pick up the rest of your money. A lot of [the pot] leaves the state."

If cannabis were legal, the growers would pay more taxes and more of the money would stay local, and the criminal networks that deal in all sorts of drugs would be edged out of one of their biggest markets.

By the time I left Greenfield, I had met several big-time pot growers. Each insisted that I take a large sample away with me. "This is much better," one of them boasted when I told him his neighbor had already given me some. My rental car smelled so strongly of pot that I was amazed I was not arrested each time I was stopped for speeding along the rest of the journey. I finished my trip in Los Angeles, visiting a friend in the film industry. I was only too pleased to hand him the entire stash, worth several hundred dollars—but not as pleased as he was to receive it.

BUILDING WITHOUT A PERMIT

Pete and Andie (not their real names) live in a house in a highly desirable part of Grass Valley. When I was there, it was still only half built—without a permit. They had bought the empty land and moved from Colorado to be closer to her family. As in Ukiah, land in this part of California is expensive because pot growers have been jacking up the prices for two decades.

To follow their dream of living closer to the land in this beautiful and mellow part of the world, they had to do more than buy bare land and risk building on it. Pete, age thirty-three, likes to smoke weed, but he prefers to make his money by legitimate means. He looked hard before he settled on the Yuba River area, and they bought land they were sure nobody else would want. The seller, a pot grower, had murdered "the wrong guy" after a drug-money double cross. He was in jail and wanted to off-load the property lest the victim's friends find him when he came out.

Unfortunately, the deed was locked in a safe-deposit box in Calgary, Canada, until he was released from prison. With a handshake, the killer pledged the house to Pete, who, for his part, took the risk of making the payments with nothing in writing to prove ownership. The gamble paid off. When the seller got out of jail, just two years later, Pete was handed his deed and he and Andie ended up with forty hilly acres in a lush corner of the Emerald Triangle, surrounded by pot growers, for well below market value.

There were already a few structures on the land: a hexayurt and a couple of greenhouses. Pete still finds black rubber hose, running for hundreds of yards, in surprising places. So far he has spent about sixty thousand dollars in renovations, and the final shape of the split-level house is beginning to emerge. The couple already have a comfortable studio apartment downstairs and a nearly finished studio upstairs, where Andie plans to practice her yoga and her art.

Andie runs a restaurant in a nearby town. She is thirty-one and as lithe as the two cats bouncing around upstairs. She said that living off grid is about being humble. "Learning to live with less. If there is no sun and no wind, then there's no power, no TV. That's fine."

"I built it," Pete said, "ninety-five percent with my own hands." Not many people could do that if they had to. He survived one fall off the roof and many cuts and grazes.

He said that he has about a year to go before they can really spread out in the place. Then he will wait for one of the irregularly scheduled but inevitable planning amnesties, designed to bring more property taxes into the coffers of Nevada County. At the time, he couldn't afford the back taxes they would charge if he turned himself in without the amnesty. He still has to spend thousands on building materials.

And he has to be polite to his rude, pot-growing neighbors. "Bad blood can cause one neighbor to turn you in." Pete is not a fan of the pot dealers. His heart sinks every harvest season, when they all flood back to the area. "One of my neighbors spends his time in Guatemala in the winter, then comes back here for the growing season. That's when you see plenty of the stereotype around here. The dirty dreads, knots in their hair, coming out of the best restaurants, getting in a really nice, brand-new forty-thousand-dollar vehicle, and you have lived here for ten years and you have never seen them work in the area. Everything they do is half-assed. These people don't really have the value of money. The money came easy to them; everything is expendable. They wouldn't think twice about a twelve-thousand-dollar generator and a tank of propane. I disagree with that whole approach—fossil fuels to run the generator. We kill people in Iraq so you can grow pot on your land?"

THE NON-IDENTITY

There are other models for a successful life in the twilight zone, away from the full glare of official recognition and databases. At STAR community, while visiting Vonnie and Pat, I met a man known simply as Ken, a happy and friendly character of about forty, very fit and fresh-looking, who is in the process of simplifying his life. His first step was selling his car and replacing it with a bicycle and trailer that he uses to travel to Taos every week. He found that the bike was "grounding" him, and that he was saving money on gas, but his food bill has gone up tremendously. "I have crashed a few times because of not eating," he told me. That led him to build an inexpensive greenhouse, both to supplement his food purchases and to provide produce to sell at the farmers market. He operates only in the cash economy, and he recently gave away his computer (although he kept his Gmail account). His mobile phone went sometime later. Vonnie told me that he has now closed his bank account and is well on his way to a life completely free of money. But he is not there yet.

In California, Kipchoge Spencer and his band, the Ginger Ninjas, are unable to drop completely off the radar, much as they would like to. Their gigs and the need to publicize their music make them relatively high profile. But they are quite unusual for a band that tours all over North America, because they travel everywhere by bicycle (carrying all their equipment). The five musicians and two crew members traveled about five thousand miles in 2009, when they toured Mexico for six weeks and then cycled back north.

Kipchoge is a striking six-footer with mid-length, shaggy light brown hair, a short beard, and a large aquiline nose. He lives in a shanty building, an archetypal ten-by-twelve-foot cabin, up in the hills near Nevada City. He calls his mission "the pleasant revolution." He tries to depend on the system as little as possible. He finds Burning Man way too mainstream. "I don't really consider myself off grid," he said. "I have wireless Internet, and I have propane for my cookstove, which I get via the grid."

Kevin used to be a stockbroker with Rocky Mountain Securities, in Denver, and he looks like a stockbroker on a casual Friday—neat haircut, rimless glasses, smart shirt. He stopped because he found it agonizing each time one of his clients went bust. "I had a couple of death threats," he said, "which didn't scare me, so much as anger me. Most of my clients didn't lose a lot of money, but every nickel they lost I hated it, felt bad for them, so I just said, 'I am going to go make pizzas till I work out what to do.' Around then I got divorced and met a woman at Pizza Hut, went to Steamboat, went to six bucks an hour. When the town shut down in April, we went for sixteen days camping in the middle of the desert. I said to myself, 'I have got to do this the rest of my life.'" He found his place in the wild outside Steamboat, and set about making seasonal money from tourism and construction work, all paid in cash. He lives in an Earthship.

I present the stories above, with little embellishment, as evidence that the all-pervasive State has not quite extended its reach to every tiny aspect of its citizens' lives. These stalwarts are usually the marginalized or the very wealthy (like the pot growers), or they actually want to come back into the fold (like Pete and Andie). But they all show that it is still perfectly possible to run your life outside the official system that most of us are fully signed up to.

12 Fear

"All men recognize the right to revolution, that is the right to refuse allegiance to and to resist the government when its tyranny or its inefficiency are great and unendurable."

Henry David Thoreau, *Civil Disobedience*

Some simplify their lives for positive reasons, and in doing so, expand upon them. Others are driven to reduce their interaction with society out of more negative emotions. A significant proportion of those who go off grid, or are considering it, are motivated by fear that the market-based system that has worked so well—for those on the right side of the tracks—may be about to break down. One variation of this fear suggests that the growth that has sustained the system until now is about to become its undoing, with raw materials, oil, and food becoming impossibly expensive, and billions dying as a result (a subset of this is the "peak oil" argument mentioned below). Another strand is that growth is now at an end, and society will collapse because our financial system cannot operate without growth. There is a grab bag of other fears too: fear of terrorism, cyberterrorism, a flu pandemic, or a natural disaster caused by man-made global warming.

That fear is glorified under the rubric of survivalism, which has been an undercurrent of American life for nearly fifty years. In the sixties and seventies, the traditional backwoods culture began to mutate into gun-toting right-wing or libertarian survivalism, spurred first by the Cold War, then by OPEC's oil-price hikes.

While the hippies were going back to the land, the survivalists were planning the first "bugout locations" (BOL)—places where one could go to endure the collapse of civilization. There were clandestine newsletters (reminiscent of Eastern European samizdats before the fall of the Berlin Wall) listing the paraphernalia one would need to survive: food rations, water, gold coins, and so forth. Long discussions appeared on the Internet bulletin boards of the 1980s, with titles such as "Fight Them or Feed Them," referring to the dilemma that a well-prepared survivalist would face in the event of a catastrophe, or as they abbreviate it, WTSHTF (when the shit hits the fan). These days there are endless slickly produced manuals defining the best BOLs and BOVs (bugout vehicles). And it's very easy to go online to buy a BOB (bugout bag) stuffed with survival gear. I sell them myself on the off-grid Web site.

That survivalist fear has now been supplemented by another strain of thinking, one that I've referred to repeatedly in this book and that ranges from a perfectly rational loss of trust in politicians and bankers to intense paranoia. The paranoia is now widespread in America, and although the credit crunch has taken over as the main focus of collective anger, it is most often expressed alongside the allegation that the 9/11 terrorist attack was carefully planned—by the Bush administration. I met three people whose principal reason for living off the grid is a fear of the coming collapse. All three are white men, highly intelligent, and loners to some extent. And each believes that 9/11 was a conspiracy carried out by the U.S. government.

LIFE'S A BEACH

At some point I heard about a surprising survivalist, a radical and by all accounts extremely liberal writer from Montauk, New York, who had moved to a Mexican beach town to await the collapse of society.

In 2001, Allan Weisbecker wrote the book *In Search of Captain Zero*. It is a "road trip beyond the end of the road," a memoir of the author's search through Mexico for a friend from his drug-dealer days, which, according to his account, had ended when he chartered a ship to carry forty million dollars' worth of cannabis to America. The ship sank, and with it his drug-dealing career.

I went in search of Allan Weisbecker.

La Saladita Beach, in Mexico, is a long, gently sweeping sandy bay known to produce some of the world's best left-hand point breaks (a wave that breaks into a rocky point, much prized by surfers). This is the reason that two of America's greatest surfers, Corky Carroll and Tim Dorsey, have each built rather grand houses here, and it's one reason that cult author and surfing fanatic Allan Weisbecker has set up residence on the beach. Literally, on the beach.

I met an American in a bar, and he sent me to see a friend of his who lives nearby, and that friend told me where to find Allan. "But he's gone crazy," I was warned. "He's wa-a-ay off the grid."

It's a beautiful beach, busy but not bustling, with gently lapping water close to the shore, too shallow for the sharks that have been terrorizing the rest of the coastline the past couple of years. There are a few bars, a small area for RVs, and a dozen fifty-dollar-a-night apartments, some with electricity, scattered around the edge of the beach in this desirable spot an hour from the Ixtapa-Zihuatanejo airport.

I tracked him down at last.

Allan was wearing purple surfer's trunks with big white

flowers. He has gray, shoulder-length hair swept back from his forehead, a gray mustache, watery, old man's eyes, an aquiline nose, and a relatively fit, tan surfer's body. He smokes filter-tip cigarettes, and ducks his head down every few minutes to light one in the wind.

His camp is both simple and sophisticated, consisting of several different elements. Closest to the sea, actually on the beach, he has a fifteen-by-fifteen-foot covered deck, the canopy tied to tent poles and overhanging trees. Next to that is a four-man tent tall enough to stand up in, a desk, and his computer in it.

The next part of the wagon circle is the small, four-wheel, custom-built Car Mate trailer that he towed down from Montauk with his 4x4. The trailer acts as a strongbox for Allan's cameras, computers, phones, three surfboards, and anything else he might consider valuable. Next to the trailer, and completing the mini-compound, is the Sun Valley Skyhawk pop-up camper that travels on top of his 4x4 flatbed pickup. This is Allan's kitchen and occasionally, on cold or wet nights, his bedroom. Most of the time it's warm and he sleeps in the tent or in a hammock on the beachfront deck.

The truck itself is parked just beyond the camp, so Allan can easily go into town or on longer journeys to more isolated surfing coves. The camp is "fenced" with cheap bamboo matting, to give him privacy. He calls it "cozy."

We sat down on the small deck, protected from the sun by a palapa, a palm-leaf thatch roof of Allan's design. He'd hired guys to build it, and has yet to winterize it for the rainy season with corrugated material. "I am really, really bad with money," he told me. "I haven't made money in the past two years." And Allan is not the kind of guy who puts savings away.

But for a guy who's hopeless with money, he has done well. He cut a rent deal for this beachfront spit nestled between a pair of cheap restaurants: $230 a month. Toilets and Wi-Fi are thrown in as part of the deal, although, he volunteered, he usually goes to the toilet in the ocean. Let's say the Wi-Fi has a value of eighty dollars a month. That means $150 a month for the campsite—five dollars a day, less than you would pay for a deck chair at a beach resort.

The place Allan lives in, and the way he lives, struck me as idyllic, a compilation of his life's wisdom. He's taken the best bits of his life on boats and Learjets and in Hollywood and put them together, and this is the result. For a decade, after he stopped being a big-time drug dealer, he was a Hollywood screenwriter—until he was ostracized for being rude to movie stars and agents.

The first thing Allan told me after I had walked off the beach and explained why I was here was that he's now finding it harder to attract women. "When you're old enough to be their father, it's OK. But when you're old enough to be their grandfather it gets tough. What gets me laid these days is the books I've written."

The three books are all memoirs. The film rights to the first two sold for six-figure sums. *Captain Zero* went to Sean Penn for four hundred thousand dollars plus a commitment that Allan would write the screenplay. But it all went horribly sour. As Allan explained it, Penn had never read the book, despite the kind things he had said about it. So the script changes Allan was asked for didn't make sense, at least not to Allan. This sort of thing happens in Hollywood all the time—is the rule rather than the exception—but instead of playing the game, Allan had asked Penn why he had not read the book or the script, stalked him demanding to know, and received an irate letter suggesting that suicide would be his best option and telling him he'd never work in Hollywood again. Not that he wanted to. "Considering my age and my habits," he laughed, "it's not like I got to worry about the next fifty years."

Disgusted by Hollywood, running out of money, he had headed back across the border.

"My problems in Hollywood were nowhere near the top of why I came to Mexico," he said, pulling miserably on a cigarette.

"I couldn't take it anymore in the states. The U.S. government was behind 9/11. The 2000 election was stolen, the 2004 election was stolen. Now, with this economic meltdown, we're on the verge of an apocalyptic change, and . . ." He looked around to sum it all up. "I feel safer where food falls on your head."

Fish and coconuts, fear *and* paranoia. This is why Allan came to this Mexican beach.

"We are talking about huge events that shaped the world, that nobody knows the truth," he said, my heart sinking in sympathy for this anguished man. He was even making a film about it, right now, filming himself telling me, and my reaction. Boy oh boy.

What makes this happen to people? I speculated. It was no idle thought. There are so many millions who also believe 9/11 was an inside job. An urgent diagnosis is required—and a cure. Otherwise America will watch its electorate change from one that merely doesn't trust politicians to one that thinks all politicians are actively conspiring against us.

"If building seven was a controlled demolition," Allan was saying, "it equals an inside job; it was set up way ahead of time."

Now I felt we were on a subject that I know a bit about. As I mentioned earlier, I made a documentary about the rebuilding process at Ground Zero for *Frontline*, and I vaguely remembered a conversation with Larry Silverstein, owner of the Twin Towers. He had told me that they had been forced to demolish the building because it was about to collapse.

Or did I remember that? It had been a long time ago, and here I was sitting on a warm beach in Mexico, but I blurted out my hazy recollection as if it was fact and immediately felt guilty. Allan's whole demeanor changed. I had suddenly become the missing link, the guy who is going to break open the whole 9/11 conspiracy. I would have to check my notes, I warned him. Had Larry told me that? I quizzed myself. Or had he simply said that he had been phoned at home to be told that building seven, a smaller office block next to the Twin Towers, had also collapsed? Hang on. Surely, even if he had been forced to demolish the building within hours of the blast, that proves nothing, right?

I shook off my reverie and returned to the present and this talented, unhappy man facing me—unhappy because nobody will listen to him; unhappy because he feels deeply that there is a terrible injustice and lie being perpetrated in the world. And he can't get anyone important to pay even a bit of attention. But mostly Allan is unhappy because he just *is* unhappy—one of those depressives who spread unease wherever they go.

"In America, people need to wake up, quit the denial, realize we are on the verge of true catastrophe," he was telling me. "I am talking about *Mad Max* stuff: riots, martial law." And then, in a moment of honesty, he said, "I do miss the United States, culturally and certain friends. I have found it difficult to be close to people who are not interested."

I asked if, somewhere deep down, he really wants to see that scenario played out.

"On a certain level, yeah," he replied after a pause. "When somebody says, 'I have my life to live,' or whatever, I say, 'I am not going to feel sorry for you when it goes down.'"

He imagines the satisfaction of telling those friends who won't listen to him now, "You are going to fucking see how stupid you are. Want to call me a nutcase? Fine." The level of denial was such that nobody would ever say he was right. "My friends had a big argument with me because I said, 'Do me a favor and put some food away.' They have a twelve-year-old kid. I say, 'The worst thing that can happen is you spend a thousand bucks and you have some food in the cellar.' They start saying, 'Well, what's three months' food going to do?' It's not like I'm asking them to move to the Canadian northwoods; I am asking them to buy a can of soup. Somehow it fucks with their denial. I say, 'Do you think there is a one-in-twenty chance that I am right? One in a hundred?' It's not fun when you are pissed off with your friends and you say, 'I hope you think of me when your family is starving.'"

Allan agrees that it would not be unreasonable to call him insane. "It drives me a little mad," he said with a nod. "If everyone believes one thing and you believe the truth, then it's not the truth anymore. Orwell hit the nail on the head about human denial and needing a constant series of victories over your own memory to believe the bullshit."

I understood this reference to *1984*, but it does seem slightly circular and self-justifying to argue that if the world disagrees with you, it's because of a mass delusion on its part. Still, plenty of Hollywood movies have been based on just that premise.

Allan was still putting forward his views on 9/11. "To me this stuff about building seven is not that different. In a leap of logic, you realize that a building coming down like that equals inside job—you'll see. I went through a stage when I knew it intellectually was one thing, but it took a while to seep into my being, and I tell you, it changed everything."

I wondered whether a coincidence of names had something to do with this obsession of Allan's: Captain Zero, Ground Zero. Had Allan identified with it in some weird, subconscious way?

"I can't have friends anymore, close friends, that don't get it. They can't be friends anymore—it's like *Invasion of the Body Snatchers*; it's like they don't have any soul."

Allan returned from this metaphysical discussion to the realities of survival in the turbulent times that he forecasts are just around the corner. "If there is no credit, they can't bring food to the stores. If things go bad, you assume it's to some extent by design, because they want martial law. You can see the advantage to the people in power—martial law, that's their dream."

I know it's Mike Reynolds's dream, but I somehow doubt that it is Barack Obama's dream, though it's possible that this is not who Allan had in mind when he was talking about the people in power.

"There are smart people who believe the plan is to get rid of about four billion of us. There is real logic to that, and I can't, in a sense, argue with it. I mean, we are going to run out of oil before too long; then they won't be able to grow food."

Here, on the beach, says Allan, it's a small community. "Somewhat tight knit, and it won't go down like if you are living in a city. I have no illusion about people coming here with guns. I don't have a gun—they catch you here in Mexico, you go to jail. But I have a club."

In Montauk, Allan has a bow and arrow, as well as hunting rifles. "There is plenty of game and fish, but in the winter it's a problem."

In the summers, when it is too hot in Mexico, Allan cautiously returns to his Montauk home and his friends, ready to flee back south at any moment—but in the event that the collapse that he forecasts actually comes to pass while he is in Montauk, there is another problem: "They would throw me into the ocean after the fourth 'I told you so!'"

Allan reckons that 9/11 was a plot to justify the Iraq war. He has lost so much faith and trust in the system, the government, the powers that run America, that he's fled to Mexico with his wagon full of stuff. It's hard to dismiss him as simply crazy. After all, he is still together enough to have a wagonload of valuable stuff. Reading his latest book, *Can't You Get Along with Anyone?*, was enough to convince me that he is a bright and witty individual, even if he does fall out with everyone he has ever worked with. He is also together enough to have clung to a piece of property at the end of Long Island, which he regards as another potential bugout location.

In the event of a genuine collapse, I asked him, would he not be faced with marauding hordes from East Hampton? "No," he replied. The sort of people who could afford East Hampton would have better plans. Steven Spielberg probably owns an island somewhere, he said. Allan had lost faith in Spielberg when he made the movie *War of the Worlds*. "Spielberg's aliens used to be so cuddly," he told me. But in *War of the Worlds*, "the aliens became threatening, menacing, hiding under the sidewalk—the enemy within, the Al Qaeda."

So Spielberg is in on it as well, I guess. Oh dear.

THE BUGOUT PALACE

Back in the United States, I was still evaluating my conversations with Allan, trying to decide whether he is sane but wrong, or crazy and right, or some other combination of possibilities, when I met another survivalist. They are opposites in some respects, but Lester Germanio is traveling on a parallel road and shares some basic beliefs with Allan.

Lester Germanio is not a total loner. He's a self-employed structural engineer who works alone, but he has a wife and family. He also happens to be one of those people who attract a variety of disputes to swirl around them, ranging in his case from squabbles with local politicians to legal battles with building inspectors.

Big, bald, jovial, paunchy, and in his late fifties, with a bright, youthful energy, Lester lives in Austin and most of his clients are local homeowners.

Lester called 9/11 a "false-strike operation—like McNamara did with the Gulf of Tonkin." (In 1964, a foreign naval attack was faked so Lyndon Johnson could use it to escalate the Vietnam War.) "I'm pretty certain it was an inside job," he said, and I have to admit that his professional background gives his words more credibility than Allan the screenwriter's.

Lester began his career designing bridges for the City of Austin Public Works Department, and then branched out on his own. For the past five years, he has been building a vast, off-the-grid stone mansion a few bricks at a time, in West Lake Hills, a very upmarket suburb a few miles outside Austin city limits. He explained, "When Bush went to war in Iraq, I was so pissed I wanted nothing to do with America after that. The idea of peace through domination and fighting wars for the last of the resources is something I just don't want to have anything to do with."

This is a slightly different wrinkle on removing oneself from the system. Lester is a believer in the theory of peak oil, which says that we are approaching the point in history at which the amount of oil consumed each year exceeds the amount of new oil found each year. This, in turn, will have consequences for how we grow our food and organize our society. Lester's unfinished home, named EarthWaterShelter, is his answer to that problem.

Before he showed me around the place, at the end of a cul de sac with a big view out over the Austin hills, he wanted to complete his peroration on the 9/11 conspiracy.

"There are some people in this country who don't believe the planes brought the towers down," he told me as we drove out to his eco-mansion. "I saw the tower leaning and then the next few seconds I saw the top thirty stories of the building leaning, then the whole thing comes tumbling down, just pulverized. The size of the plane compared to the size of the building . . . I don't know how they did it, but it didn't happen the way they say. The core of the building should not have collapsed. Even if the floors pancaked around it, the core should not have come down, especially at the speed of gravity. I don't know how they did it, but I suspect that they did it.

"As soon as the towers came down, we were in there talking about going into Afghanistan as a retaliation, and soon afterwards George Bush and Colin Powell and a whole bunch of them had put together a plan to do a bit of Middle East domination . . . and that's what got this project started, and I'm still working on it."

Here was another disaffected member of society voicing his doubts about 9/11, suggesting that because events moved swiftly, there must be something to hide.

Lester cited all sorts of indications that it had been a government plot. "Homeland Security was all ready to go and went into effect after 9/11. A whole bunch of stuff was already prepared, waiting on that event. SEC investigations were taking place in building seven—so that was a gift for the big shots.

"It's not like I don't like this country," he concluded. "I am doing this because this is my country, and I don't want these bastards to take it away from me, and I do not want to partake in the spoils."

America has what Lester and others call a "fiat currency," meaning the value of the dollar is dictated by the U.S. government (in conjunction with the global financial system), rather than being backed up by gold or some other store of value.

Now we were getting to the point where I agree with Lester. For the fiat currency system to work, and the whole system of debt and mortgage repayment and interest and bank loans to work, he said, "there has got to be growth to keep it afloat. And without cheap energy, growth is gonna quit and we're seeing the pain. As I see the grid, it depends on them (by which I think Lester meant the military-industrial complex) and their control over us. I am trying to cut the cord, be nearly sustainable in water and shelter and not need the grids, whether that be grocery stores, agribusinesses, sewer, water, and electricity—that's the purpose of this project, to get off the grid."

This entire conversation had been a prelude to our tour. We walked along a short path from the street to one of biggest and most grandiose houses I had seen. It rivals Mike Reynolds's Phoenix House, which had been built as a model home and small conference center, in size. It marches up the hillside on multiple split levels. All the steel is already in place, more steel than I had seen in all the other off-the-grid homes put together. "There's going to be a dressing room here, a bathroom there, a living area here," he said, although there were several roofs and walls awaiting financing, including the roof of the main structure, overlooking a huge valley with views stretching at least fifteen miles. The building is designed to house a total of eight people in four thousand square feet. But another eight souls could probably be squeezed into the multiple courtyards and terraces, as the house climbs up three levels of steep hillside.

A second, smaller building does have a roof. It will eventually be the guesthouse, but for now Lester and Mrs. Germanio plan to make use of it. This will save them money in these difficult economic times.

Lester graduated from Louisiana State University with a degree in architecture, and then became a licensed structural engineer. But this doesn't appear to have helped when it came to building his house. It is not the lavish scale of the building that was the problem; that is perfectly in keeping with the tone of the area; his main crime was trying to live off-grid. "After a year I ended up with seven stop-work orders, but never had a code violation. They shut me down for a year and I was in criminal court for fourteen months.

"The last mayor lived in a five-million-dollar house right up this little hill," he said, pointing upward. "And if he walked through his backyard he could see what I was doing. A fringe nut building within his view. Why in the world would somebody want to build off grid in the city of West Lake Hills? It's a small town of three thousand people, about 1,050 houses. The mayor was there for twelve years. A small group ran the town."

When Lester bought the land in 1979, West Lake Hills was not the upscale neighborhood it is now. The median price for a home here is eight hundred thousand dollars, and some are in the two- to five-million-dollar range. In May 2009, Lester's building permit expired. He needed to extend it, but it was $1,257 for the extension permit, and then there was a whole review process that he had to comply with, and new ordinances affecting the way he will have to build, or rebuild, his unfinished home.

So it is possible that Lester will never actually put a roof on his new home, which would be a shame. Perhaps this story shows that the building regulators are deeply unsympathetic and that it does not pay to be overambitious when building off the grid. As Andie said of her unpermitted home in Northern California, "It's about being humble."

ONLY DISCONNECT

The third 9/11 survivalist I met is Brett Butler, the young man who had been tending the fire while I chatted man-to-man with Eustace Conway at Turtle Island. He is an appropriate-technology major at Appalachian State University, in Boone, North Carolina, and the antithesis of Allan Weisbecker. Whereas Allan is wacky and creative, Brett is buttoned down and analytical. Whereas Allan is old, Brett is twenty-three. Whereas Allan surfs, Brett shoots. Whereas Allan smokes, drinks, and likes to play with the ladies, Brett was a clean-living Eagle Scout with the expectation that he would have very few monogamous relationships. But, like both Allan and Lester, Brett is certain that 9/11 was a "false operation—a complete conspiracy by the government." He believes the bumper-sticker slogan implicitly, he said: "9/11 *was* an inside job."

I suggested that if it was, then surely the *New York Times* and the *Washington Post* would have detected the plot.

"They are part of the conspiracy—part of the problem, not the solution," Brett said.

"What about Watergate? They stuck it on the government then."

"That was a different era," he said.

Like Allan, Brett has constructed a belief system that cannot be challenged by evidence—any suggestions to the contrary are just part of the conspiracy.

Brett is about six feet tall with short blond hair, the hint of a beard, and clear eyes. He is also a fluent conversationalist. Unlike Daniel Staub's stereotype, he does not drink at all. He is what some call a "straight edge," which is unusual for a university student. Brett is another of those who read *The Last American Man* as a teenager and became inspired to follow the Eustace Conway way of life.

He invited me to spend a night in his tepee, a few miles outside Boone.

I pulled my SUV out of the lot at Earth Fare and we drove south, ten miles out of Boone. Brett had found his home a year earlier, by placing an ad on Craigslist saying he was a college student looking for a place to put a tepee, that he was "clean and quiet and an Eagle Scout." That one mention of Eagle Scout is what attracted the only reply to his ad, from another former Eagle Scout, whom he has never met, a man who has no interest at all in living on the land.

Brett doubts that the Boy Scouts are training a generation that will want to live off the grid. "The Scouts were too lax—it's the leadership that determines the values coming out of the Scouts. The quality of leadership has gone down because the number of strong, reliable men has decreased." We were back on Eustace's territory. "I wish they were straighter and stricter and kept the kids more in line. When I was a Scout there were no radios, cell phones, or Game Boys allowed." On a recent backpacking trip, Brett said in outraged tones, "The adults were smoking and listening to a Walkman during a hike. Of course you are going to have weak boys, out committing crimes, when you give them role models like that."

Following Eustace Conway, he said, is something that runs deep in American culture. "The quality of masculinity in our culture has diminished—you have this whole crop of soft boys playing video games about camping in the woods, instead of actually camping in the woods."

By now it was dark and we were skidding up a heavily rutted road in drenching rain toward Brett's home, or, more accurately, his campsite. During the brief run from the car to the shelter of the tepee, I could see we were on a plateau beside a steep slope, overlooking a heavily wooded valley. At the bottom of the hill is the silvery glint of the blacktop we had traveled along. Although it's pretty close to civilization, it was spookily quiet during the occasional breaks from the pounding rain.

Brett pulled on a head-mounted LED light, made a fire, and cooked dinner as we talked. Although his initial interest in off-the-grid living was spurred by reading about Eustace Conway, it was eventually supplanted by a broad fear of coming social collapse. Brett thinks part of the solution to the present crisis is gun ownership. He told me that it's not the American flag that is the symbol of democracy; it's the rifle. "The Second Amendment guarantees the right to bear arms, to protect us from an evil and tyrannous government. Basically it was put in place to make sure none of our other rights and freedoms were impinged upon. I think every American has a duty to exercise that right, to have at least one gun—a .22 caliber rifle is the most widely used. The ammunition is cheap—a hundred rounds for six bucks, and that's the good stuff. It's a great hunting tool. You can teach anyone to shoot a .22, because the recoil is so light.

"People argue that guns cause violent crime," he continued. "That's true—but if you enact laws to limit ownership, it's the criminals who would break that law. So the law-abiding citizens would not have guns—only the criminals would have guns. The problem is not that everybody has a gun. If more people had guns, then crime would be lower. If you had, by law, to keep ammunition and a gun in working order, then every time you went to someone's house, you [would know] there was a gun in that house. Crime would be drastically lower."

The next morning, before breakfast, Brett took me for some target practice, first with a handgun, then with a semiautomatic M14. My shots were all so tightly bunched around the bull's-eye that at first I thought I had missed altogether. It was undoubtedly a good rifle.

In addition to eight handguns, Brett has a blowgun, a hollow tube that fires a dart made of bamboo, fletched with thistle-down plucked from the flower, with animal sinew attaching the down to the dart.

As Brett prepared breakfast, I sat in the tepee looking at his books. It's worth listing some of the main texts. As I mentioned earlier, survivalism was originally a samizdat-based movement, and a selection of the book titles I saw on his shelf offers an insight into the mind of a survivalist:

Patriots: A Novel of Survival in the Coming Collapse, by James Wesley Rawles

Welcome to the Machine, by Derrick Jensen and George Draffan

SAS Survival Handbook, by John "Lofty" Wiseman

Tom Brown's Guide to Wilderness Survival, by Tom Brown

The *Foxfire* series, by Eliot Wiggington

The Encyclopedia of Country Living, by Carla Emery

The Good Life, by Helen and Scott Nearing

Iron John, by Robert Bly

Brett's next plan is to build a small office nearby, so he can move his computer, books, and desk out of the tepee, making room for his girlfriend and her daughter. Sarah is a geography student at ASU, and once she is relocated, the two will begin making plans for the ultimate bugout location and draw up a list of those who will be invited to join them.

Since starting college in Boone, Brett has met several locals with a similar outlook, living off the grid because they believe that society is heading rapidly toward total social breakdown. One is a woman who teaches dance and lives off grid with her husband. They "have a lot of guns," Brett told me, and she is an excellent gardener.

"It's not a question of if—just a question of when," he said. "It could range from the economy, collapse of the dollar, or mega-hyperinflation. Or it may have something to do with China—owing them a lot of money. Or North Korea shooting missiles. Most Americans don't have a friggin' clue what's really going on."

13

Getting There

"We shall be reduced to gnawing the very crust of the earth for nutrient."

Henry David Thoreau, *Chesuncook*

WHY IT MATTERS

Most of the people I met on my tour of America are losing faith in the grid, in both its literal and metaphorical sense. They don't feel a sufficient advantage to being inside the fabric of society.

This led me to conclude that living off the grid is more than a lifestyle choice. It is a political act, with benefits way beyond the individual off-gridder. And compared to listing environmental problems or complaining about the oil industry, it is a positive act, one that adds to social diversity and is good for the species.

For one thing, if off-the-grid building permits were easier to come by in more parts of America, hundreds of thousands would be allowed onto the property ladder, including many who have been in foreclosure or who are trapped in mortgages they cannot afford.

The depopulation of rural America has left a vast countryside where highways speed us through a near-empty landscape and horses outnumber humans in some of the lushest and most livable areas. Many city-dwellers would prefer to live in the country, but are prevented by the artificially high price of real estate.

The zoning laws operate in favor of existing homeowners by excluding others from building on the most desirable locations. Even when they are allowed to build, the code can be onerous if all one can afford is a small wooden cabin but the code calls for brick and double glazing. "The entire system," says Robert Bruegmann, a professor of urban planning at the University of Illinois and the author of *Sprawl: A Compact History*, "is designed to protect the kind of urban neighborhoods in which [the advocates of the current planning system] live, and the country houses where they vacation, while the problems fall most heavily on other parts of the population."

As well as cheaper housing, living off the grid reduces energy bills (after the initial outlay on power generation equipment). That benefits the wider energy security of the nation. In the event of disruption of energy supplies, whether for economic reasons or due to peak oil or to natural disaster, a sizable off-grid population would increase the resilience of society as a whole and its ability to continue to supply power to those who need it.

Whether consciously or by accident, off-the-grid households in the United States are firmly part of the larger environmental movement. Living off the grid just happens to be good for the environment, fostering lower energy consumption and increased awareness of the natural forces shaping our planet and introducing a radical approach to cutting consumption of everything in our domestic lives, not just energy and water. Although climate-change science has been partly discredited, that is no reason to stop protecting the environment from corporate polluters and overexploitation of dwindling resources. To me, that is what environmentalism has always been about.

Policies favorable to off-the-grid living would bring hundreds of thousands back to the land, revive dying communities, and nurture long-forgotten skills needed to grow food and live self-sufficiently.

Smaller, more mobile, and more efficient versions of existing products—batteries, phones, solar panels, wind turbines, computers, and much more—are being developed at an incredible rate. Fuel cells may soon entirely replace our century-old battery technology. Other innovations aimed at marine and camping communities have given us the means to live luxuriously in the middle of nowhere, with all the standard household appliances, from fridges and TVs to computers and lighting systems. And wireless broadband Internet allows us to surf the Web or check e-mail almost anywhere.

Thanks to this technology, the off-gridders don't need to turn away from society as drastically as their sixties and seventies back-to-the-land forebears did (only to return as lawyers or real estate agents, or, in Northern California, as wine and pot growers). They can keep writing, or making craft items, or telecommuting, earning their living from home in a variety of ways.

To me, the most heartening aspect of the off-grid movement is its opposition to overconsumption—the bane of American health and wealth.

During the eighties and through the long boom, we were all lulled into thinking of ourselves as consumers. But the "consumer" will seem like a tired, outdated concept in the future, with its overtones of slurping up scarce resources.

As individuals, some of us are ashamed of our previous high levels of consumption. We've had enough of brand names and shopping-as-entertainment; we'll never lose interest in dressing to the latest trends, but many resist *buying* the latest trends. These days we are as likely to "shop the closet" as we imitate magazine spreads on the latest must-have color or hemline.

Houses became the essence of the consumer society, to an absurd degree. Bigger houses, gated communities, marble-topped kitchens, heated pools—by the time the crunch came,

Americans had overhoused themselves to the point that the home became not an asset but a liability, so high are the utility, tax, heating, and maintenance costs.

A place like Greenfield Ranch, where this journey began, could seem like a hopeless relic of the 1970s, but in fact it is a harbinger of the future. Young Lita Jarboe is a bubbly valley girl, the antithesis of a solemn eco-campaigner, not yet twenty-one when her late uncle bestowed the intractable property upon her and her brother and sister, neither of whom has yet shown any interest in it.

She is somewhat daunted by the task ahead of her, so she tends to sit in the crumbling home on the lot with her boyfriend, Joe, laughing and letting the days go by. He works at the local garden center in addition to cultivating his six plants. She does a little babysitting, and waitresses from time to time. They hardly embody the next generation that the groundbreaking hippies might have envisioned as they struggled to raise their children in the woods.

Her uncle (who was not actually her uncle but a close family friend) had owned the twenty acres with his late wife, who on her deathbed had made him promise that their place would remain a retreat, in its natural state. So he'd had to look long and hard for someone willing to accept this condition.

As long as Lita and Joe stay stoned, the property is likely to remain in its natural state. But what if a freak mold invasion destroys an entire year's crop and leaves them clearheaded? They may decide that their only option is to develop the place.

Sequoia, whose wake I attended, also had strong views about the plot she had nurtured for thirty-six years. "She asked me to take care of the land," her former land partner, Jim, told me over the phone a few months after the wake. He had been just five when Sequoia arrived at Greenfield. "She wanted to see the re-wilding of the earth," he said. "She didn't want Greenfield to become like a suburban setup."

He told me he isn't really doing much with the land. For him, there is little point, since "the world will end with the Mayans," a reference to the Mayan prophecy that all human life will end in 2012. "We are about to witness the boiling off of the oceans."

It remains to be seen whether Sequoia chose wisely when she chose Jim. He is truly committed to the lifestyle. For now. But suppose the oceans do not "boil off" in 2012, and Jim decides that the Mayans want him to build condos instead?

All over America, aging landowners are confronting the same problem that Lita's uncle and Sequoia faced late in their lives: They want to honor their pact with nature. They feel that their land is something more than just a plot of soil; it is something special. They don't want it to be sold off only to provide foundations for hunting lodges or condos.

Children of these landowners may be hoping to inherit parcels bought for a few thousand dollars and now worth hundreds of thousands, in some cases millions. Or there may be no children to inherit the land. Or there might be children who have no interest in the land itself. No matter what the specifics of the scenario, these aging landowners are all asking the same question: What will happen to our land after we go?

As the baby-boomer generation ages and dies in the next two decades, this problem will intensify. Hundreds of thousands of acres that were used to "go back to the land" will come onto the market, and the developers will be there waiting. But there are options. Earlier I hinted that I have a potential solution to this problem.

JED is the collective in Maine that owns the land its residents build and live on. They are working on ways to help others do the same, and central is the idea of land trusts devoted to keeping the land in its natural state and bringing owners and future residents together. As the JED members will attest, this represents the best hope in terms of providing ample amounts of quality land for the next generation of off-gridders. The average age of the JED members is about twenty-seven, and it is this generation that is most likely to adopt the values of their 1970s forbears.

At the same time as back-to-the-landers are dying or going back on the grid (in order to be nearer to doctors and just to have an easier life), the current crop of college graduates are facing very bleak prospects. I forecast that a sizeable minority will see going off the grid may be their least bad option, and doing so under the patronage and tutelage of their elders may be a great opportunity for both parties. The elders gain a role and a status that have been denied them for several generations. The youngsters gain a community and the means to make a living without joining the rat race.

There are endless ways in which the sort of deal that Carolyn Chute is hoping to work out with the JED collective can go wrong. Suppose a young caregiver moved in with the promise of looking after an elderly landowner and then just plain refused to do any caring, and refused to move out? Suppose an aging landowner dangled the possibility of future ownership of the land in front of a needy group of youngsters but then failed to follow through with the deal? Let's face it, young people who want to go off the grid usually cannot afford $150,000 or even fifty thousand for a few acres.

Nevertheless, a younger generation of people who want to live what one might call "noncommercial" lives is emerging. The ever-rising cost of land (caused partly by the number of urbanites who want their weekend homes or bugout locations in the country) combined with other obstacles—such as work shortages, difficulty in subdividing, and opposition from neighbors—makes it hard for most of them to get a start. They could always migrate to the Taos mesa or Big Bend, but those locations have the drawbacks already described.

The solution could take the form of small, localized non-profit groups that take control of land and ensure that the original owners' wishes are followed. These nonprofits would have three functions: 1) to take ownership of the land and thus be fully empowered to see that the original owners' desires are adhered to; 2) to introduce landowners to land seekers; and 3) to provide legal advice and help draft land-use agreements.

But before I fully endorse the establishment of these nonprofits, I'd like to address a pair of criticisms of living off the grid that have arisen in recent years. First, some environmentalists are cautious and even skeptical of living off the grid. They say that exurban scatter is bad for the environment in general and relies on excessive car travel, and that batteries are dirty because they are made from lead and contain sulfuric acid, and heavy use, whether in an urban or rural setting, is dangerous and harmful. It's a common argument, but it doesn't stand up to closer scrutiny.

I am not convinced that big, dense cities are greener than low-density cities such as L.A. or lower-density towns and suburbs, where the bulk of Americans live. Using the subway or bus is greener to a certain extent than driving, and city homes tend to be smaller and therefore easier to heat or cool, but cities generate huge amounts of heat and carbon. Vast amounts of gas are used to bring in food from around the country, and the same buses and trains that liberate commuters from their cars are still energy intensive and somewhat polluting. What's more, lead-acid batteries are in reality fully recyclable. About ninety-five percent of automobile batteries are already recycled. The fancy new lithium-ion batteries used in electric cars, on the other hand, have a higher carbon footprint in the way they are manufactured and maintained.

Environmentalists tend to say they would prefer to use the grid as their battery, meaning that they feed back any renewable energy they generate into the grid, thereby reducing their bill, hopefully down to zero. This approach may make people feel better about maintaining their current lifestyles while being able to call themselves "green," but it conveniently ignores the huge "embodied" costs of both solar panels and the grid—a term referring to the carbon generated during the production process in the case of solar panels, and the manufacture and distribution of electricity in the case of the wasteful and antiquated grid. In addition, there are the continuing expansion costs anticipated for the so-called smart grid that may cost trillions.

I think environmental campaigners are being too strategic for their own good when they dismiss the off-grid life. Perhaps they fear being dismissed as wacky if they support such a marginal lifestyle. The green leaders want to be part of the mainstream, but the whole (oft-overlooked) point of the green movement is that it is totally at odds with the mainstream desire to consume and to fund our credit-dependent lives through everlasting economic growth. It could be argued that only the off-grid population is living a truly twenty-first-century, low-carbon eco-lifestyle. Most environmentalists who live standard grid-connected lives are doing less to reduce global warming than an off-gridder who gives scarcely a thought to the environment. And often so-called environmentalists are simply fearful homeowners, worried that encroaching developers will damage their property values. They are the type that oppose wind farms near them on environmental grounds, then drive their new Prius to the mall to buy a designer composting bin.

The second most common criticism of living off the grid is that it's a kind of selfishness, a battening down of the hatches and withdrawal from society, the "cold and selfish isolation" I have referred to throughout. Yes, it can be selfish. For some hermits, religious groups, and old-style survivalists it is exactly that—but it doesn't have to be. Many hundreds of people who live off the grid, or aspire to, have contacted me via my Web site, and most of them have conveyed that they appreciate the lifestyle not because they want to live like hermits, but because it represents an alternative community to the consumer-driven state that most Western people now live in. They are not alone; they are simply apart, together with other like-minded folks.

Earlier I hypothesized that Americans are losing faith in the grid, both in the literal sense (beginning to doubt that the power supply will be entirely reliable in the future) and in the wider, more metaphorical sense (losing trust in the system as a whole). Our energy needs are a source of possible conflict and crisis in the years ahead, and those who downplay or ignore the benefits to society of an off-the-grid segment are doing the whole country a disservice. On a wider, national level, the collapse of trust is a critical threat to the functioning of democracy. Without the belief that elected leaders and their civil servants are both capable of considering and actively working in the people's best interest, there is what political philosophers call a legitimation crisis, which is every bit as dangerous as the credit crisis or the environmental crisis.

The collapse in trust in the government to protect its citizens is closely related to the loss of faith in the financial system, where it became quite clear to everyone that the politicians and shareholders had lost control of their profit-crazed brokers and banksters. The trust crisis also covers more mundane things, such as the food-distribution system. Bob and Wretha, for example, are so concerned about this that they've stockpiled a year's supply of canned chicken and dumplings. Allan in Mexico has a six months' supply of canned and dried goods.

Finally, it extends to the value system that guides American society, and there again I found a widening disconnect. Melinda was led off the grid not only because of her financial hole but also because of her concerns and hopes for her children. She felt they were in moral and physical danger in the crumbling Rust Belt town she had escaped when she could no longer pay the mortgage. Caleb and Rebecca told me that their decision to go off the grid would bring them closer to their kids. And both Lynn Padgett and Carlos Proffit badly wanted to live somewhere they could be proud of but that wasn't going to break the bank.

I have described the various forces and impulses leading all these ordinary yet extraordinary, decent, hardworking Americans off the grid. They range from a desire for tranquility to a furious rage against "the machine." And if I am correct, then the hundreds of off-gridders I met are representative of hundreds of thousands more Americans.

The role of government, both national and local, should be to remove the obstacles and allow people to go about their lives in the way they wish. First and foremost this means amending land-use and zoning laws across the country. Based on everything I've heard and seen in the process of researching and writing this book, here are my suggestions:

Noncommercial, low-density, low-impact off-grid developments in parts of the countryside (places such as Grass Valley or Mendocino County) that are currently protected by rules limiting the subdividing of forty-acre lots or barring low-density home building need to be allowed, *on condition that they stay off the grid in perpetuity.* Like architect Robert Bruegmann, I would give the needs of the landless and poor a higher priority than the wants of the landed and wealthy.

Single homes should be permissible on lots that are only, say, half the size of the existing land minimum. For example, Mike Riddell's forty-acre lot in Greenfield could be split in half so that another home could be built. I do, however, recognize the legitimate need to defend nature so that all can enjoy her. So the crucial condition: All of the newly liberated land should be restricted to off-grid structures. And once developed, it must stay off the grid forever. That should help keep it affordable.

Those who already own forty acres and a mini-mansion would plead that their roads and water resources could not withstand a few more residents. This is mere nimbyism and can be disregarded, as long as the environmental benefit could be proven. Unlike Mike Reynolds, I do not think it is necessary to call for martial law. But there does need to be an agreed-upon standard for what kind of structures justify waiving the current environmental-protection rules. An off-grid home could be profligate in use of energy and water if its owners were wealthy enough, and there would have to be limits on the size of home that could be built on these newly liberated lots. Limiting the size pretty well limits the power and water consumption.

The same elite homeowners that Bruegmann identified earlier would oppose this reform, either because they paid full price for their land or out of a concern for nature and water shortages.

But if it should be pushed through it would, I believe, help reduce some of the problems afflicting America, including the housing shortage, or at least the shortage of affordable housing in areas where people actually would be able to successfully and comfortably live the low-impact life. There are also the social benefits, including energy security, strengthened rural communities, and revitalized rural skills. To that could be added something that is on the agenda of many off-gridders I spoke to: an end to the growth economy, a realization that the engine of global growth is shifting to Asia, that America, and the West in general, can now develop other priorities.

I would like to see Energy Secretary Steven Chu fund half a dozen experimental off-grid developments. They may cost a few million each—not much compared with the billions Chu has handed out for research into carbon capture and the smart grid. Each could have a few hundred inhabitants, and each could be limited to using, for example, only ten percent of the energy used per capita in the rest of the country. The speed and enthusiasm with which these places would be taken up would determine, once and for all, the level of demand for this lifestyle. And if the experiment proved that the technology works, then this once-maverick section of American society would be widely imitated by mainstream society, because my hunch is that deep down millions feel the same way.

Most of the off-gridders I met simply do not believe that there is a sufficient advantage to being inside the fabric of society. But if enough people join the off-grid movement, then society may just have to shift slightly in their direction.

I hope it is not fear or a sudden crisis that provides the impulse for a growth in the off-grid population. I want to see the rural population growing again, enabled by new technology. I want to see rural America teeming with life, rather than an empty place we drive through along the freeways.

A sense of joy is what attracted me to life off the grid, not an inward-looking survivalist scenario. It's about taking nature back into our lives, even in an urban context—looking outward, regaining our freedom and control over our own destiny.

Acknowledgments

I want to thank all the off-gridders who allowed me into their homes and hearts. I visited many more locations than I wrote about, and the generosity and hospitality I received wherever I went was deeply appreciated.

My thanks also to my editor, Tom Roberge, for having the vision to bring this book to fruition, and to Michael Edge and Helen Edwards for their help and encouragement when I was first developing the idea.

Henry Shawdon kindly read and commented on an early draft, and Nick Osborne provided essential historical research in Chapter 2. Any errors that remain are mine.

I was grateful to Nigel Carr for his generous advice and Felix Unger-Hamilton, Mark Larkin, and Anne-Katrin Spiess for logistical support. Marcus Ottmers, Ted Norris, Shannon Conley, Pat from Skywalker Farm, Teo Kermeliotis, and Lisa Botter also helped on the research.